International Perspectives on the Goals of Universal Basic and Secondary Education

Routledge Research in Education

International Perspectives on the Goals of Universal Basic and Secondary Education

Edited by Joel E. Cohen and Martin B. Malin

American Academy of Arts and Sciences
Cambridge, Massachusetts

Routledge
Taylor & Francis Group
New York   London

First published 2010
by Routledge
270 Madison Avenue, New York, NY 10016

Simultaneously published in the UK
by Routledge
2 Park Square, Milton Park, Abingdon, Oxon OX14 4RN

Routledge is an imprint of the Taylor & Francis Group, an informa business

Typeset in Sabon by IBT Global.
Printed and bound in the United States of America on acid-free paper by IBT Global.

Library of Congress Cataloging-in-Publication Data
International perspectives on the goals of universal basic and secondary education /
   edited by Joel E. Cohen and Martin B. Malin.
      p. cm. — (Routledge research in education ; 22)
   Includes bibliographical references and index.
   1. Basic education.   2. Education, Secondary.   3. Education—Aims and objectives.
I. Cohen, Joel E.   II. Malin, Martin B.   III. American Academy of Arts and Sciences.
   LC1035.I58 2009   2010
   370—dc22
   2008035693

ISBN10: 0-415-99766-6 (hbk)
ISBN10: 0-203-88214-8 (ebk)

ISBN13: 978-0-415-99766-9 (hbk)
ISBN13: 978-0-203-88214-6 (ebk)

Contents

PART IV
Empowering Children through Art and Science

PART V
The Special Role of Skepticism as Universal Educational Goal

Figures and Tables

FIGURES

TABLES

Acknowledgments

Since 1998, the project on Universal Basic and Secondary Education (UBASE) of the American Academy of Arts and Sciences has sponsored and reviewed research on what it would take to provide an education of high quality to every child in the world who is between the approximate ages of six and seventeen, and what the consequences would be. The project produced *Educating All Children: A Global Agenda* (edited by Joel E. Cohen, David E. Bloom, and Martin B. Malin; published by MIT Press, 2007), Occasional Papers of the American Academy of Arts and Sciences, other documents and data on the web at www.amacad.org/projects/ubase.aspx, and this book.

We are grateful to those who have given their time, talent, and financial support to make this work possible. David E. Bloom has been the UBASE project co-director and our co-conspirator throughout. This book is in part his idea. We thank him for his leadership and wise counsel. Alice Noble, program officer at the American Academy, ably steered this book to publication and the first stage of the UBASE project to completion. Helen Curry provided indispensable project coordination, copy-editing, and intellectual content.

The UBASE project received generous financial support from several sources. Many of those who offered or facilitated the financial support also contributed significantly to the project's content. The project received major support from the William and Flora Hewlett Foundation, and particular encouragement from Paul Brest, Tamara Fox, and Marshall Smith. Generous support was also received from John Reed, the Golden Family Foundation, Paul Zuckerman, the Zlinkoff Fund for Medical Research and Education, an anonymous donor, and the American Academy of Arts and Sciences. Leslie Berlowitz, the Academy's chief executive officer, supported and encouraged the UBASE project from the outset.

We thank this volume's authors and others who participated in a workshop to develop it: Mallam Zaki Abubakar, Mallam Bala Ahmed, David E. Bloom, James Carroll, the late Mohamed Charfi, Kai-ming Cheng, William Cummings, John Daniel, David Hansen, George Ingram, Rebecca Jacobsen, Ana Carolina Letichevsky, Beryl Levinger, Claudia Madrazo, Kishore Mahbubani, Deborah Meier, Mary Joy Pigozzi, Stephen Provasnik, Vimala Ramachandran, Hamadi Redissi, John S. Reed, Fernando Reimers, Richard

Rothstein, Laura Salganik, Marcelo Suárez-Orozco, Margot Stern Strom, Adam Strom, Martin Sleeper, and Camer Vellani.

The authors of *Educating All Children* taught us much about the rationales, the history, the means, the assessment, and the consequences of providing basic and secondary education of high quality to all children. We thank Aaron Benavot, Eric Bettinger, Melissa Binder, David Bloom, Henry Braun, Claudia Buchmann, Javier Corrales, Paul Glewwe, Emily Hannum, Anil Kanjee, Michael Kremer, Julia Resnik, and Meng Zhao.

Members of an advisory committee to the UBASE project provided valuable guidance on peer review and other matters for which we are grateful. The committee consisted of Leslie Berlowitz, Nancy Birdsall, Joan Dassin, Howard Gardner, George Ingram, Kishore Mahbubani, Katherine Namuddu, Kenneth Prewitt, John S. Reed, Jeffrey Sachs, Gene Sperling, and Paul Zuckerman.

We received valuable comments from several anonymous reviewers and from Howard Gardner. We thank each reviewer for his or her insights.

In addition to Alice Noble and Helen Curry, American Academy staff members Anthony Baird, Phyllis Bendell, James DiFrancesca, Jennifer Gray, Elizabeth Huttner, Leigh Nolan, Corinne Schelling, and Carolyn Yee helped keep the project on track. Jim Miller, at the time the editor of *Daedalus*, edited the manuscript of Chapter 12 by Charfi and Redissi with great skill and understanding.

Joel E. Cohen recalls gratefully the late William T. Golden's firm belief in the value of the UBASE project and thanks him and his family for their hospitality. Cohen also thanks Priscilla K. Rogerson for her skillful, genial help.

In a commentary in *The New York Times*, March 12, 2002, the former president of the Tunisian Human Rights League and Tunisia's minister of education from 1989 to 1994, Mohamed Charfi, wrote of the need for Muslim states "to begin a new phase of engagement with the world." He suggested that "educational reform needs to be at the heart of this effort." Charfi was the first person we contacted to contribute to this volume. His words and deeds as a reformer of education, and as a human rights advocate, encouraged our ongoing exploration of the goals of universal basic and secondary education. Sadly, Charfi died June 6, 2008, at the age of seventy-two, just three weeks before the final manuscript of this book went to the publisher. We hope this book will honor his memory by stimulating vigorous cross-cultural discussion of the purposes and values of educating all children.

This volume has been a collective effort from start to finish. It has been a tremendous privilege to work with each of those named above in producing this work.

—*Joel E. Cohen*
Rockefeller and Columbia Universities

—*Martin B. Malin*
Harvard University

Part I

Introduction

1   Goals of Universal Basic and Secondary Education

Joel E. Cohen

What should be the goals of basic and secondary education of high quality? Which, if any, of these goals should be universal? What does "universal" mean? What happens when educational goals conflict? What are the meanings of "high quality" in basic and secondary education? Who decides these questions, and by what process do they decide? How should the quality of decisions about educational goals be evaluated?

Attention to educational goals is intrinsic to achieving educational quality. Knowing where one wants education to go, ultimately or incrementally, facilitates deciding whether one is getting there effectively. In the final decades of the twentieth century, the international movement toward universal primary education focused on expanding access to schooling and largely sidestepped trying to define goals. Yet the same international community promoted educational assessments as a means to improve educational quality. Such assessments are most useful if they measure what education is trying to accomplish.

The project on Universal Basic and Secondary Education (UBASE), based at the American Academy of Arts and Sciences, recognized a lack of consensus within and among countries and a lack of focused international discussion on the desired content and aims of basic and secondary education. Acting on the conviction that questions of educational goals were too important to leave unargued and unanalyzed, the project invited individuals from different geographic, cultural, professional, and religious backgrounds to address these questions. These individuals wrote from different levels of analysis, reflecting their backgrounds as, among others, teachers and headmasters of schools, a diplomat, a philosopher, a statistician, an economist, a lawyer, a minister of state, a physician, an artist, a journalist and novelist, and professionals related to the study and administration of education—and from cultures and geographical locations in Africa north and south of the Sahara, Arab regions, East and South Asia, Europe, North America, and Latin America. Some of their written responses are the following chapters of this book.

The purposes of this volume are to stimulate attention to educational goals on the part of individuals, families, educational professionals, community leaders in business, religion, and politics, local governments, national governments, and international organizations, and to provide some starting points for future discussions among the different groups with different agendas that compose any society. Educational goals are at the heart of contests of values and interests at most times in many societies. The diversity of educational goals in the chapters of this volume illustrates the challenges local communities, nations, and the international community will face in trying to set educational goals. Although the proposed goals vary with their authors' political, economic, social, and religious contexts, the multiple voices reflected in these chapters provide valuable material for an informed discussion. This volume may be the only place in recent decades where divergent, insightful views of the goals of primary and secondary education from around the world confront one another between the same covers.

This introduction reviews the context and content of the following chapters. I first identify some difficulties in establishing and evaluating educational goals. I then sketch the history of educational goals. The second half of this introduction summarizes the educational goals of basic and secondary education proposed by the authors of this volume.

This volume leaves major questions unanswered. It will have succeeded if it contributes to broadening and deepening conversations about the goals of education. Rich countries and poor, and rich people and poor, should devote more attention to the goals of basic and secondary education, and to what universal education should mean.

WHY DEFINING EDUCATIONAL GOALS IS DIFFICULT

The chapters in this volume collectively do not indicate a single set of educational goals. Specifying educational goals and agreeing on them are difficult for multiple reasons. Stating some of these reasons may help to avoid naive optimism and may encourage sustained attention to the challenge.

A society's goals for education and a society's goals for schooling (when these goals can be defined) may differ. For example, a society that wants its youth and adults to be trustworthy, courageous, and patriotic may sponsor youth movements outside of formal schooling. How a society encourages or regulates newspapers, magazines, the Internet, popular music, radio, television, film, political and commercial advertising, and video games reflects a society's implicit educational goals for its young people and adults. If there are differences between a society's goals for education (what kind of young people and adults does the society want?) and a society's goals for schooling, there may also be differences between high-quality education from a broad social perspective and high-quality schooling.

Goals for schooling may pertain to educational inputs, processes, immediate outputs, or long-term outcomes. Educational budgets and physical facilities are inputs. Hours of instruction per year are both inputs and processes; pedagogical techniques and procedures of discipline and administration are processes. The fraction of primary school entrants who complete primary school and the fraction of primary school graduates who know their multiplication tables are both immediate outputs. Long-term outcomes could be measured by the fraction of young adults who are able to compete in global labor markets and who participate in national political debates on an informed basis, or by progress toward national political and economic goals.

Goals for educational inputs, processes, and immediate outputs may affect the possibility of reaching goals for long-term outcomes but do not determine what those long-term goals should be. A goal of increasing the use of computers in classrooms or incorporating art, music, or science into primary schools does not specify the long-term outcomes of education. Ranking educational goals for schooling requires some definition of long-term educational goals, and that definition is the responsibility of the society at large. A society may find it difficult to face or fulfill that responsibility if the views or interests of powerful actors within the society are too divergent.

A society's broad educational goals usually pertain to long-term outcomes but may often also affect the resources for and content of educational inputs and processes. For example, a society's goals for freedom of speech may influence the freedom of speech permitted in schools; a society's goals for democratic participation may influence the democratic participation permitted students in schools.

In short, what the society wants for itself affects the goals of schooling. The goals of schooling affect the long-term goals a society can hope to achieve. In the two-way causal interactions between the goals of schooling (regarding educational inputs, processes, and immediate outputs) and a society's broad educational goals (regarding long-term outcomes), there is a large margin of indeterminacy in both linkages. For example, in rulings on June 25, 2007, the United States Supreme Court forbade one kind of free speech to a high school student and authorized a greater range of free speech in political campaign advertisements (Stout, 2007).

Long-term outcomes may be specified at multiple levels, for example, the individual learner; the population of teachers (their training and orientations toward tolerance, the diversity of student needs, and technological innovation in education, for example); the educational system (for different age groups or tiers of education); the population reaching the age of 18; the adult population; and the society and economy. Goals at one level are not necessarily sufficient to determine goals at all levels. For example, a goal that the individual learner realize his interests and potential to the fullest extent possible, regardless of gender and urban or rural location, does not determine whether the population reaching the age of eighteen has the distribution of academic, vocational, commercial, and interactive skills and political loyalties required for a viable society. Hence it seems necessary to specify educational goals at multiple levels. The UNESCO goals for individual learners and for the educational system (Mary Joy Pigozzi, Chapter 18, this volume) are a start in this direction of multi-level specification of goals.

Educational goals are subject to influence at multiple geographic or spatial scales, and may be determined differently at each scale from international to individual. Different spatial scales of influence interact in a complicated network. International organizations have goals for education based on their understanding of the reasons for providing education. For example, the United Nations Convention on the Rights of the Child says that education is a basic human right, while some multinational businesses promote education where they want an educated labor force. Nongovernmental organizations and organized religions also attempt to influence education internationally. Educational goals are promoted by national governments, which may listen to the international community, and by national ministries, unions, and professional associations. State, provincial and local school boards, religious groups, and home-schooling parents may set goals for children's education in countries where the central government does not preempt that right. The parents in a family set educational goals and standards for their own children that need not coincide with those of the local or national community. Finally, individual children within a family may set themselves differing educational goals and standards.

Current discussions of the quality of education largely overlook the challenge of defining educational goals when means are limited (George Ingram, Chapter 19, this volume):

> . . . presentations on quality education most often describe what is required to produce quality education in ideal circumstances—strong political commitment, adequate resources, supportive and involved parents and community, trained teachers and systems to support them, healthy students, etc. (p. 149).

But how do you maximize quality in less favorable circumstances?

> Missing is a systemic analysis of what would define quality education and how it would be maximized in a resource-poor environment— crowded classes, poorly trained and compensated teachers, inadequate materials, and unengaged parents (p. 250).

When Mexican sixth-grade students who were the first in their families to go to school had teachers they rated as consistently effective, they acquired literacy skills at the same level as students with educated parents; but the first-generation students were handicapped in acquiring literacy when they perceived their teachers as ineffective (Reimers, 2006). This empirical finding underlines the importance of Ingram's emphasis on the quality of teaching. Ingram also suggests a second missing ingredient: examination of the definition of an education of quality for students who are not in school, are vulnerable, or are hard-to-reach, such as "street children, rural dwellers, disabled children, HIV/AIDS orphans, dropouts, child laborers, night travelers in Uganda, and children with mental, physical and emotional disabilities" (p. 250). He notes that although interventions are currently directed toward these groups, basic questions of quality are not being addressed. He asks, "[W]hat are realistic, relevant goals? What type of learning is relevant for such groups?" (p. 250).

These questions can create tensions within countries as well as between or among them. Does universal education include students who are learning disabled or severely emotionally or physically disabled? If so, how are they to be reached, and how should a society decide how much to spend on educating them at the possible expense of educating others who learn more readily? In the public schools of the United States, for example, according to the National Education Association (2004):

> The current [2004] average per student cost is $7,552 and the average cost per special education student is an additional $9,369 per student, or $16,921. Yet, in 2004, the federal government [was] providing local school districts with just under 20 percent of its commitment rather than the 40 percent specified by the law [Individuals with Disabilities Education Act], creating a $10.6 billion shortfall for states and local school districts.

The 5.3 billion people in the less developed regions with 2004 average Gross National Income of $4,450, let alone the roughly 2.7 billion of those 5.3 billion people who were living on less than two U.S. dollars per day, cannot afford such expenditures for students with special needs. How can the educational needs of such students be respected?

I have spoken of "a society's goals for education" as if a society were to have unified goals for education. But societies are usually composed of different groups with different agendas and interests. Attaining agreement throughout a society on goals for education and schooling can be expected to be a difficult political process in which power, compromise, and self-restraint are complexly mixed. Many individual people want to influence educational goals within schools and more broadly, including, among others, children, parents, teachers, education officials, policy makers, religious leaders, labor leaders, business leaders, politicians, and members of the community at large. In addition to individuals, many organized groups of people, which we may call corporate interests, seek to influence educational goals, for example, labor unions (including teachers' unions), organizations of industrialists, organized religious groups, political parties, and governments. All these have an interest in what goes on wherever education takes place, in and out of schools, and their interests may concur at some of the levels and scales identified previously and may differ at others.

International economic requirements and international comparative educational assessments can powerfully influence decisions about the goals of education within a country. At present, no international body has the authority to establish international goals or standards for schooling. If de facto standards emerge from international requirements for commerce and scientific and technological exchanges, an institution devoted to formalizing the emergent standards may be found useful in the future.

A related difficulty in establishing goals concerns assessment. Once goals are established, individuals (students, teachers, parents) and authorities (school administrators, nongovernmental organizations, and ministries of education, finance, and defense) have an interest in tracking progress toward those goals. In the process of measuring progress, questions arise that are important for the determination of goals. When a verbal statement of goals is proposed or adopted by an educational authority, are the goals sufficiently well defined to make assessment possible? What are the implications of goals for methods of assessment? What are the implications of available methods of assessment for the choice of goals? How can the educational effects of media and institutions outside of schools be assessed? New collaborations or new institutions may be required to improve the coupling between educational goals and educational assessments.

The evolution of evaluations from checking students' rote mastery of facts to measuring the capacity for value judgments requires the development of criteria of excellence in judgment (Ana Carolina Letichevsky, Chapter 16, this volume). When different stakeholders have different values about excellence in judgment, the task of evaluation and assessment becomes complicated by the requirement that values be negotiated among those who require the evaluation, those who carry out the evaluation, and those who are affected (positively or negatively) by its results. Letichevsky writes, "Discussions of educational evaluation require a discussion of how the results will be used to improve education and a discussion of the standards to be adopted" (p. 216).

Eisner (2005) argued that new methods of assessment should be developed to correspond to more ambitious and less tidy goals. Camer Vellani (Chapter 7, this volume) reports an effort in Pakistan to develop new forms of assessment for secondary-school leavers that would favor the ability to reason and solve problems over rote memory. He acknowledges that, even with a successful implementation of the new form of examination, it will take many years to determine whether the new examinations will shape education to achieve the long-term goals favored by the new examination.

The Organisation for Economic Cooperation and Development (OECD) launched in 1997 the Programme for International Student Assessment (PISA) "to measure how far students approaching the end of compulsory education have acquired some of the knowledge and skills essential for full participation in the knowledge society" (OECD, no date, p. 4). In 2000, when PISA first went into the field, forty-three countries participated in the assessment. In 2006, fifty-seven or fifty-eight countries participated. Participating countries or areas that were not members of OECD were Argentina, Azerbaijan, Bulgaria, Colombia, Hong Kong, Indonesia, Macao, the Russian Federation, Slovenia, Tunisia, Croatia, Estonia, Kyrgyzstan, Lithuania, Qatar, Serbia and Montenegro, Taiwan, Uruguay, Brazil, Chile, Israel, Jordan, Latvia, Romania, and Thailand.[1]

PISA is designed to monitor progress toward goals defined by OECD and is administered to fifteen-year-olds in schools, 4,500 to 10,000 students in each country. The assessments compare what students know and can do in reading, mathematics, science and problem solving. PISA suggests that students also need "literacy" and "lifelong learning." Literacy is defined as "the capacity of students to analyze, reason and communicate effectively as they pose, solve and interpret problems in a variety of subject matter areas." Lifelong learning is students' "motivation to learn, beliefs about themselves and learning strategies."[2] Further,

> Reading literacy [is] [t]he capacity to understand, use and reflect on written texts, in order to achieve one's goals, develop one's knowledge and potential, and participate in society. . . . Mathematical literacy [is] [t]he capacity to identify and understand the role that mathematics plays in the world, make well-founded judgments, and use and engage with mathematics in ways that meet the needs of one's life as a constructive, concerned and reflective citizen. . . . Scientific literacy [is] [t]he capacity to use scientific knowledge, identify scientific questions and draw evidence-based conclusions, in order to understand and help make decisions about the natural world and the changes made to it through human activity.[3]

Whatever PISA's success in measuring all of these components, the articulation of goals and continued effort to improve monitoring of their achievement across countries is an important step. That it is also a contentious and internationally tenuous process is illustrated by the fact that the United States elected not to participate in the PISA 2007 assessment, presumably to avoid drawing attention to the comparatively mediocre performance of U.S. students, even as progress toward the goals expressed in "No Child Left Behind" should by now be evident.

A further difficulty in choosing educational goals is the challenge of understanding and measuring the consequences of education (Hannum and Buchmann, 2006). In principle, adopting economic growth as a goal to be produced as a result of investing in universal education is defensible if evidence shows that economic growth is, or can be, a consequence of universal education. Such consequences are in fact very difficult to measure. If education is incapable of producing a desired long-term consequence, it makes little sense to invest in education toward that particular end. A closer intellectual and practical linkage between education's demonstrable consequences and proposed goals might add realism to reflections about educational goals.

In defining goals for universal education, another question arises: What does "universal" mean? Does it demand that all children have access to education of some kind or kinds, with uptake optional, whether uptake is free or dependent on payment? Or does it mean that all children finish a full course of education? UNESCO's 2006 *EFA* (*Education for All*) *Global Monitoring Report* states that universal primary education "will be achieved only when all children have access to and complete primary education" (UNESCO, 2005, p. 48). The UN Millennium development goal likewise describes universal primary education as completion of primary education by every child.

Less has been done to address questions about the universality of educational content, which varies across countries and regions. Universal could mean that all children get the same education. Or it could mean that all children get some education, but the content differs by place, type of school, or technology of instruction. Or it could mean that there are universal principles that apply everywhere but that the implementation and specification of these principles in practice depend on the local context. If content differs, there may be some or no common elements for all children. Or it could mean that education is the same for everybody except for those children who are disabled, remote, rural, minority, or otherwise handicapped.

Conflicts of values are a fundamental difficulty in choosing educational goals. Between and within cultures, choices based on values must be made about the priority of goals. For example, values differentiate the orientation of Deborah Meier's Mission Hills School (described in Chapter 13, this volume) to prepare children for democracy from the orientation of Mallam Bala Ahmed's Qur'anic school (Chapter 6, this volume) to inculcate traditional moral values, and values differentiate both of these from the orientation of Kai-ming Cheng's proposal (Chapter 2, this volume) to prepare students for global commerce.

One of the most difficult questions posed at the beginning of this introduction is: How should the quality of decisions about educational goals be evaluated? To amplify slightly, by what process, using what criteria, and over what time span could one decide whether a society is better off adopting one set of educational goals versus another? Rothstein and Jacobsen (Chapter 17, this volume) find a large discrepancy between what people in the United States currently say they want from public schools and what federal education laws seem to be promoting. But who is to say which alternative set of educational goals for the public schools is better for the United States to pursue in the long run? Suppose I have my prejudices about the goals of education and you have different prejudices about the goals of education. What objective evidence could you and I agree in advance to consider decisive about the relative merits of our prejudices? Using what information and by what process could you and I and others collaboratively design educational goals that are superior to those favored by my prejudices and by yours? The educational goals that are best for the United States may turn out to depend on the educational goals adopted elsewhere in the world, for example, in Brazil, China, Japan, Saudi Arabia, or Russia; may depend on the time span chosen (what is best for the next five years may differ from what is best for the next fifty years); and may depend on who within the United States is defining "best." I have found little or no discussion of how to evaluate choices of educational goals.

Modesty requires recognition that, however desirable may be the goals chosen for education, external conditions constrain the effectiveness of any school system in realizing those goals. Case studies in this volume include a girl in a village in West Africa (reported by Beryl Levinger, Chapter 5, this volume), and a boy in the remote mountains of Pakistan (reported by Camer Vellani, Chapter 7, this volume). More generally, what basic and secondary education can hope to accomplish is constrained, Vellani recognizes, not only by the capacity learners bring to school, but also by "operational and political reasons. Chief among the former are the paucity of appropriately trained teachers and managers, adequate physical facilities, geographic access, and finance. These issues are compounded by the enormous school-age population and public perception of value, especially for girls, in underprivileged communities" (p. 102). The goals of schooling and of education broadly, no matter how wise and enlightened, are not the only factor in the ultimate effectiveness of education.

Even when it is possible to choose educational goals for today, a further difficulty is that the choice is never final and, until the world stops changing, can never be final. Even those who believe that inculcating tradition is the primary goal will have to concede, upon critical scholarly study, that traditions change in response to changing circumstances. The difficulty of adapting educational goals to changing circumstances locally and globally will never disappear. The absence of systematic attention to procedures and institutions that could facilitate changes in educational goals exacerbates the difficulty.

The next section gives a brief overview of some historical highlights in thinking about educational goals. The section after that reviews ideas about the goals of basic and secondary education proposed by the following chapters of this book.

HISTORICAL PERSPECTIVES ON THE GOALS OF EDUCATION

The following survey of the history of thought on educational goals is necessarily superficial and incomplete because it must be brief. This survey shows that many of this book's authors are picking up threads with a long history. Up to the middle of the twentieth century, the goals of education, especially in the West, shifted gradually and incompletely from a focus on elites to a focus on all citizens (initially narrowly defined by gender and race), and then nominally to all children, although different children continue to receive very disparate levels of education. The major changes were, not surprisingly, driven by changes outside of educational systems: the rise of nation-states in Europe, the rise of democracy in North America, the widespread demand for skilled labor associated with the Industrial Revolution, and the availability of cheap books and newspapers as a result of the invention and diffusion of printing. As the need to educate more people grew in the United States and Europe, the institutional model of education by means of scheduled and graded classes in schools largely locked into nationally or locally prescribed curricula triumphed over earlier models. Political and economic interests usually dominated the goals of schooling.

Ancient Perspectives

People have been worrying about the purposes of education for at least 2,500 years, from the times of the Buddha, Confucius, and Plato until today (Bailey, 1976; Curtis and Boultwood, 1977). Often commentators espoused one view and neglected or dismissed all others. Beliefs about the purposes of education influenced who was educated and how education was offered.

The nominal purpose of education for Plato (approx. 427 BCE–approx. 347 BCE) in *The Republic* was knowledge of the good. Education, Plato wrote, aimed to remove the veil from people's eyes so that they could see the reality of pure ideas. Plato's educational vision was not universal. Not everyone was supposed to receive an education, and no educational content was common to all who were supposed to be educated. Education fitted people for their class. The guardians, or the philosopher-kings, received one kind of education, the soldiers another, and the citizens a third. The slaves did not receive an education. The prescribed education had the political or civic purpose of creating the city-state Plato thought perfect. The discrepancy found in Plato's *Republic* between the announced purpose of education and the effective purpose the prescribed education serves is an early instance of a discrepancy that persists to today.

According to Plato's *Republic*, primary education for the guardians lasted until age twenty. Primary education included basic intellectual development, extensive physical training on the Spartan model, and musical performance to develop the sense of harmony and proportion in the individual. Secondary education continued to age fifty, covering first arithmetic, geometry, and theoretical (not observational) astronomy; then philosophy and apprenticeship in governance. The people who rose to the top in these areas became the guardians, who governed the country. Those who did not rise to the top became the soldiers. For Plato, it was important to censor all arts, because poetry and drama could mislead people through stories about the passions and revenges of the gods; the models created by these stories were not useful for government. Plato's argument in favor of state censorship of the arts reveals clearly his political mission for education. Because men and women did not differ in their capacity for guardianship, even though they differed in their capacity to be soldiers, future guardians received equal education regardless of gender.[4]

Confucius (551 BCE–479 BCE), whose influence on Chinese thought was comparable to that of Socrates and Plato on Western thought, regarded morality as the most important subject of education (Zalta, 2006). In addition to morality, he taught proper speech, government, and the refined arts (ritual, music, archery, chariot riding, calligraphy, and computation). Natural understanding was not sufficient to learn any subject; long and careful study was required. Study consisted of imitating the words and deeds of a good teacher familiar with past ways and ancient practices. Confucius was willing to teach any eager and tireless student regardless of social origin or standing. In the millennia since Confucius emphasized right behavior and transmitting the heritage of the past, these themes have recurred in subsequent discussions of educational goals in all parts of the world.

Buddhist monasteries in India and China served as schools, centers of higher learning, and refuges from persecution during the early centuries of the Buddhist religion (400 BCE–800 CE). Women and untouchables were permitted to join these Buddhist communities and to receive instruction there. Enlightenment was to be attained by means of the Middle Way between self-indulgent sensual pleasure and pointless self-torture. Enlightenment consisted in knowing the four Truths. The fourth Truth was a program of training required to obtain an understanding of all of the Truths. This program, which may be viewed as the educational agenda of Buddhism, consisted of the Noble Eightfold Path: right views or right understanding, right intention or right thought, right speech, right action, right livelihood, right effort, right mindfulness, and right concentration. This essentially ethical training required giving up a household life in favor of residence in a strictly regulated monastery. Although anyone, male or female of any caste, could aspire to enlightenment, only the monks and nuns of the monasteries were seen as having taken the necessary steps to achieve it. This educational system appeared to be open to all in principle but was elitist in practice.

Early Western Perspectives on the Goals of Education

Western perspectives have come to have a dominating influence in many, though not all, parts of the world. With the decline of feudalism, Protestant Prussia and Catholic Austria initiated universal education as a consequence of the rise of the concept of the individual (Salganik and Provasnik, Chapter 20, this volume). The leaders of the Protestant Reformation and the Catholic Counter-Reformation in the sixteenth century sought to use schools to train their subjects to save their own souls and to be loyal to the state of their own volition. The goal of education was indoctrination in religious dogma that would generate piety and loyalty. After the end of the wars of religion, the religious importance of the state-supported schools declined and the political importance increased. States increasingly viewed universal education as an instrument to produce citizens with the motivation and skills required to serve the purposes of the state (initially militarily; more recently, economically). For further elaboration of the history, see Benavot and Resnik (2006), Corrales (2006), and Rothstein and Jacobsen (Chapter 17, this volume).

Early Western treatises on education reveal changing views of the purposes of education, from suiting students to the tasks of their class to preparing young adults for the workforce, from instilling moral and civic virtues in individuals to promoting democracy. All of these purposes continue to be present in discussions of educational goals today.

The English philosopher John Locke (1632–1704) argued that education should further the knowledge and morals useful for both the pupil and the community. Locke shared Plato's assumption that different kinds of education were appropriate for different social classes. Locke's two later books on education described education for the elite and education for the working classes. His 1693 volume, entitled *Some Thoughts Concerning Education*, collected letters to a friend in England about how to educate the friend's son. Locke suggested that elite education was for boys, not girls, and that good morals and good manners were more important than knowledge. Any knowledge taught should be usable and practical. As there were no schools at the time, instruction was by tutors, with the involvement of parents. In *On Working Schools* (1697), Locke wrote that education should teach children of the masses to work, and to become useful and God-fearing people not dependent on charity so that they would not have to be supported by the upper classes.[5]

Some early American thinkers, following Locke, included moral and civic purposes among the goals of education as well as the fundamental skills of reading and computation. Thomas Jefferson (1743–1826), for example, specified the objects of primary education in his 1818 *Report of the Commissioners for the University of Virginia*:

> The objects of this primary education . . . would be,
>   To give to every citizen the information he needs for the transaction of his own business;
>   To enable him to calculate for himself, and to express and preserve his ideas, his contracts and accounts, in writing;
>   To improve, by reading, his morals and faculties;
>   To understand his duties to his neighbors and country, and to discharge with competence the functions confided to him by either;

To know his rights; to exercise with order and justice those he retains; to choose with discretion the fiduciary of those he delegates; and to notice their conduct with diligence, with candor, and judgment;

And, in general, to observe with intelligence and faithfulness all the social relations under which he shall be placed.

To instruct the mass of our citizens in these, their rights, interests and duties, as men and citizens, being then the objects of education in the primary schools, whether private or public, in them should be taught reading, writing and numerical arithmetic, the elements of mensuration, (useful in so many callings,) and the outlines of geography and history. (p. 434 of the printed version)

In this report, "citizen" referred only to white males. Only citizens who owned enough property could vote at the time.

For Horace Mann (1796–1859), who promoted public education in Massachusetts before the Civil War, the "common school" had a purpose beyond teaching morals and basic knowledge. Mann saw the common school as an instrument to unify the diversity of Americans, create social harmony and promulgate common, non-sectarian values (Cremin, 1961). He thought that the schools would promote social harmony if state legislatures and local boards of education, rather than professional educators, assumed political control over the schools. Mann advocated putting control in lay hands because he believed that the public should be entrusted with the task of defining what would be taught in the common schools. He rejected private tutoring of individuals, as Locke had recommended for the elite of England. For Mann, the goal of unifying Americans could be achieved only by bringing together heterogeneous students in common schools. Mann recognized differences among children in interests and abilities and advised that the lessons be adapted to such differences. To reconcile values of individuality with teaching children in groups, Mann called for self-control and self-discipline. Teaching children self-discipline was the common school's way to prepare its students for freedom.

By 1860, the majority of states in the United States had public school systems. Free public education had been extended to secondary schools in a few states like Massachusetts, New York and Pennsylvania.

Educational reformers and leaders after the Civil War were guided by William Torrey Harris (1835–1909), superintendent of the St. Louis public schools, United States Commissioner of Education, founder of the *Journal of Speculative Philosophy*, and devotee of the German philosopher Georg Hegel. Harris conceived a purpose for common education even grander than Mann's aim of social harmony. Harris saw the public school as the means of enabling all people to participate in civic and civilized life, a life of order, self-discipline, civic loyalty, and respect for private property (Cremin, 1961).

Harris's schools confirmed a social order that Mann helped create and shape. Elementary schools were to stress discipline and orderly behavior while giving mastery of the "five windows of the soul," as Harris called them: mathematics, geography, literature and art, grammar, and history. High schools and colleges were to concentrate on mathematics, languages, and the classics. The desired final product was a reasoning person who exercised freedom in the context of his own civilization (Cremin, 1961). Harris emphasized order over freedom, work over play, effort over interest, prescription over election; he emphasized regularity, silence, and industry as the foundations of civil order. He strongly resisted demands for vocational education and training for trade, setting the stage for the protests and educational reforms of the succeeding generation.

Vocational skills became an aim of education in some institutions, despite Harris. The Philadelphia Centennial Exposition of 1876 emphasized the relation between education and the progress of the nation (Cremin, 1961). An exhibit to demonstrate the teaching of the mechanical arts in the instructional workshops of the Moscow Imperial Technical School caught the attention of John D. Runkle, then president of the Massachusetts Institute of Technology, who saw in it "the philosophical key to all industrial education" (Cremin, 1961, p. 25). By August 1876, the trustees of MIT established a School of Mechanic Arts for manual training of future workers in industry.

Calvin M. Woodward of Washington University, St. Louis, adopted, generalized, and abstracted the ideas from Moscow and MIT. He created the Manual Training School of Washington University in 1879 as a three-year secondary program that combined mental skills (mathematics, drawing, science, languages, history, literature) and manual skills (carpentry, wood turning, patternmaking, iron chipping and filing, forge work, brazing and soldering, and bench and machine work in metals). The emphasis was on education and principles rather than production and narrow skill. Woodward was critical of the existing educational system that trained only for the learned professions and neglected the working classes. In a famous phrase, Woodward urged schools: "Put the whole boy in school" (Cremin, 1961, p. 28). The slogan echoed not only in the United States but throughout Latin America through the reporting and writing on educational theory and pedagogy of José Martí (1853–1895), leader of the Cuban independence movement of the late 1800s (Martí, 1979).

In the United States, opponents (with Harris) and proponents (with Woodward) debated the desirability of manual training hotly within the National Education Association. Meanwhile, manual training generalized to home-making in high school and to arts and crafts in elementary school (Cremin, 1961). A parallel conflict developed at the end of the nineteenth and beginning of the twentieth century. The National Association of Manufacturers denounced organized labor's opposition to trade education, while the American Federation of Labor favored apprenticeship under union control and opposed, initially, the mass training of competitors for union jobs as a result of cooperative arrangements between manufacturers and school administrators. But from 1910 onward, the Federation proposed a bill for federal support of secondary-school instruction and teacher training in agriculture, home economics, and the trades. If vocational training would be offered, the Federation wanted to be involved in determining how it was offered.

From its founding in Philadelphia in 1857 to the end of World War I, the National Education Association was the meeting place and forum for leaders of American education from universities, colleges, academies, normal schools, and public primary schools, without distinction by level.[6] The National Education Association's 1918 report, *Cardinal Principles of Secondary Education,* was supported by representatives of the entire educational system. It listed seven aims: (a) health; (b) command of fundamental processes; (c) worthy home membership; (d) vocation; (e) civic education; (f) worthy use of leisure; and (g) ethical character. One twenty-first-century commentator wrote that this report "would become one of the most influential education documents of the twentieth century." Another wrote: "The downfall and undoing of education in America can be said to have commenced upon the release and implementation of the Cardinal Principles here set forth and submitted for your disapproval." At least in definition, if not in reality, the universal educational system in the United States came to embrace goals for work and for home, and for moral, intellectual, and civic life.

The leading educational thinker of the United States during the first half of the twentieth century was John Dewey (1859–1952), founder of the Laboratory School at the University of Chicago and author of *The School and Society* (1899) and *Democracy and Education* (1916), among other influential works. Dewey, elected honorary life president of the National Education Association in 1932, believed that education could embrace multiple and changing aims as required by a changing society. Like Socrates as reported by Plato, Dewey rejected authoritarian teaching methods. Contrary to Plato, Dewey's philosophy of instrumentalism held that truth has no reality apart from human purposes but is an instrument humans use to solve their problems. For Dewey, the problems that affect most people have educational priority: "The things which are socially most fundamental, that is, which have to do with experience in which the widest groups share, are the essentials. The things which represent the needs of specialized groups and technical pursuits are secondary" (Dewey, 1916, p. 225). Dewey devoted Chapter 8 of *Democracy and Education* to pointing out "the futility of trying to establish the aim of education—some one final aim which subordinates all others to itself" (p. 225).

> [S]ince general aims are but prospective points of view from which to survey the existing conditions and estimate their possibilities, we might have any number of them, all consistent with one another. As [a] matter of fact, a large number have been stated at different times, all having

great local value. For the statement of aim is a matter of emphasis at a given time. And we do not emphasize things which do not require emphasis . . . a given epoch or generation tends to emphasize in its conscious projections just the things which it has least of in actual fact (p. 225).

Some Recent Perspectives on the Goals of Education

In the second half of the twentieth century, the rise of international institutions concerned with primary and secondary education led to confrontations between Western educational thinking and the goals and values of some non-Western societies. The results were sometimes friction at points of contact and sometimes reluctance to engage in contact where friction would be expected to follow, especially in international institutions governed by consensus. These cross-cultural contacts stimulated some people to desire that education prepare people to deal with cross-cultural contacts and conflicts.

When international institutions did espouse educational goals, the goals were sometimes stated at a level of abstraction insufficient to guide action. I now examine this process in greater detail.

Carl Ransom Rogers (1902–1987), a theologian turned clinical and educational psychologist, was influenced by the writings of John Dewey. In 1969, with explicit reference to the atmosphere of crisis in education produced by widespread conflicts over the Vietnam War, he described the goal of education as giving learners the capacity to adapt to continual change and to learn under conditions of freedom. He states his view of the goal of education in terms of the individual and of the society:

> Here then is my theoretical model of the person who emerges from therapy or from the best of education, the individual who has experienced optimal psychological growth—a person functioning freely in all the fullness of his organismic potentialities; a person who is dependable in being realistic, self-enhancing, socialized, and appropriate in his behavior; a creative person, whose specific formings of behavior are not easily predictable; a person who is ever changing, ever developing, always discovering himself and the newness in himself in each succeeding moment of time. Let me stress, however, that what I have described is a person who does not exist. . . . What I have described is my version of the goal in its "pure" form (p. 295).

At the social level, Rogers wrote, "The goal of education must be to develop a society in which people can live more comfortably with *change* than with *rigidity*. In the coming world the capacity to face the new appropriately is more important than the ability to know and repeat the old" (p. 295). This perspective contrasts diametrically with that of Confucius.

Other recent definitions of educational goals have focused on the intellectual, moral, and physical characteristics of the individuals shaped by the ideal education. Charles Slater (2005) proposed that students (and teachers, parents, administrators, and staff) should be: (a) readers of literature; (b) poets whose words envision new ways of being; (c) writers who reflect thoughtfully; (d) problem solvers who can use mathematics; (e) observers who sense the wonder of science; (f) citizens who study history and take action; (g) speakers of at least two languages who cross cultural borders; (h) workers who can create with their hands and use technology; (i) artists who sculpt, draw, or paint; (j) musicians who sing or play an instrument; (k) athletes who exercise for a lifetime; and (l) leaders who recognize the moral dimension.

The goals of Rogers and Slater touched tangentially on the role of education in promoting cross-cultural understanding. That role was stressed above others when educational goals were discussed internationally. The Convention on the Rights of the Child, which entered into force (in United Nations' language) in 1990, proposed educational obligations in article 28 and educational goals in article 29. All countries of the world have adopted the Convention on the Rights of the Child by ratification, accession, or succession, except Somalia and the United States of America, which signed but had not ratified it as of 9 June 2004.[7] The Convention calls for universal primary education and encourages the development of "different forms of secondary education, including general and vocational education." It also details the aims of education to which participating states have agreed:

(a) The development of the child's personality, talents and mental and physical abilities to their fullest potential;
(b) The development of respect for human rights and fundamental freedoms, and for the principles enshrined in the Charter of the United Nations;
(c) The development of respect for the child's parents, his or her own cultural identity, language and values, for the national values of the country in which the child is living, the country from which he or she may originate, and for civilizations different from his or her own;
(d) The preparation of the child for responsible life in a free society, in the spirit of understanding, peace, tolerance, equality of sexes, and friendship among all peoples, ethnic, national and religious groups and persons of indigenous origin;
(e) The development of respect for the natural environment (United Nations, 1990, article 29).

However desirable these aims may appear to some eyes, their operational effect in primary and secondary education is often unclear. John Daniel, then head of the education sector at UNESCO and former rector of the Open University, wrote bluntly (Daniel, 2002):

> If declarations and exhortations alone could produce textbooks that are suffused with respect for human rights, universal values and fundamental freedoms[,] we should have got there a long time ago. Sadly, . . . Respect for human dignity and difference is in short supply in many parts of the world. UNESCO is frequently asked to prevent textbooks being vehicles for intolerance and hatred.

Textbooks in many countries present views of in-groups and out-groups that are controversial for some in-groups and some out-groups. Recent examples may be drawn from many countries, including Japan (International Movement Against All Forms of Discrimination and Racism Japan Committee, 2001; Onishi, 2006; Kyodo News, 2006), Bosnia and Hercegovina (Low-Beer, 2001), Pakistan (Ansari, 2004; Sarwar, 2004), Croatia (Kovac, 2002), and Saudi Arabia (Shea, 2006). Such problems are serious wherever they occur.

For example, in Japan, a middle school teacher "was dismissed on March 31 [2006] from her position at a public school run by Tokyo's Chiyoda Ward for describing a member of the Tokyo Metropolitan Assembly and a history text publisher as 'history distorters' last year. . . . The teacher believes remarks by the assembly member and the history textbook contradict the government's recognition of Japan's wartime aggression, and that telling her students about them was therefore not inappropriate" (Kyodo News, 2006).

In another example, according to a report issued in May 2006 (summarized by Shea and introduced by Ackerman, 2006),

> . . . a study conducted in 2003 by former Saudi judge Sheikh Abd Al-'Aziz Al-Qassem and Saudi author and journalist Ibrahim Al-Sakran, . . . examined three curricula for Saudi middle and high schools—*Al-Hadith*, a general curriculum on Islamic traditions, *Al-Fiqh*, a curriculum on matters of religious law and ritual, and *Al-Tawhid*, a curriculum on matters of belief. This study was presented at the Second Forum for National Dialogue, held in Saudi Arabia in late December 2003 under the patronage of then-Crown Prince Abdallah Ibn Abd Al-'Aziz and published early the following year. It noted that the Kingdom's religious studies curriculum "encourages violence toward others, and misguides the pupils into believing that in order to safeguard their own religion, they must violently repress and even physically eliminate the 'other'" (p. 8).

On May 18, 2006, the Saudi foreign minister, Prince Saud Al-Faisal, in a joint appearance in Washington, DC, with Secretary of State Condoleezza Rice, told journalists that Saudi Arabia had overhauled its textbooks. However, the Shea–Ackerman (2006) review of twelve textbooks[8] for Islamic studies published by the Ministry of Education in Saudi Arabia and apparently in use during the 2005–2006 school year in Saudi Arabia and in Saudi-supported Islamic academies in other countries (including the United States) found that

> . . . the Saudi government continues to propagate an ideology of hate toward the "unbeliever," which includes Christians, Jews, Shiites, Sufis, Sunni Muslims who do not follow Wahhabi doctrine, Hindus, atheists and others. . . . We do not know with certainty what is taught on a daily basis in the Saudi schools. What we know is what these textbooks contain (Ackerman, 2006, pp. 8–9).

According to two American observers of Saudi Arabia (Bronson and Coleman, 2005), "over the longer term nothing will benefit U.S.–Saudi relations more than tackling educational reform." They referred to educational reform in Saudi Arabia. But these problems are limited neither to Saudi Arabia nor to Islam, nor are they universal in all parts of Saudi society or all parts of Islam.

In her 1961 doctoral dissertation at Saint Louis University, a Jesuit university, Sister Rose Thering[9] found that Catholic textbooks widely used in United States parochial schools calumniated Jews and Judaism (Thurber, 2006). Her findings were introduced in Catholic Church councils through Augustin Cardinal Bea and contributed to the Vatican's pronouncement *Nostra Aetate* (Declaration on the Relation of the Church to Non-Christian Religions) on October 28, 1965:

> . . . what happened in [Christ's] passion cannot be charged against all the Jews, without distinction, then alive, nor against the Jews of today. Although the Church is the new people of God, the Jews should not be presented as rejected or accursed by God, as if this followed from the Holy Scriptures. . . . Furthermore, in her rejection of every persecution against any man, the Church, mindful of the patrimony she shares with the Jews and moved not by political reasons but by the Gospel's spiritual love, decries hatred, persecutions, displays of anti-Semitism, directed against Jews at any time and by anyone.[10]

This pronouncement called for the reversal of the Church's then-standard teaching of hostility toward Jews, a reversal that required substantial rethinking within the Church and among some of its followers (Carroll, 2001, pp. 41, 568, and elsewhere).

Like the Convention on the Rights of the Child, the report to UNESCO of the International Commission on Education for the Twenty-first Century, *Learning: The Treasure Within* (henceforth the Delors report; Delors, et al., 1996), affirms the role that education should play in promoting cross-cultural understanding. The report was chaired by Jacques Delors, former President of the European Commission (1985–1995) and former French Minister of Economy and Finance. Its opening chapter asserts:

> We must be guided by the Utopian aim of steering the world towards greater mutual understanding, a greater sense of responsibility and greater solidarity, through acceptance of our spiritual and cultural differences. Education, by providing access to knowledge for all, has precisely this universal task of helping people to understand the world and to understand others (Delors, et al., 1996, p. 34).

The report describes "four pillars of learning":

- learning to know, by combining a sufficiently broad general knowledge with the opportunity to work in depth on a small number of subjects. This also means learning to learn, so as to benefit from the opportunities education provides throughout life.
- learning to do, in order to acquire not only an occupational skill but also, more broadly, the competence to deal with many situations and work in teams. It also means learning to do in the context of young peoples' various social and work experiences which may be informal, as a result of the local or national context, or formal, involving courses, alternating study and work.
- learning to live with others, by developing an understanding of other people and an appreciation of interdependence—carrying out joint projects and learning to manage conflicts—in a spirit of respect for the values of pluralism, mutual understanding and peace.
- learning to be, so as better to develop one's personality and be able to act with ever greater autonomy, judgment and personal responsibility. In that connection, education must not disregard any aspect of a person's potential: memory, reasoning, aesthetic sense, physical capacities and communication skills (Delors, et al., 1996, p. 37).

The Convention on the Rights of the Child and the Delors report indicate an international consensus that education could serve international political purposes, a belief shared by some scholars of education. Martha Nussbaum elaborated a "model of education for democratic citizenship" (Nussbaum, 1997; I rely here on her summary in Nussbaum, 2005, p. 4). She proposed that three capacities are essential for such citizenship: first, "the capacity for critical examination of oneself and one's traditions"; second, "an ability [for children] to see themselves as not simply citizens of some local region or group but also, and above all, as human beings bound to all other human beings by ties of recognition and concern"; and third, "narrative imagination . . . to think what it might be like to be in the shoes of a person different from oneself, to be an intelligent reader of that person's story, and to understand the emotions and wishes and desires that someone so placed might have" (p. 7).

As Nussbaum pointed out, each of these capacities is related to the idea of freedom, a key to successful democratic societies:

> At the heart of all three . . . capacities is the idea of freedom: the freedom of the child's mind to engage critically with tradition; the freedom to imagine citizenship in both national and world terms, and to negotiate multiple allegiances with knowledge and confidence; the freedom to reach out in the imagination, allowing another person's experience into oneself (2005, p. 9).

Nussbaum illustrated the desired freedoms with anecdotal comparisons of non-governmental and governmental schools in India. In some democracies, people who practice the freedoms that she advocated may be vulnerable to others with greater power who may have different interests. For example, in nominally democratic Indian villages with highly unequal distributions of wealth and power, wealthy landowners may not always respond kindly or justly to children who exercise too vocally their school-taught freedoms. How to survive with dignity and integrity in the face of hostile power may be a useful skill along with the three freedoms Nussbaum identified as appropriate for an equitable democracy.

In the United States of America, educational goals have received insufficient attention in the view of some critics, and too much thoughtless attention in the view of other critics. In 1994, President William J. Clinton signed into law the "Goals 2000: Educate America Act" (P.L. 103–227). In this law, Congress added two educational goals to six goals adopted in 1989 by President George H. W. Bush and U.S. governors. According to the Act,[11] by the year 2000:

1. All children in America will start school ready to learn.
2. The high school graduation rate will increase to at least 90 percent.
3. All students will leave grades 4, 8, and 12 having demonstrated competency over challenging subject matter including English, mathematics, science, foreign languages, civics and government, economics, the arts, history, and geography, and every school in America will ensure that all students learn to use their minds well, so they may be prepared for responsible citizenship, further learning, and productive employment in our nation's modern economy.
4. United States students will be first in the world in mathematics and science achievement.

5. Every adult American will be literate and will possess the knowledge and skills necessary to compete in a global economy and exercise the rights and responsibilities of citizenship.
6. Every school in the United States will be free of drugs, violence, and the unauthorized presence of firearms and alcohol and will offer a disciplined environment conducive to learning.
7. The nation's teaching force will have access to programs for the continued improvement of their professional skills and the opportunity to acquire the knowledge and skills needed to instruct and prepare all American students for the next century.
8. Every school will promote partnerships that will increase parental involvement and participation in promoting the social, emotional, and academic growth of children.

Richard Rothstein wrote in 1999:

> We can now declare defeat, having flunked all eight goals we were to reach by the millennium. . . . Some "Goals 2000" were ridiculous in the first place. Others required substantial resources to accomplish, and these were not provided. Still others required far more than 11 years to achieve. . . . Policy makers' lack of candor about the irresponsible way the goals were set can breed local educators' contempt for the entire standards movement.

A contrast with an excess of unachievable or inadequately funded educational goals is an absence of educational goals. According to the United States Department of Education,[12] "On Jan. 8, 2002, President George W. Bush signed the *No Child Left Behind Act of 2001* (P.L. 107–110) into law with overwhelming bipartisan support. . . . No Child Left Behind ensures accountability and flexibility as well as increased federal support for education." The announced "four pillars" of NCLB are described as "stronger accountability for results, more freedom for states and communities, proven education methods, and more choices for parents." Educator Nel Noddings (2005) criticized NCLB for its broad "failure to address, or even ask, the basic questions . . . : What are the proper aims of education? How do public schools serve a democratic society? What does it mean to educate the whole child?" (p. 8).

Noddings argued that educational policy in the United States failed to address significant social needs by not considering goals beyond literacy and numeracy. She wrote, "Unfortunately, public policy in the United States today concentrates on just one of the Cardinal Principles proposed by NEA in 1918: 'command of the fundamental processes.' Although reading and math are important, we need to promote competence in these subjects while also promoting our other aims [the NEA aims listed earlier in this chapter]" (2005, p. 11). Noddings noted that broadening educational policies to include the other NEA aims could address school-level and national concerns:

> We will not find the solution to problems of violence, alienation, ignorance, and unhappiness in increasing our security apparatus, imposing more tests, punishing schools for their failure to produce 100 percent proficiency, or demanding that teachers be knowledgeable in "the subjects they teach." Instead, we must allow teachers and students to interact as whole persons, and we must develop policies that treat the school as a whole community. The future of both our children and our democracy depend on our moving in this direction (Noddings, 2005, p. 13).

Elliot Eisner (2005), in an article immediately following that by Nel Noddings, agreed with her on the importance of holistic education. He proposed that "Our schools, teachers, and students might be a lot better off if schools embraced the idea that education means learning what to do when you don't know what to do" (p. 17). He proposed a return to the vision of education for "the whole child" provided by the progressive education movement (see Calvin Woodward's contribution, mentioned earlier). He pointed out that this approach had implications not only for methods of teaching and for content, but also for assessment. He argued that where education addressed the needs of the whole child, "assessment should . . . be concerned about more than the measurable. Not everything that matters is measurable, and not everything that is measurable matters. . . .the social and emotional life of the child needs to be as much a priority as measured academic achievement—perhaps an even greater priority" (Eisner, 2005, p. 18).

The distinguished psychologist Howard Gardner proposed his own ambitious goals for basic and secondary education (Gardner, 2001) and tertiary education (Gardner, 2005).

Many of the debates over the goals of education in the second half of the twentieth century could have taken place in the second half of the nineteenth century with only small changes. Where late nineteenth-century educational thinkers wanted public schools in America to build a tolerant civil society from the diverse immigrant and native cultures gathered in the United States, many late twentieth-century educational thinkers wanted schools, public and private, all over the world to build tolerant civil societies everywhere. The change from the nineteenth to the twentieth centuries was that the tolerance was expected to extend across wider cultural and geographical gaps. At the same time, the debates between technical education for specific skills versus education of the whole child continued. The change from the nineteenth to the twentieth centuries was that new technical skills were required, especially those related to the handling of information and the provision of services and collaborating with culturally diverse co-workers. The continuing strands of discussion from the nineteenth and twentieth centuries are reflected in the chapters in this book.

PERSPECTIVES ON THE GOALS OF EDUCATION FROM THE UNIVERSAL BASIC AND SECONDARY EDUCATION (UBASE) PROJECT

The chapters in this volume were commissioned to address the question "What should be the goals of basic and secondary education of high quality?" Diverse themes emerged in the answers. The chapters are organized under seven broad headings, though few of these chapters fit neatly into just one of these categories: educational goals for tomorrow's society; educational priorities in poor countries; empowering children through art and science; the special role of skepticism as a universal educational goal; educating global citizens; defining educational quality as a basis for educational policy; and perspectives on assessment and educational goals. This ordering is one of many ways of organizing these chapters. Moreover, few if any of the topics presented here are comprehensively addressed. Our purpose was to initiate an international examination of the goals of education in hopes of providing a starting point for further investigation. If this book succeeds in its aim of stimulating additional discussions of the goals of universal basic and secondary education, it is to be hoped that other, still richer ways of structuring the issues will emerge.

Educational Goals for Tomorrow's Society

Several chapters acknowledge that yesterday's goals—and yesterday's means for pursuing them—may not be appropriate for tomorrow's world. Kaiming Cheng (Chapter 2) discusses education to enable students to understand and participate gainfully in the increasingly globalized economy of the twenty-first century. For him, a principal educational goal is to enhance economic and work-related success. Cheng argues that if people are not educated for the world economy, then they are excluded from the benefits of the world economy. Education has to respond to the needs of the economy, and those needs include technical skills as well as skills in teamwork. The world economy requires students who know how to negotiate with people and how to specialize while also being aware of the bigger picture. Cheng paints a rich picture of what it takes to survive in the world economy.

Kishore Mahbubani (Chapter 3) argues that "The huge challenge for the twenty-first century will be to weave in some universal elements that will remind children all over the world that they belong to a single common humanity. . . . [O]ne key stream of Western civilization, the spirit of Socrates, could well provide some key universal threads to weave humanity together" (p. 67). Mahbubani here suggests that the pedagogical methods of Socrates—the questioning, the critical reasoning—may be a more important legacy for education in the twenty-first century than the political and philosophical agenda of Socrates' scribe and interpreter, Plato.

Mahbubani's perspective on China's principal educational need in the coming century—namely, cosmopolitanism rather than Sinocentrism—complements and reinforces (but for very different reasons) the emphasis of Kai-ming Cheng on giving all students, including Chinese, the capacity to engage productively in the world economy. Mahbubani suggests that changing the methods of the Chinese educational system is essential, not because it will better prepare students for the world economy, but because it will promote international understanding. Mahbubani suggests that "Traditional Islamic education has suffered from the same handicap as traditional Chinese education: an emphasis on rote learning. Just as China will have to rise to the challenge of the twenty-first century by introducing a heavier emphasis on questioning and critical reasoning in its educational system, the Islamic world will have to do the same" (p. 68). Mahbubani warns "educational policymakers that if we enter the twenty-first century on auto-pilot using existing conventional wisdom, we may be delivering a prescription for both misunderstanding and disharmony" (p. 71).

William K. Cummings (Chapter 4) observes that because education on the recent Western model (with school buildings, teachers, textbooks and other equipment) has become increasingly expensive and because transnational entities failed sufficiently to share the costs of the educational models they asked the developing countries to emulate, the willingness of developing countries to accept the Western educational model with all its expenses has declined while the educational ambitions of developing countries have increased. A comparison of national educational plans in 2001 with those of 1982 shows that governments now want to eradicate illiteracy rather than merely extend literacy, want education to reduce specific inequalities (gender, regional, rural-urban, poverty, and historical injustices), view technology both as an asset for learning and as a means for social development, and emphasize promoting values through education such as democracy, religiosity, and tolerance—but also national unity and the need to counter extremism and terrorism.

Cummings envisions a future of education in which computer-assisted technology takes over many of the duties and burdens of teaching "such as the presentation of materials, the facilitation of exercises, the evaluation of student performance, and the analysis of student learning difficulties" (p. 78). He argues that "there are ways to design education that reduce dependence on the modern props of school buildings, the uniform curriculum, textbooks, trained teachers, and one-time national examinations. Focusing on the goals of education as contrasted with the modern means is the key to the elaboration of these possibilities. Educational technology opens up many of these possibilities" (p. 79).

Educational Priorities in Poor Countries

Determining educational priorities in poor countries, particularly those in Africa and South Asia, raises daunting challenges. Describing the daily struggle of a typical ten-year-old West African girl, who lives in a village 5 kilometers from the nearest school, Beryl Levinger (Chapter 5) defines an education of quality as an education that "enable[s] learners to dramatically surpass the full range of limitations imposed by the circumstances of their birth" (p. 87). Such an education is the key to disrupting cycles of poverty in developing countries. If the billion people or more who live on less than one U.S. dollar per day are to earn a living, protect their environment, contribute to family life, and be enlightened citizens, they

> will need the instrumental skills of reading, writing, and basic computation as well as content-driven knowledge in the natural sciences, social studies, health, and nutrition. But [their] education must also focus on . . . values, processes, and attitudes. Three building blocks that form the core of "quality education" lie within this realm[:] metacognitive skills that contribute to the transfer of knowledge and to the solution of novel problems. . . . skills that prepare learners to avail themselves of development opportunities. . . . [and] processes that add to the store of social capital in the community (pp. 84–86).

Education must enable poor children and their cities and nations to integrate into the world economy, she argues. Thus she links personal capacities and economic consequences.

Nigerian schoolmaster Bala Ahmed (Chapter 6) reports that the leadership of UNESCO and the support of international donors have redirected the aims of education toward participation in society, particularly in the workforce. Ahmed writes that the goals of universal primary and secondary education have been extended beyond reading, writing, and teaching of morals to include life skills. He mentions four specific skills: the ability to communicate in both Arabic and English; the ability to keep records of events in both Arabic and English; preparation to qualify Islamiyya primary and secondary school leavers for employment as teachers, judges, agriculturists, and in other relevant professions; and knowledge of trade and commerce.

Ahmed lists eighteen specific and pragmatic measures to ensure a basic and secondary education of high quality in Nigerian Islamiyya schools. These measures include the adoption of standard curricula, secure classrooms, hygienic bathrooms, clean drinking water, nutritious food, teacher training, and compensation. The task of meeting these prerequisites must be shared, he says, by governmental and religious authorities, parents, teachers, and local communities.

Camer Vellani (Chapter 7) describes an encounter he had with a seventeen-year-old boy from Pakistan's North West Frontier Province. The boy perceived insurmountable political, economic, and cultural barriers to his professional advancement, despite having completed ten years of schooling. Acknowledging the powerful influence of social environment, Vellani looks beyond economic circumstance and stresses the importance of nurturing learning ability, a crucial property of the brain developed during infancy and early childhood, when it is affected by nutrition, health, and the stimuli provided by the social environment (Young, 2002). In one study of the development of 1,200 children aged zero to three years in urban and rural Sindh (B. Iqbal, 2003, unpublished data), the proportion of children in their first, second, and third years of life who had delayed psychomotor development increased from 14 percent to 22 percent to 37 percent, associated statistically with various elements of the social environment. Since psychomotor performance reflects development of the brain and nervous system, the delay in development of higher orders of function of the nervous system in almost two children in five by the age of three years is astonishing.

Vellani proposes the goals of basic and secondary education broadly as an understanding of "one's . . . identity in a global context" (p. 99), acquisition of "attitudes and skills that are relevant to responsible citizenship" (p. 99), and moral reasoning. He concludes that "perspectives on the purposes of education should be broadened to consider a holistic, interdependent view of human development, encompassing early childhood and development of society. No investment in formal education alone will reverse long-term limitations in learning, health, and behavior that are established in the early stages of life as a result of insufficient child nurture" (p. 103).

Vimala Ramachandran (Chapter 8) examines the inadequate access to and quality of primary and secondary schooling in India. She argues that educational quality is at the heart of India's national struggle for equality and justice. She writes, "There is an urgent need to re-imagine education, overhaul the system and link education to life, livelihood, peace and social justice. While striving for equality, the education system should respond to aspirations and opportunities while enhancing choices. . . . The education system should have the depth as well as the range to span different worlds that people live in and also create bridges" (p. 108).

Empowering Children through Art and Science

Many educators have argued for a long time that education in the arts can be a very important ingredient of an education as a working example of integrating knowledge, skills, attitudes, and values (Eisner, 2002; Read, 1943). Madrazo (Chapter 9) presents one example of how it has been possible to bring the goals of integral education with the *dia* (Development of Intelligence through Art) program to more than thirteen thousand classrooms in Mexican schools in the last decade, providing teachers with useful and specific tools as they develop the necessary didactic abilities to become mediators who can focus on their students' affective, social, communicative, and cognitive abilities. Because all humans have an immense inner potential to feel and think, to integrate and balance these two fundamental elements, art is an excellent stimulus for human development in other contexts (besides schools). Madrazo writes, "Since 1999 we have worked with underprivileged groups such as life-term prisoners, children with Down syndrome, indigenous communities, migrant workers and homeless children. In these spaces, new questions emerge along with new possibilities for mediating through art" (p. 123).

My Chapter 10 emphasizes that nurture is physical, intellectual, and emotional. I propose that basic and secondary education should support making a bigger pie (better technology), bringing fewer forks to the table (lower fertility, rational consumption), and practicing better manners (less violence, less corruption, fewer barriers to economic rationality, more equity within and between societies, and more acceptance of other societies and cultures) by cultivating the intellectual and emotional capacities of all children. On the intellectual side, sophisticated primary and secondary education in the arts and sciences offers substantive, developmental, civic, and personal benefits. On the emotional side, love is a crucial ingredient of the inputs, processes, and results of education. In agreement with the recommendations of Charfi and Redissi, I stress the importance of providing children with at least two different perspectives—for example, two languages, intimacy with the arts and sciences, differing religious traditions—to give depth and contrast to children's understanding of the world. The educational importance of binocular vision precedes and extends beyond formal education.

The Special Role of Skepticism as a Universal Educational Goal

James Carroll (Chapter 11) distinguishes two meanings of universal: one imperial and imposing, the other inclusive, tolerant, and endlessly skeptical even of itself. His chapter shows that conflicts arising from claims of universality have afflicted the Abrahamic religions for not less than the last two millennia and recognizes that some of the same conflicts arise with respect to the pursuit of universal education. To avoid "the pitfalls that that have turned previous efforts at 'universal' education into exercises, however nobly defined, of imperial triumphalism" (p. 144), Carroll writes, it is necessary to acknowledge that the ideal of universality is itself problematic. Such an approach to universal education would be "consistently self-critical, aware of the implications of power," and focused on teaching "intellectual humility" (p. 144).

Mohamed Charfi and Hamadi Redissi (Chapter 12) describe the struggle over educational goals in the Arab-Muslim world. In balancing secular versus religious values in the curriculum of the Arab world, they argue that education must enable people to read their sacred texts along with the texts of Freud and Darwin, to think critically about the texts and the history of their own culture, and to incorporate into their own worldview the world-views of others and initiate a conversation. They write that if a society is going to coexist with other societies, critical thinking about one's own and other cultures is necessary. They ask that students become citizens of their own culture and of the world.

Deborah Meier (Chapter 13), an outspoken critic of state-mandated standards and tests, argues that the purpose of basic and secondary education is to prepare students to use their minds for democratic governance, specifically "to develop in our young strong democratic habits of heart and mind—appropriate intellectual skepticism and informed empathy for others unlike ourselves" (p. 178). With John Dewey, she recommends: "[E]very potential voter needs the education that was once reserved for the ruling classes . . . people [should] see school as a tool for enlarging the intellectual . . . life of our citizens, as, above all, the place where everything must be justified by how it prepares people to be decision-makers in the larger society, how it allows them to join the debate on the future of their community, state, nation and planet. . . . That most of these habits may be useful in the job market is at best a lucky coincidence. If it fails the latter test, then we need to insist that K–12 schooling is not the place to make it up" (p. 177). ". . . The litmus test of each and every reform is whether it provides more, not fewer, opportunities for the adults who surround kids to be taken seriously, to exercise judgment, to show off knowledge in public settings, and to bear witness to the problems of democratic decision making. The litmus test of good reforms is whether they encourage respect for the power of one's own and other people's ideas" (p. 179).

Educating Global Citizens

Globalization's consequences for education are not only economic and pedagogical, as Cheng and Mahbubani emphasize, but also political and social. Fernando Reimers argues that schools should teach global civility: to tolerate and appreciate individual and cultural diversity and to settle conflicts through peaceful negotiation. For Reimers (Chapter 14), global civility competes with three other contenders to be the principal goal of education: economic competitiveness, nationalism, and local relevance (religious, cultural, or political). Global civility renders its adherents vulnerable to those who are more belligerent and aggressive unless this goal is promoted universally or nearly so. Hence, the cooperation of an appropriate transnational organization would facilitate the widespread simultaneous adoption of global civility as a goal. UNESCO, originally chartered to promote the teaching of global civility, instead devoted its energies to promoting literacy and access to school. The World Bank's agenda for education is to promote economic competitiveness and reduce poverty, not to promote global civility. A promising avenue is to scale up successful local efforts that now educate children for global civility. By building sufficient grassroots support among individuals and institutions, it may eventually be possible to engage the support of governments and international institutions.

Marcelo M. Suárez-Orozco (Chapter 15) proposes a program of research to improve understanding of how to prepare children to engage globalization. Like Cheng, he focuses on the effects of globalization on education, but emphasizes the cultural as much as the economic consequences of globalization. He suggests that globalization requires successful children in the twenty-first century to have "(a) . . . autonomy and creativity of thought and the capacity to work with others on complex problems that often cut across disciplinary traditions; (b) the ability to communicate and understand others across cultural boundaries; and (c) the development of hybrid identities indexed by the ability to navigate across discontinuous or incommensurable linguistic and epistemic systems" (p. 208).

Suárez-Orozco calls for research on several areas of interaction between globalization and basic and secondary education. For example, migratory flows of unprecedented magnitude ". . .generate new identities and ways of belonging. How would reforming education in Arab countries be relevant to the seven million Muslims being educated in Europe today?" (p. 209).

Defining Educational Quality as a Basis for Educational Policy

Increasing access to education has been a long-standing goal of national and international agencies that fund and provide education. Access is relatively easy to define as a target, though achieving that goal has eluded the world for decades. Far more difficult, and increasingly crucial, is defining what is meant by educational quality. Mary Joy Pigozzi (Chapter 18) provides a perspective from UNESCO on the goal of improving educational quality. Each school, in her account, includes individual learners, teachers and administrators, and schools collectively constitute a system. Pigozzi spells out ten dimensions—five system-related—required for a country to provide an education of high quality for all its children. Her first five suggestions are administrative or organizational goals that are focused on learners. They include seeking out learners; responding to what the learner brings from experience and endowment; providing a safe environment; providing appropriate content; and recognizing that the processes of education are part of the learner's education. Her second five suggestions focus on the educational system. They include structuring management and administration around the learner with fair, transparent and approachable procedures implemented by responsive people; communicating educational policies to the classroom, supporting the policies by mechanisms of implementation, and coordinating educational policies with policies in other sectors of the society; facilitating changes in the education system through an enabling legislative framework; providing resources of money, human capability, and time; and monitoring educational outcomes and attuning monitoring more closely to the evolving goals of education.

Laura Salganik and Stephen Provasnik (Chapter 20) take a Western perspective elaborately developed under the auspices of the Organisation for Economic Co-operation and Development (OECD). They suggest that "a successful life and a well-functioning society" are universal goals; "a successful life" includes individual fulfillment and economic sufficiency, while "a well-functioning society" includes political and economic functioning of the society.

The OECD's project on the definition and selection of key competencies (Rychen and Salganik, 2001, 2003) asked, "What competencies do we need for a successful life and a well-functioning society?" Here, "we" refers to individuals in OECD countries, but Salganik and Provasnik argue that their conclusions apply equally to individuals in developing and transitional countries. According to the project, "Each key competency must: contribute to valued outcomes for societies and individuals; help individuals meet important demands in a wide variety of contexts; and be important not just for specialists but for all individuals" (OECD DeSeCo Project, 2005, p. 4). As defined by the OECD, "competencies [are] understood to cover knowledge, skills, attitudes and values" (OECD DeSeCo Project, 2005, p. 4).

Individuals (regardless of age, but beginning in primary school and continuing through secondary school and adulthood) should acquire competence in three broad areas. They should be able to (a) "use . . . tools for interacting effectively with the environment: both physical ones such as information technology and socio-cultural ones such as the use of language. [They] need to understand such tools well enough to adapt them for their own purposes—to use tools interactively"; (b) "engage with others . . . from a range of backgrounds . . . in heterogeneous groups"; and (c) "take responsibility for managing their own lives, situate their lives in the broader social context and act autonomously" (OECD DeSeCo Project, 2005, p. 5).

These competencies contribute to individual capability. Whether increased individual capability leads to individual fulfillment and supports societal goals of education depends on political, economic, and social circumstances. Under favorable circumstances, individual competencies are likely to contribute to economic self-sufficiency for the individual and prosperity for the society. Under unfavorable circumstances, individual competencies may conflict with national political goals (e.g., Romania under Ceausescu, the Chinese Cultural Revolution, and Prussia under militarism). A recent review of the evidence (Hannum and Buchmann, 2006) found

> . . . considerable controversy surrounding the effects of educational expansion on the democratization of societies, though expansions of primary and secondary education are likely to improve the informed citizenship of individuals. . . . democratization, perhaps more so than

other outcomes, may hinge directly on the hard-to-measure content of education. . . . the consequences of expanding universal basic and secondary education for political democratization remain an empirical question (p. 522).

George M. Ingram (Chapter 19) reviews many diverse proposals (including UNICEF's and UNESCO's) about "what is required to produce an education of quality" (p. 248). If any theme is common to all the proposals for what constitutes an education of quality, Ingram suggests, "it is the concept that education should prepare a student to be a constructive, contributing member of society by delivering a minimum quality of competence in literacy, numeracy, life skills, and problem solving. . . . Many educational systems also are expected to deliver values, but there is a wide range of differences in what those values should be" (p. 248). Ingram notes that education of high quality has yet to be defined for hard-to-reach and very poor populations.

Perspectives on Assessment and Educational Goals

Ana Carolina Letichevsky (Chapter 16) describes how evaluation is helping to improve primary and secondary education in Brazil, raising questions and challenges that apply much more broadly. Although educational evaluations originally focused on the performance of individual students, evaluation is now used to create and implement new educational policies, to estimate the proficiency of students, to improve educational processes and schools, and to justify education to society. Brazil has made strenuous efforts to use evaluations, not to punish or reward, but to aid learners in identifying their own educational strengths and educational deficiencies with a view to further learning.

Richard Rothstein and Rebecca Jacobsen (Chapter 17) examine the shortcomings of educational assessments in the United States. They compared what four samples of Americans say they want education to achieve with what the school system is being required to achieve by recent legislation. The announced goals of samples of adults, school board members, state legislators, and school superintendents were surprisingly consistent across all four groups and were much broader than basic academic skills in core subjects, such as reading, writing, mathematics, and knowledge of science and history. Most individuals surveyed gave weight to critical thinking and problem solving, social skills and work ethic, citizenship and community responsibility, physical and emotional health, the arts and literature, and preparation for skilled work that does not require a college degree. Rothstein and Jacobsen conclude, "This gap between the preferences for educational goals expressed in our survey and the educational standards established through political processes reflects a widespread policy incoherence" (p. 231). According to Rothstein and Jacobsen, schools are sacrificing

history, civics, science, the arts, literature, physical education, social studies, and civics in favor of reading and arithmetic in efforts to meet the standards imposed by the tests. They report that the sacrifice of educational
breadth is greater in schools with large proportions of poor and minority
groups than in schools for the wealthy and the white.

UNANSWERED QUESTIONS

I began with a set of questions. The chapters in this book address mainly
the first two: What should be the goals of basic and secondary education of
high quality? Which, if any, of these goals should be universal? Still mostly
unanswered are the remaining questions: What does "universal" mean?
What happens when educational goals conflict? What are the meanings
of "high quality" in basic and secondary education? Who decides these
questions, and by what process do they decide? How should the quality of
decisions about educational goals be evaluated? These questions deserve
discussion and answers.

Discussions of these questions would benefit from empirical research
into why different educational systems are more or less effective in meeting the explicit aims and purposes they have set for themselves and into
the conditions (organizational, legal, and political) that enable specific
educational goals to be met. Comparing goals, achievements, and assessments case by case, country by country, is a massive undertaking for the
future. Globally, setting targets and tracking achievements is an explicit
function of UNESCO's yearly *EFA (Education for All) Global Monitoring Report* (e.g., UNESCO, 2005). However, the targets to date have been
more concerned with enrollment, attendance, and completion of schooling
than with the aims, content, and quality of education offered.

The original proposal for the UBASE project called for an integrated
working group on the goals and assessment of efforts toward universal
education. Only discussions of assessments (Bettinger, 2006; Braun and
Kanjee, 2006; Kremer, 2006) appeared in the initial volume of the UBASE
project (Cohen, Bloom, and Malin, 2006). The present volume was organized to initiate a response to the difficult challenge of setting targets for
content and quality.

ACKNOWLEDGMENTS

This introductory essay benefited from the skilled editing of Helen A.
Curry and from the constructive comments of Sissela Bok, Rachel Bronson, Walter Feinberg, F. Gregory Gause, Claudia Madrazo, Martin Malin,
Mary Joy Pigozzi, Stephen Provasnik, Fernando Reimers, Richard Rothstein, Laura Salganik, Martin Sleeper, Camer Vellani, Rosanna Warren,

and anonymous publishers' readers. James Carroll provided helpful background. I thank the late Mr. and Mrs. William T. Golden and their family for hospitality during this work.

NOTES

1. PISA, 2006—*List of Participating Countries,* http://www.pisa.oecd.org/do cument/13/0,2340,en_32252351_32236225_33666189_1_1_1_1,00.html (accessed February 1, 2006).
2. PISA Definitions. www.pisa.oecd.org
3. Ibid.
4. For a digital version of Plato's *Republic* (Book II and Book III), see http://www.philosophypages.com/hy/2g.htm; http://www.ilt.columbia.edu/publications/Projects/digitexts/plato/the_republic/book02.html; http://www.ilt.columbia.edu/publications/Projects/digitexts/plato/the_republic/book03.html.
5. http://www.socsci.kun.nl/ped/whp/histeduc/locke/locke_intro.html; http://www.ilt.columbia.edu/publications/digitext.html
6. http://www2.nea.org/he/roots.html (accessed October, 16 2006).
7. http://www.unhchr.ch/pdf/report.pdf (accessed June 11, 2006).
8. For excerpts from *Saudi Ministry of Education Textbooks for Islamic Studies: Arabic with English Translation,* see Center for Religious Freedom of Freedom House with the Institute for Gulf Affairs (2006).
9. "Sister Rose Thering" (2006, July 19). In Wikipedia, The Free Encyclopedia, http://en.wikipedia.org/w/index.php?title=Sister_Rose_Thering&oldid=64572060 (accessed July 28, 2006).
10. See "Declaration on the Relation of the Church to Non-Christian Religions *Nostra Aetate,*" http://www.vatican.va/archive/hist_councils/ii_vatican_council/documents/vat-ii_decl_19651028_nostra-aetate_en.html (accessed July 27, 2008).
11. For Sec. 102. National Education Goals, see http://www.ed.gov/legislation/GOALS2000/TheAct/sec102.html (accessed June 24, 2008).
12. http://www.ed.gov/nclb/overview/intro/guide/guide_pg12.html#history (accessed January 4, 2006).

REFERENCES

Ackerman, Peter. 2006. "Foreword." In *Saudi Arabia's Curriculum of Intolerance: With Excerpts from Saudi Ministry of Education Textbooks for Islamic Studies,* ed. Nina Shea. Washington, DC: Center for Religious Freedom of Freedom House. http://www.hudson.org/files/publications/CRF_SaudiReport_2006.pdf.
Ansari, Massoud. 2004. "Newsline Special: Lessons in Intolerance." *Newsline,* May 1. http://www.newsline.com.pk/NewsMay2004/NewsspMay1.htm (accessed June 10, 2006).
Bailey, Stephen. 1976. *The Purposes of Education.* Bloomington, IN: Phi Delta Kappa Educational Foundation.
Benavot, Aaron, and Julia Resnik. 2006. "Lessons from the Past: A Comparative Socio-Historical Analysis of Primary and Secondary Education." In Cohen et al. 2006, 123–230. http://www.amacad.org/publications/ubase_GlobalExpansion.aspx (accessed June 4, 2006).

Bettinger, Eric. 2006. "Evaluating Educational Interventions in Developing Countries." In Cohen et al. 2006, 355–388. http://www.amacad.org/publications/braun.pdf.

Braun, Henry, and Anil Kanjee. 2006. "Using Assessment to Improve Education in Developing Countries." In Cohen et al. 2006, 303–354. http://www.amacad.org/publications/braun.pdf.

Bronson, Rachel, and Isobel Coleman. 2005. "Saudi System Is the Problem." *Dallas Morning News*, May 7. http://www.cfr.org/pub8083/rachel_bronson_isobel_coleman/saudi_system_is_the_problem.php (accessed May 14, 2005).

Carroll, James. 2001. *Constantine's Sword: The Church and The Jews: A History.* New York: Houghton Mifflin Company.

Center for Religious Freedom of Freedom House with the Institute for Gulf Affairs, ed. 2006. *Excerpts from Saudi Ministry of Education Textbooks for Islamic Studies: Arabic with English Translation.* http://www.freedomhouse.org/uploads/special_report/ArabicExcerpts.pdf.

Cohen, Joel E., David E. Bloom, and Martin B. Malin, eds. 2006. *Educating All Children: A Global Agenda.* Cambridge, MA: MIT Press.

Corrales, Javier. 2006. "Political Obstacles to Expanding and Improving Schooling in Developing Countries." In Cohen et al. 2006, 231–299. http://www.amacad.org/publications/ubase_GlobalExpansion.aspx.

Cremin, Lawrence A. 1961. *The Transformation of the School: Progressivism in American Education, 1876–1957.* New York: Alfred A. Knopf.

Curtis, Stanley J., and Myrtle E. Boultwood. 1977. *A Short History of Educational Ideas.* Slough, England: University Tutorial Press.

Daniel, John. 2002. "Wanted: Better Learning Materials and Textbooks." Opening remarks at Expert Meeting on Textbooks and Learning Materials: Components of Quality Education that can Foster Peace, Human Rights, Mutual Understanding and Dialogue. http://portal.unesco.org/education/en/ev.php-URL_ID=11416&URL_DO=DO_TOPIC&URL_SECTION=201.html (accessed June 10, 2006).

Delors, Jacques, et al. 1996. *Learning: The Treasure Within: Report to UNESCO of the International Commission on Education for the Twenty-First Century: Highlights.* Paris: UNESCO. http://www.unesco.org/delors/delors_e.pdf.

Dewey, John. 1916. "Natural Development and Social Efficiency as Aims." In *Democracy and Education.* New York: Macmillan. http://www.ilt.columbia.edu/publications/dewey.html.

Eisner, Elliot W. 2002. "The Arts and the Creation of Mind." In *What the Arts Teach and How It Shows*, 70–92. New Haven: Yale University Press. http://www.naea-reston.org/tenlessons.html (accessed June 4, 2006).

Eisner, Elliot. 2005. "Back to Whole." *Educational Leadership* 63 (1): 14–18.

Gardner, Howard. 2001. An Education for the Future: The Foundation of Science and Values. Unpublished manuscript, Harvard Graduate School of Education, Cambridge, MA. Available at http://pzweb.harvard.edu.

Gardner, Howard. 2005. "Beyond Markets and Individuals: A Focus on Educational Goals." In *Degrees of Mediocrity: Higher Education at Risk*, ed. Richard Hersh and John Merrow, 97–112. New York: Palgrave-Macmillan.

Hannum, Emily, and Claudia Buchmann. 2006. "Global Educational Expansion and Socio-Economic Development: An Assessment of Findings from the Social Sciences." In Cohen et al. 2006, 495–534. http://www.amacad.org/publications/monographs/Ubase.pdf.

International Movement Against All Forms of Discrimination and Racism. Japan Committee. 2001. "Statement Against the Approval and Adoption of Textbooks Made by the Japanese Society for History Textbook Reform, 7 August 2001, To Mr. Prime Minister Junichiro Koizumi From Kinhide Mushakoji, President,"

IMADRJC. http://www.imadr.org/tokyo/statement.textbook.html (accessed June 11, 2006).

Jefferson, Thomas. 1818. "Report of the Commissioners for the University of Virginia." [machine-readable transcription], Electronic Text Center, University of Virginia Library, 1995, from *Early history of the University of Virginia, as contained in the letters of Thomas Jefferson and Joseph C. Cabell.* The e-text comes from Appendix I: J. W. Randolph, Richmond, VA, 1856 at p. 434 of the printed version. http://etext.virginia.edu/etcbin/toccer-new2?id=JefRock. sgm&images=images/modeng&data=/texts/english/modeng/parsed&tag=publi c&part=1&division=div1.

Kovac, Vlasta. 2002. "New Study Questions Values Taught in Croatia's Textbooks." *Jewish Telegraphic Agency*, December 18.

Kremer, Michael. 2006. "Expanding Educational Opportunity on a Budget: Lessons from Randomized Evaluations." In Cohen et al. 2006, 389–412. http://www.amacad.org/publications/braun.pdf.

Kyodo News. 2006. "Middle School Teacher to Sue Tokyo Over 'Illegal' Dismissal." *Japan Times*, September 15.

Low-Beer, Ann. 2001. "Politics, School Textbooks and Cultural Identity: The Struggle in Bosnia and Hercegovina." *Paradigm* 2 (3). http://faculty.ed.uiuc. edu/westbury/Paradigm/LOW-BEER.PDF (accessed June 10, 2006).

Martí, Jose. 1979. *On Education: Articles on Educational Theory and Pedagogy,* and *Writings for Children from the Age of Gold.* Trans. E. Randall and ed. Philip S. Foner. New York: Monthly Review Press.

National Education Association. 2004. Special Education and the Individuals with Disabilities Education Act. https://www.nea.org/specialed/index.html (accessed June 4, 2006).

Noddings, Nel. 2005. "What Does It Mean to Educate the Whole Child?" *Educational Leadership* 63 (1): 8–13. http://www.ascd.org/authors/ed_lead/el200509_noddings.html.

Nussbaum, Martha C. 1997. *Cultivating Humanity: A Classical Defense of Reform in Liberal Education.* Cambridge, MA: Harvard University Press.

Nussbaum, Martha C. 2005. "Education and Democratic Citizenship: Capabilities and Quality Education." Paper delivered at the second annual conference of the Human Development Capability Association, September 14. Paris: UNESCO.

Onishi, Norimitsu. 2006. "Japan's Conservatives Push Prewar 'Virtues' in Schools." *New York Times*, June 11. http://www.nytimes.com/2006/06/11/world/asia/11tokyo.html (accessed June 13, 2006).

Organisation for Economic Cooperation and Development (OECD). No date. *PISA—The OECD Programme for International Student Assessment.* www. pisa.oecd.org (accessed January 15, 2009).

OECD Definition and Selection of Competencies: Theoretical and Conceptual Foundations (DeSeCo) Project. 2005. *The Definition and Selection of Key Competencies: Executive Summary.* http://www.oecd.org/dataoecd/47/61/35070367.pdf.

Read, Herbert. 1943. *Education through Art.* New York: Pantheon Books.

Reimers, Fernando. 2006. "Teaching Quality Matters: Pedagogy and Literacy Instruction of Poor Students in Mexico." In *International Education for the Millennium: Toward Access, Equity, and Quality*, ed. Benjamin Piper, Sarah Dryden-Peterson, and Young-Suk Kim, 195–214. Cambridge, MA: Harvard Education Press.

Rogers, Carl R. 1969. *Freedom to Learn: A View of What Education Might Become.* Columbus, OH: Charles E. Merrill.

Rothstein, Richard. 1999. "'Goals 2000' Score: Failure 8, U.S. 0." *New York Times*, December 22. Republished under the headline "'Goals 2000' Scorecard: Failure

Pitches a Shutout." http://www.epi.org/content.cfm/webfeat_lessons19991222 (accessed May 25, 2006).

Rychen, Dominique S., and Laura H. Salganik, eds. 2001. *Defining and Selecting Key Competencies.* Göttingen, Germany: Hogrefe & Huber.

Rychen, Dominique S., and Laura H. Salganik, eds. 2003. *Key Competencies for a Successful Life and a Well-Functioning Society.* Göttingen, Germany: Hogrefe & Huber.

Sarwar, Beena. 2004. "Jehad and the Curriculum." *Countercurrents.org*, April 3, http://www.countercurrents.org/ipk-sarwar030404.htm (accessed June 10, 2006).

Shea, Nina. 2006. "This Is a Saudi Textbook (After the Intolerance Was Removed)." *Washington Post,* May 21. http://www.washingtonpost.com/wp-dyn/content/article/2006/05/19/AR2006051901769.html (accessed June 10, 2006).

Slater, Charles L. 2005. "What Does It Mean to Be an Educated Person?" *The School Administrator.* http://www.aasa.org/publications/saarticledetail.cfm?ItemNumber=2894&snItemNumber=950.

Stout, David. 2007. "Justices Loosen Restrictions on Campaign Ads." *New York Times,* July 25. http://www.nytimes.com/2007/06/25/washington/25cnd-scotus.html?hp=&adxnnl=1&adxnnlx=1182823652-eMODBJn9PH2YNEmSCrz/DA.

Thurber, Jon. 2006. "Obituary of Sister Rose Thering, 85; Catholic Scholar Battled Anti-Semitism." *Los Angeles Times,* May 9.

United Nations, Office of the High Commissioner for Human Rights. 1990. Convention on the Rights of the Child, Adopted and opened for signature, ratification and accession by General Assembly resolution 44/25 of 20 November 1989, entry into force 2 September 1990, in accordance with article 49. http://www.unhchr.ch/html/menu3/b/k2crc.htm.

United Nations, Office of the High Commissioner for Human Rights. 2004. *Status of Ratifications of the Principal International Human Rights Treaties as of 09 June 2004.* http://www.unhchr.ch/pdf/report.pdf (accessed June 4, 2006).

United States Department of the Interior, Bureau of Education: Commission on the Reorganization of Secondary Education, Appointed by the National Education Association. 1918. *Cardinal Principles of Secondary Education.* Washington, DC: United States Government Printing Office, 1928. http://tmh.floonet.net/articles/cardprin.html (accessed July 28, 2006).

UNESCO. 2005. *EFA Global Monitoring Report 2006.* Paris: UNESCO.

Young, Mary E., ed. 2002. From Early Child Development to Human Development. *Proceedings of a World Bank Conference on Investing in Our Children's Future.* Washington DC: World Bank. http://www-wds.worldbank.org/external/default/WDSContentServer/WDSP/IB/2002/04/26/000094946_02041304004942/Rendered/PDF/multi0page.pdf.

Zalta, E. N. 2006. "Confucius." *Stanford Encyclopedia of Philosophy.* http://plato.stanford.edu/entries/confucius/.

Part II
Educational Goals for Tomorrow's Society

2   Education for All, but for What?

Kai-ming Cheng

PREAMBLE: QUESTIONS

"Education for all" has been a world mission since the 1960s. There were, in the early 1960s, visionary targets of achieving universal nine-year education in twenty years.[1] The failure in achieving such goals prompted the Jomtien meeting in 1990, which revitalized the international community's attention to the education of our next generation, which is so dear to the general advancement of humankind.

The general situation of Education for All in the early twenty-first century is rather different from what it was in the 1960s and even 1990. While for many countries in the less developed world, enrollment and access to basic education are still the major concern, there is also a legitimate concern about what kind of basic education should be provided. The concern in many countries, developed and developing, has gone beyond universal attendance. Parents used to ask, "When will my child have a place in the school?" Now that their children are in schools, they ask, "What has the school done to my child?" This underpins the general sentiments in many jurisdictions where people decide to reform for *quality education*.

This poses a deeper question: What quality of education should we aspire to? In a society that has undergone fundamental changes, what should happen to our education, and basic education in particular? Should we improve our education by doing more and better of what we have been doing? Or should we rethink the fundamentals of education and reform for a different notion of education? Even in societies that have yet to face fundamental developmental changes, global challenges are imminent, and one has to ask: Is the basic education that we provide indeed preparing our young people for a different future, and for an ever-changing future?

Once we started asking these questions, we faced two further questions. First, what in the real world would have implications for the development of education? Second, given the sweeping process of globalization, to what extent are these implications commonly shared by all countries, including those in the least developed world?

I do not pretend that this small chapter could answer all these questions. However, I hope the observations in this chapter might yield some meaningful hints.

In the following, I will start by looking at the workplace as a window on society. The changes in the workplace have created rather different expectations of individuals, and hence of education. I conclude that education should undergo some fundamental revisions so that we might fulfill our responsibility of preparing our young people for their future.

THE PYRAMIDS

Perhaps I should clarify from the outset that the word *workplace* is chosen on purpose. I am not referring to the job-market or employment, which belong to the realm of economic analyses. What I am trying to achieve is a kind of anthropological understanding of human lives in work. I have not chosen to use the word *organization,* because as it will soon become clear, there are people who do not work in organizations.

Let me start with the case of Hong Kong. In at least two ways, Hong Kong is atypical. It is an economy with almost no agricultural sector. Even its manufacturing sector operates outside Hong Kong.[2] In 2007, the service sector contributed to 91 percent of Hong Kong's economic growth (Census and Statistics Department, Hong Kong, 2007). It is a small city of around seven million people, with limited flow of people across its borders. However, these characteristics have also made Hong Kong almost an ideal case to study what a place would be like where the economy is largely post-industrial. The choice of the descriptor "post-industrial" is again deliberate. I have refrained from using "knowledge society" because that would require a rather solid definition.

In 2007, there were more than 305,000 registered companies in Hong Kong. Of these companies, 99.3 percent were organizations with less than one hundred people. They are what are called SMEs, or small and medium enterprises. This may not be totally unexpected, but 94.0 percent of all the companies in Hong Kong in the same year had fewer than twenty people, and 86.5 percent had fewer than ten people (Census and Statistics Department, Hong Kong, 2008). The Hong Kong case would be seen as less atypical if we compare it with the United States, which is a much larger society. Of all the business enterprises in the U.S., in 2002, 96 percent employed fewer than one hundred people, and 86 percent employed fewer than twenty (U.S. Census Bureau, 2001, p. 483).

However, one would be surprised to find that even in Shanghai, which still has a substantial component of manufacturing in its economic sectors, 99.7 percent of the registered enterprises were classified as SMEs. Their employees constitute 86.8 percent of all employees in the municipality (Coordinating Office for the Promotion of Small and Medium Enterprises, Shanghai, 2005).

The implications are tremendous. This is no longer the kind of society that we were familiar with in the industrial era. It is not the kind of society that was there even fifteen years ago.

A typical industrial society is a pyramid. Let us consider a typical workplace organization in a manufacturing factory. It would be a pyramid. In a garment factory in Swaziland,[3] there are 3,000 workers at the front-end production lines. These are so-called "raw laborers" or "unskilled workers" who were expected to perform simple, routine, repetitive and manual tasks. Such tasks are dictated by the overall production plan, which fully exploits the principles of *division of labor*, so that each worker is required to perform a simple action, as just a small part of the complex production process. In so doing, these workers are to follow strictly prescribed procedures, and are governed by rules and regulations in a rigorous structure. These three thousand workers are organized in production lines each served by fifty workers. For the approximately one hundred production lines, there are one hundred supervisors with a decent understanding of the production procedures and some skills of supervision. In order to manage these one hundred supervisors, there is a layer of middle managers who possess higher level management skills, or technicians who are equipped with higher level expertise. Additional layers of technical and management personnel undertake higher levels of supervision and management, and so forth, until, at the apex of the pyramid, there is the Manager and a few leading engineers who form the mastermind of the entire production process in the factory. These are the few people who decide what should happen at the lower levels of the factory (i.e., design) and who make sure that they do happen according to the design (i.e., management). This was the case in the majority of factories and in other large commercial firms in the industrial era.

Because of the pyramidal structure of most workplaces in an industrial society, *society* as a whole was a pyramid. The largest majority in society were the front-line workers. They were the blue-collars who form the "cheap labor" and take care of the minute manual tasks. Then there were the middle managers and mid-level technicians who formed layers of the administration. There were only a few chief engineers or managing directors who stayed at the top of society. It was a pyramid of manpower.

The pyramid was also a pyramid of knowledge. The chief engineer had to be highly educated, and was supposed to be the one who had the greatest amount of knowledge and highest wisdom in the entire factory. The managers and technicians at the lower levels possessed less knowledge, and their expected education decreased at lower levels of the pyramid. The front-line or grass-roots workers were manual workers who were not supposed to exercise their brains. The best worker at the front-end production lines followed instructions strictly. They were therefore also called "operatives," "unskilled laborers," or simply "raw laborers," just to indicate the non-necessity of knowledge or skills.

Because people in industrial society were typically ranked according to their formal qualifications and credentials, the education system was also a pyramid. The largest majority of the populace did not have any education beyond basic education, or simply were illiterate. Moving up the pyramid, there were layers known as *craftsmen* who had received training in vocational school or had undergone apprenticeship; *technicians* who had acquired a dose of technical education in technical institutes or some kind of post-secondary education; *senior technicians* who received sub-degree diplomas; and finally *engineers* with higher education degrees, or further training attained through membership in a professional body.

The education systems in most countries still reflect the industrial era, and are pyramids.

In sum, in a typical industrial society:

- There were fine divisions of labor, an array of departments, layers of administration, well-defined structure and hierarchy of qualifications, which were best summarized in Max Weber's (1947) notion of a *bureaucracy* in the neutral sense of the term.
- People were classified also as layers of manpower. They were classified vertically as operatives, craftsmen, technicians and engineers,[4] for example in a manufacturing set-up.
- Unless they were front-line manual laborers, people worked in specific occupations, in specific jobs and on specific tasks. They were classified horizontally by occupation. They worked with specialized expertise in specialized departments. In other words, people owned distinct occupational identities.
- People worked separately according to specific job descriptions and pre-set procedures, under well-defined rules and regulations specific to their jobs. Such procedures, rules and regulations were designed from the top and handed down to workers at lower levels.
- Echoing the pyramids in the workplace, education systems were designed in a manner that ranked people according to their levels of knowledge and skills, and labeled people with different occupational identities. Below is a schematic representation of the workplace–education match.

Industrial Society: Manpower and Qualifications Pyramid

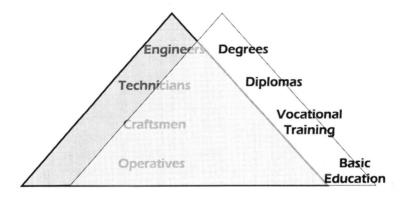

Figure 2.1   Industrial society: manpower and qualification pyramids.

For the discussions that follow, it is essential to reiterate that the pyramidal manpower structure was matched by the education system, which was, and still is, also a pyramid. The education system screens people, allowing only a percentage to move on to upper levels of the system. At each transition, the system exits a certain percentage of people (called graduates). They are supposed to possess the different amounts or levels of knowledge that match the expectations of such knowledge at the workplace.

THE PROJECT-TEAMS

When one looks at societies where most of the work units are small, such as Hong Kong, Shanghai and the United States, the situation is different. A small organization of nine people, for example, could afford few layers and few departments. The division of labor is no longer the primary principle for organizing people in a small workplace.

In most of the small organizations I studied, people are assigned tasks according to the needs of clients, rather than according to the nature of the task. The size of the unit is only the tip of the iceberg. It is a symbol of the fundamental change in the nature of the workplace. People who work in small units face very different environments and expectations when compared with those who work in pyramidal organizations.

A member in a typical department in a large pyramidal industrial organization serves a special purpose. In a manufacturing factory, members in a department perform their specific responsibility, without necessarily knowing the whole picture of the final product. In a large commercial firm in the industrial model, each department serves a special dimension of every transaction, but the department is not required to have the knowledge of the entire transaction.

In a post-industrial society, the organization of the workplace is typified by what is called a "project team" or, in other variations, a "taskforce," "production group," "client unit," "deal team" or "account team."[5] A project team works in ways that contrast those in an industrial organization, even if the project team is part of a large organization such as a consulting firm or investment bank with a few hundred members.

A project team typically works exclusively on one single project. It faces one client or caters to one product. This is fundamentally different from a department in an industrial organization, where each department faces many clients and each client has to face many departments. A conventional hospital set-up, for example, follows an industrial style where each patient has to face many departments to complete one visit: registration, temperature and blood pressure tests, inspection by the clinical doctor, injection or other minor operations, pharmacy, cashier, appointment reservation and so forth. In a typical investment bank or consulting firm operation, which is often the most representative of a post-industrial organization, one project team takes care of one client, providing total solutions to the client. Such solutions are meant to be holistic and comprehensive. The client does not have to turn to any other part of the bank to receive services.

A crucial element is that such project teams are at the front line, but they do not work according to any design handed down from above. The project team directly works with the client. It faces the requests and problems. It has to provide answers and solutions, and hence it has to design and innovate. If we walk into an insurance firm, most likely we find members discussing in small groups. They are agents who bring home clients' requirements, and they are creating "customized products," as they would say. The front-line workers in a post-industrial organization are no longer routine, low-skill, manual laborers. They have to possess the knowledge, expertise and mentality that belonged to middle managers or even leaders in a typical pyramidal organization in the industrial era.

A project team is also temporary. It ends when the project is complete. A member of such an organization often serves more than one project team as required by circumstances. Most likely, the role of each member in the project team is vague and could vary over time. What is treasured in the teamwork is the collaboration among members and integration of expertise. Members work as a generic team, rather than as specialists confined to certain knowledge and skills.

Such characteristics of the workplace are not specific to large organizations. The very small enterprises are basically themselves project teams. The only difference is perhaps that the same team (i.e., the organization) will be handling different projects.

It would be too sweeping to say that all organizations are working in the same mode, but it is safe to say that the trend is unmistakable and irreversible. It is also safe to say that quite a few are working in "matrices" that allow departments and project teams to co-exist. They could be regarded as intermediate between bureaucracy and post-industrial structures.

Implicit in the preceding discussions is the change in the economy or in the mode of production. In the industrial era, products and services used to aim at the large-scale market with large quantity. Products and services now, in a post-industrial economy, are customized and tailor-made for clients, and are provided more directly to the users. Attention focuses now on quality, and producers face a market of diversity. Hence, the overall trend is to have many more designs of products, but a smaller quantity is produced in each. "Selling less of more" is perhaps a succinct description of the mode of productions in a post-industrial society (Anderson, 2006). Translated into the work force, there is an increasing need for designers rather than simple producers, and there is a gradual disappearance of middle-level administrators, but more front-line managers. Accordingly, there is also a diminishing layer of "blue collar" operative manual workers.

The picture is not complete if we ignore the expanding sector of free-lancers. Even now, it is not always easy to have statistics on freelancers in a society. Freelancers work as independent individuals. They may either register themselves as a one-person firm, may be employed by multiple organizations at one time, or may be classified as unemployed and do not appear on an economic census. An estimate was that in 2003, there were 220,000 free-lancers in Hong Kong,[6] comparing with a total of 2,200,000 employees in all the registered companies in that year. Freelancers could be seen as further developments in the move from large bureaucracies to small work units. Freelancers could be seen as one-person "project teams" that are free from assigned procedures, rules and regulations, yet provide effective and innovative total solutions to their clients.

Such trends are not limited to metropolitan cities or to the most developed cities. In the various places where I made a presentation of this theme, there are enthusiastic echoes that similar trends exist, though in different degrees. The trend is spreading very rapidly from the most urban and international centers to other, less developed regions. In China, which could be seen as a microcosm of the world, the spread of the economy from the more to the less developed regions has also brought changes in the workplace. Places which have not experienced such changes will be affected in the near future. Since the cause of the change lies with the mode of production, such changes affect all economies, even those at the early stages of industrialization, in an era of globalization. For example, the factories in Swaziland, mentioned earlier, face changes in the demand of the consumers in North America and may disappear in a few years time because of change in the import quota system.

INDIVIDUALS

Changes in the workplace strongly affect individuals' career lives. In an industrial society, individuals were typically employed by an organization because of their credentials. Credentials provided the employers a convenient assessment of the individuals' level of knowledge as reflected by academic study. Such credentials have lifelong currency. Most likely, such individuals are appointed to large organizations and to specific departments according to their specializations. The individuals are expected to move up the hierarchy when they grow older and become more experienced in the organization. When they enter the organization, they could legitimately expect promotion through the ranks, with continuous elevated ranks and statuses, accompanied by escalating incomes. As such, they develop loyalties to the organization and commitment to their respective specialization. They could then also safely look forward to retirement at their advanced ages with well-defined benefits.

This is no longer the reality. In a post-industrial society, individuals are appointed increasingly because of their personal attributes rather than their credentials. Although good credentials are still necessary and beneficial, they are no longer sufficient.

In a leading multinational investment bank in Hong Kong that I studied, the Managing Director is himself a political scientist. The person in charge of human resources is a graduate of English Literature. The Managing Director explained to me why their recruitment did not aim at trained accountants. "For us, the required level of expertise could be attained in a matter of four weeks." This was confirmed in their recruitment plans every summer. "What we are interested in are young people who have had some aims to strive for, have experienced some difficulties and competition, and eventually succeeded. We are looking for 'winning personalities.'"[7]

A retired senior partner of Deloitte and Touche in Hong Kong, in a newspaper interview,[8] commented that what are essential for the auditing profession are integrity and human skills. The accounting skills could be learned after recruitment. This was confirmed by a Physics graduate, who joined a leading multinational accounting firm, undertook training, and obtained his Public Accountant license in six months.[9]

We may well argue that there are other specialized knowledge and skills that are not attainable in four weeks or six months, but the important message is that learning on the job is a general expectation in the workplace.

In other words, the workplace is interested in what the recruits could learn in the future in the workplace, rather than what they have learned in the past in educational institutions. It expects their members to learn on-the-job, on-demand and just-in-time, because whatever is learned could soon become obsolete and is short-lived. The members should have the capacity and willingness to learn. The tasks in the workplace are so rapidly changing that individuals have to learn continuously in order to fulfill their responsibilities. Knowledge in any specific area becomes renewed so quickly that whatever one has learned will soon have to be renewed.

New knowledge is also required because individuals' job situations change rapidly. A recent survey reveals that an average adult between eighteen and forty in the United States experiences 10.5 jobs (U.S. Department of Labor, 2006). A similar survey in the United Kingdom indicates that an average individual experiences thirteen jobs in a lifetime.[10]

The contemporary workplace undergoes constant reengineering, downsizing, de-layering, outsourcing, closures, mergers and acquisitions (Deal and Kennedy, 1999). It is no longer realistic for an individual to expect long-term appointment in any particular organization. There is decreasing room for organizational loyalty. Such loyalty could easily be overtaken by the disappearance of the organization because of closure, merger or acquisition. Even if individuals stay in the same organization, changes in the market, technology, client or partnership could require them to change their position, status and specialization. They have to learn to do new things in the same organization. However, what is also likely to happen is that the individuals have to leave the organization, very much against their own wills. Circumstances might require them to change their jobs, or even change their careers.

During such changes, individuals no longer can anticipate long-term continuity in their careers. They can no longer expect good planning of their career developments. Disruptions in career paths, fluctuations in incomes and lifestyles, and switches to new careers are commonplace in the contemporary world. It is not unusual for an individual to experience several careers in one's lifetime. It is also not unusual for an individual to work across occupations or work in areas with blurred career boundaries, multi-skilling or cross-skilling. Many more people are temporarily unemployed (or "between-jobs") or undertake early retirement,[11] willingly or unwillingly. It is increasingly difficult to maintain job stability, organization loyalty and occupational identity. In their place, waiting for our young people are personal insecurity and career uncertainty,[12] a future that is no longer predictable.

However, the challenges to individuals are not limited to their careers. What the workplace requires has also changed. A simple scan of surveys of employers' expectations or workplace requirements would agree with the list of attributes of preferred appointees in business organizations as well as NGOs:

- Ability to communicate effectively
- Ability to work as a team member
- Flexible human relations
- Preparedness to face changes and challenges
- Preparedness to solve problems
- Willingness to take risks

- Capacity in analysis and conceptualization
- Capacity and willingness to learn new things
- Ability to question, to query, to challenge and to innovate
- Willingness and capacity to assume personal responsibility
- Capacity for self-reflection and self-management

It may surprise educators that, with almost no exception, such lists do not include elements of the "subject matter" of the job. It would not be sensible to assume that such "subject matters" are not important. The workplace would not tolerate poor language skills, for example. There are knowledge and skills, such as those for clinical medical practices, that have to be learned before engaging in practice. Scientists, as another example, have to be equipped with profound knowledge in their respective disciplines before they could even be admitted to laboratories. In most jobs in the service industries, some kind of special knowledge is required, although much of such special knowledge could be learned on the job on demand. Perhaps it is not that such substantial knowledge is not necessary, but it is not the determining factor for success in the workplace. This is fully understandable when we look at the modes of activities in a contemporary workplace.

In a typical contemporary work unit, which I tried to delineate earlier in this chapter, human interactions have become more intensive than ever. Teamwork, collaboration, integration and partnership have replaced strict division of labor, prescribed procedures and rigid rules and regulations. Typical activities in the workplace are communications, presentations, brainstorming, demonstrations, negotiations, debates, lobbying, seminars, teleconferences, videoconferences, and retreats; all amount to human–human interactions. Technologies have also changed the format and intensity of interactions among people. Audio and video telecommunications through mobile telephones and the Internet are replacing written or printed documents and other formal paperwork. Moreover, with the workplace becoming more fluid, individuals now face various and varying teammates, clients, partners, social networks and employer–employee relations. This change is perhaps best reflected in the practice of 360-degree appraisal, where individual performances are no longer assessed by the bosses, but evaluated by all parties who are related to the specific individual in one way or another.

In such close human interactions, individual behaviors are less governed by bureaucratic and hierarchical requirements, but are more a reflection of the individuals' attitudes, values, emotions, ethics, principles and personalities. There is much more reliance on individuals' moral standards and value judgments in the workplace. Furthermore, because the outputs rather than processes are being monitored, individuals are expected to exercise their discretion most of the time, but are also expected to bear personal responsibility and "carry things through" as an individual undertaking.

Because of the loose nature of the work organizations, individuals are expected to be self-confident, and have to have a rather strong capacity for self-management and self-reflection.

There is no pretense that the flatter society would be more equal or fair, only that the disparity (in terms of status and income) is no longer a matter of organizational or manpower structure, neither is it determined by the amount of knowledge or experience one possesses at the time. It is a competition of a different nature, and the rule of the game changes over time and varies according to situations. As individuals are now less protected by their work organizations, they also have to be more capable of understanding the larger context in which they live and work, more autonomous in planning their future, and more conscious of protecting their own rights and their families.[13]

Because of the frequent changes in the products, clients and their own careers, individuals seldom do things that they have done before. Therefore they have to have a strong capacity to learn everywhere at all times, to avoid inertia, to question the conventions, to query the status quo, to "think outside the box" and to create and innovate almost every day.

It is perhaps necessary to say that the preceding discussions concentrate on the workplace, but people's cultural, social, political, religious and family lives are also facing unprecedented challenges in a post-industrial society.

UNDERSTANDING SCHOOLING

The preceding observations are just a brief scan of what is happening around us. Many of those observations are perhaps commonsense in the larger society. However, they should be more than enough as a starting point for renewing our understanding of education.

In most jurisdictions, apparently, most workplace expectations mentioned earlier are not the target goals of the education system. It is safe to assume that in almost all education systems, high examination scores are de facto the one major goal of school education, although there are always some lofty goals in theory. This is reflected not only in teachers' actual daily practice, but often in the emphasis of government policies. It is also almost taken for granted in many academic investigations, where examination scores are conveniently used as the proxy for education outcome or student achievements. As a matter of reality, in most systems, the largest portion of resources for education is used for classroom teaching of academic subjects.

It would be unfair to say that schools and universities do not care for a student's personal development, but it is fair to say that relatively few resources are allocated to non-academic matters. One should perhaps be sympathetic with educators, because they are under tremendous pressure to prepare young people for the next stage of education, or for immediate employment. For example, a secondary school could not survive if its graduates were not admitted to good universities. In many parts of the world, a primary school is judged by the admission of its graduates to good secondary schools. Educators are left with little room to prepare young people for their longer-term future.

The picture becomes clearer when we understand that schooling as a national system was started in Europe in the mid-nineteenth century. It emerged as a necessity for many industrial societies. Cynics would condemn the schools as a system to sift and select human beings.[14] But even the most constructive interpretation regards schools as a place to transmit knowledge and skills, to train people's ability to work and fit them into the appropriate position in the manpower structure.[15]

The manpower approach to education, which prevailed over educational planning for almost three decades since the early 1960s, overtly assumes horizontal classification and vertical ranking of human beings in order to match the manpower structure in society. Although manpower planning is seldom a central theme now, most countries still practice manpower forecasting as a means of safe planning, and education is still supposed to play a crucial role to balance the supply and demand in manpower.

Human capital theories, based very much on rate-of-return analysis, assume that a hierarchy of incomes will match a hierarchy of abilities. Such abilities are assumed to be related to education. "Higher learning leads to higher earning," goes the dictum. Here, both learning and earning are supposed to be a *lifelong* phenomenon, where the benefit or return in the analysis refers to the added financial income due to the education credential obtained from formal education. Rate-of-return analysis could be a subject of continuing academic debate in the context of a post-industrial society.

However, when we look into the practice in education, we see that schools are very much the machinery for processing ("teaching") the massive number of students. Schools are large organizations, and they practice a division of labor. Teachers are subject specialists. Students are taught selected lumps of knowledge ("subjects"). All students are given more or less the same amount of knowledge (the "curriculum"), and they follow the same paths (moving through yearly "grades"). Each day, each specialist ("subject teacher") supplies the students with a dose of a particular subject at the specified time slot (according to the "time table"). The process is complete when all the required doses of knowledge are taught (according to the "syllabus") and the quality of acquisition of such doses (called "learning") is tested (in "examinations"). Teachers are virtual "quality controllers" of the process.

PARADIGM SHIFTS

Such a delineation of the school system might sound cynical. I wish I could argue against such an interpretation. In the following, I try to identify the paradigms underlying the practice of education in our present school system, and I suggest that shifts in paradigms are necessary if we are to fulfill our responsibility for preparing our young people for their future.

The Paradigm of "Teaching"

The paradigm of teaching pertains to the understanding of learning. This is a matter of paradigm as well as a matter of knowledge and understanding. The following discussion is no stranger to educators who are familiar with the contemporary theories of human learning.[16]

What is learning? There is a general belief that learning is the transmission of knowledge from those who know to those who do not. Therefore, students do not "learn" unless they are taught. Education is about teaching. Good "learning" means absorbing as much as possible from teachers. Learning in this sense takes place only in institutions such as schools where teaching takes place.

Hence, it is for the teachers to decide wisely what students should learn. Every student can and should learn in the same manner. Students' brains are like containers of knowledge. Learning happens in individual brains by filling these containers. Learning is assessed by how much knowledge such containers have or are able to hold. Those who can hold more get higher scores and hence are better students.

There are also assumptions that learning is about what is known. It is not about creation. Learning is about understanding, which is separate from application and use of knowledge. Learning is basically about knowledge and skills that can be taught. Learning outside the curriculum is extra and optional, and learning beyond the campus is often seen as illegitimate and deserves no recognition.

However, it is now commonly agreed that learning is the active construction of knowledge by the learner. What happens in the learner's brain is due to the learner's interactions with the external world. Meaningful activities bring about the construction of meaningful knowledge, or meaningful learning. Education is therefore a matter of *learning experiences*. Learning experiences are useful when the activities are useful applications of the knowledge being constructed. This is reflected in the rather simplistic saying "learning by doing."

The corollaries of this notion of constructive learning include several dimensions, all very significant to education. All students can learn, but they learn differently. They learn from a whole spectrum of activities that they encounter every moment. Human beings also learn from peers. In this sense, teachers are senior co-learners. But teachers also have the responsibility of building a framework or "scaffolding" for students, so that students do not have to repeat their ancestors' learning.

If we believe that student learning is the core business of education, then the shift of paradigm in human learning should have tremendous implications for education.

The Paradigm of "Screening"

Implicit in the education system in the industrial era is the paradigm in education that "there are smart kids and dumb kids."[17] Some can learn; some cannot. Only smart kids deserve more education, and school helps control the gate to higher learning. Hence, education is providing society the noble service of classifying and ranking human beings.

This system is not consistent with the current understanding of learning. It is not supported by any theory in the entire literature about learning. The notion of intelligence quotient (IQ), for example, is a convenience that hinges upon the type of intelligence we measure.[18] If we accept Gardner's (1999) notion of multiple intelligences, then students should well be measured by multiple quotients that could better reflect their development in various intelligences. But if we accept that learning is not an accumulation of knowledge, then there are dimensions of learning that do not lend themselves to quantitative measurement.

However, the quantitative measurement of "learning" has been well supported by society in the industrial era. The manpower pyramid reflects a fine division of labor among the departments and layers, where human beings are classified according to occupational identity and ranked according to levels of education qualifications. Society needed a legitimate way to classify people and discriminate people by their ability, and education became the best candidate for that function. This is where credentials came into play. As some economists would argue, credentials provide a convenient signal for both individuals and employers to find appropriate matches in the job market (see Spence, 1973).

In the post-industrial society, it is doubtful that the possession of knowledge can remain the primary means for discriminating among human beings. This is partly because most tasks require knowledge and learning and there is no room for the less educated; it is also because the acquisition of knowledge, thanks to technology, is now so convenient that it no longer can be used as a means for discrimination.

Again using Hong Kong as an example, despite basically universal attendance in both primary and secondary schools, youth unemployment consistently stays high regardless of the fluctuations in the economy.[19] In 2002, 19 percent of fifteen- to nineteen-year-olds suffered from "double-disengagement": these young people were not able to study or to work (Commission on Youth, 2003). With a life expectancy of eighty-four years among females and eighty-one years among males, what will these people do in the next sixty years? It has become a major social problem. The case of Hong Kong invites a question: When education is massively sifting out those who are supposed to be of low ability, and when many of those losing out are not given an opportunity to survive, does the problem lie with the students or the system?

Indeed, many countries have seen a dramatic expansion of higher education in the past decade. Many societies, particularly in the urban centers, have made it possible for every young person to have some kind of post-secondary education. According to Organisation for Economic Co-Operation and Development (OECD) figures, one third of youths were admitted into all types of tertiary education in 1996 (OECD, 1998, p. 174). In 1999, three years later, 40 percent of youths were admitted to Type A tertiary education (full-time degree-bearing programs; OECD, 2001, p. 148). In 2006, the Type A enrollment further rose to 56 percent, with another 16 percent in Type B places (sub-degree programs) (OECD, 2008, p. 58), hence a total of 72 percent in all types of higher education. East Asia provides a further example. In Korea, Taiwan and Japan, there is an oversupply of higher education places vis-à-vis secondary school graduates. In major cities such as Shanghai and Beijing, the enrollment ratios for higher education have exceeded 75 percent. Singapore is moving toward 80 percent, and Hong Kong has achieved 65 percent higher education enrollment. The admissions mechanisms to higher education are also evolving accordingly in these societies. If admissions to higher education are no longer highly selective, why should secondary schools be keen in screening their students?

It seems inevitable that educators have to accept that everybody can learn and should learn, for life. That shift in the paradigm would drive reforms in the curriculum, in assessment, and in the entire role of schools. Such reforms are emerging, but they are not widespread. Some are half-hearted. Nonetheless, the trend is unmistakable.

The Paradigm of "Specialization"

The preceding discussion also highlights the role of specialization. Educators commonly believe that human beings are prepared for their future only when they have acquired some occupational status. This has also developed into a belief that a higher level of learning should result in a higher degree of specialization.

On two counts, specialization in education is facing challenges. The first comes from the change in the workplace where, as is mentioned earlier, specialization is blurred because of the retreat from a strict division of labor. It is true that long-term specialist training is essential in occupations such as medical doctors, scientists and engineers. But there are many more others in which the specialist requirements are acquired either on the job or in a relatively short training program. Among a good percentage of graduates, there is a general "mismatch" between what students study and what they do after graduation. The frequent change of jobs and careers has also challenged the notion of specialist training, particularly at the undergraduate level.

The second challenge comes from within the education system. There is a general trend in higher education toward programs that either reduce the specialist elements or delay the specialization to a later stage.

A typical example of the former is the Washington Accord, where six Institutes of Engineers came together in 1989 and agreed, among other things, to devote 30 percent of the undergraduate engineering program to non-engineering areas of study.[20] In some newly reorganized undergraduate journalism programs, only 30 percent are on journalism per se. The idea is to train journalists with a broad knowledge base.[21] This, of course, challenges the entire notion of a "major." In the United Kingdom, where the higher education system has been known for its specialized programs, there has been a call to install a two-year generic Foundations Degree followed by three-year Masters degree program.[22] Consistent with this trend are numerous efforts to introduce double degrees (where two disciplines merge at the undergraduate level),[23] to de-specialize entrance requirements[24] and to keep the first years of undergraduate study as general programs.[25]

The most significant example of delayed specialization is obviously the Bologna Process,[26] which calls for a unification of European higher education to follow a three-year generic undergraduate program, leaving specialization to the second and third degrees. This is already practiced in many countries.

The Paradigm of "Study"

The paradigm of "study" begins with the assumption that learning in education is the academic study of theories in classrooms, libraries and laboratories. It has developed to such an extent that academic study is taken as the proxy for student learning.

However, expectations in the workplace show that academic study is only one type of learning. Much of what is expected in the workplace is beyond what can be learned though academic study. First, what is learned in academic study is limited to the few subjects often dictated by the examination syllabuses. Second, because of the intensive human interactions in the workplace, there is a general expectation of good character and personality. There is the demand for good human relations and social competencies. There is also a renewed attention to attitudes, values, emotions, ethics and principles. These values are not acquired automatically from academic study. This has given rise in Western education systems to the call for values education, civic education, ethics education, tacit knowledge,[27] character education and social competence, beside the traditional emphasis on "moral education" among Asian societies.

In established universities, students are readily learning from a variety of experiences such as student organizations, internships, mentorships, fellowships, team sports, community services, volunteer work, music and arts activities, service learning and overseas exchange. In most cases, these activities are not part of the academic curriculum, and students most likely do not receive any credit for their involvement. Such experiences are seldom examinable, but are nonetheless important as part of the students' personal formation.

Baseline Competence

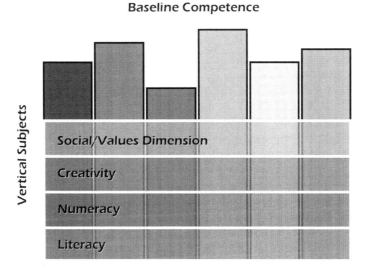

Figure 2.2 Baseline competence.

Most recently, in the realm of arts in education, it has been advocated that apart from literacy and numeracy, creativity should be included as one of the baseline competencies in basic education (UNESCO, 2006). This proposal opens up a very good framework to consider student learning in terms of baseline competencies, which are different from what could be called vertical subjects.

This reminds us of the UNESCO call for "learning to know, learning to do, learning to live together and learning to be" (Delors, et al., 1996). A comprehensive framework for learning is also presented in the OECD study of Key Competencies[28] as is reflected in Chapter 20 of this book. The OECD study raised three dimensions of key competencies in contemporary societies:

- Interacting in socially heterogeneous groups
- Acting autonomously
- Using tools purposively and interactively

These could be interpreted, if we use a Chinese education framework, as learning how to face people, learning to face oneself and learning to face practical tasks. It echoes very well the analysis of expectations in the post-industrial workplace. However, if we use this as a mirror and look at our school curricula, they are at best taking up only part of the third dimension, on using tools.

If we follow this argument, there are indeed many attributes in people that are important for human lives but are neglected in school, yet are achievable during the school years. These include: optimism about life, passion about nature, commitment to society, commitment to nation, perseverance against odds, readiness to expand one's capacity, experience in organizing, appreciation of arts and music, attitude of helping and caring, seriousness about the details, eagerness to interact with people, love for peace, sense of justice, consciousness of equity, awareness of the deprived, comfort with other cultures, basic understanding of sex and family, understanding and facing moral dilemmas, belief in rationality, tolerance of diversity and plurality, and so forth. The list could be much longer.

The world would be different if schools provided more learning experiences that attended to such dimensions. In some Western cultures, the teaching in these affective or values dimensions is left to the church or the family. In other cultures, such dimensions are subsumed under "knowledge and skills,"[29] but are not earnestly taken care of by schools, public schools in particular.[30] In many systems, these are the privilege of the private schools, and are inherited from their religious past. The large variety of student organizations, sports teams and community services in such schools has provided rich learning experiences for the students in the human and social dimensions.[31] In many oriental cultures, however, such dimensions are indeed a serious part of school education. Even in these cases, the kind of "moral education"[32] in East Asian cultures, for example, is inherited from the pre-industrial era, and its contents and methodology have to be revisited in order to catch up with developments in society. In still other cultures, education and religion are intertwined concepts,[33] and developments in the affective and values domains are part of the process of personal religious formation. Overall, human learning in these dimensions is understudied. Good practices are not seriously analyzed and theorized, and cross-culture awareness is minimal. A lot has to be done in order that these affective and values dimensions receive their deserved attention on the policy agenda.

Nonetheless, in reality, teachers have to struggle with the paradigm that only academic studies count, only examination scores are reliable proxies for learning outcomes, and only those that are quantifiably measured are valuable.

CONCLUSION

I began this chapter with observations about fundamental changes in the workplace in a post-industrial society and their implications for individuals and education. The change in society is so comprehensive that it challenges the basic assumptions of the system of education established at the height of the industrial era.

A change of paradigms is by no means easy, but I have collected many examples, of which I am able to present only a few in this chapter, where reforms are emerging and beginning to undermine conventional assumptions about education. Many such reforms are still in their embryonic stage, but are nonetheless precious.

The fundamental question is: If the basic function of education is to prepare young people for their future, are our education systems doing them justice? I believe that educators are mostly kind-hearted, and they are committed to helping our young people. However, do teachers know what our young people will face when they leave school? Do teachers know what is already quietly happening in the larger society that surrounds our schools?

What is presented in this chapter is based on common sense and public knowledge. It is only when we look underneath the surface that we discern the profound challenges to education. If this chapter confuses our readers and provokes queries, I have served my purpose.

Much of what I have discussed here is happening in societies where "education for all" is not seen as a problem, because they all enjoy near universal enrollment. Many of these societies are in the process of widening the participation in higher education. If my observations are valid, then it indeed poses a challenge to these systems: Education for all, but for what?

This change in the workplace will also pose a more serious question to so-called "less developed" countries that are in the process of achieving "Education for All" and are trying to catch up with the system of education that prevails in the so-called "more developed" nations. Do we really think that education systems should follow a linear model? Do we think that all countries should construct their educational systems based on an industrial model, until they find that such a model does not work for their future?

In this context, perhaps it is essential to mention that the coming of the post-industrial era is not limited to the more industrialized societies. Because of globalization, many of the less-developed economies are tightly geared to developments and markets in the developed economies. The changes in the mode of production and the notion of organization, for example, are taking place everywhere regardless of the economic status of the nation.

If the entire human society is gradually moving out of the industrial model, so should education!

NOTES

1. These were the themes of the meetings in Addis Ababa, Lima, and Karachi for the respective continents in the early 1960s.
2. Basically, Hong Kong, with a population of around seven million, runs a manufacturing sector in Mainland China across the border. Such a manufacturing sector comprises around 80,000 enterprises under Hong Kong investments, hosting around thirteen million workers. The vast majority of these workers are from within China. Presentation made by Andrew Leung, Chairman of Hong Kong Federation of Manufacturers, February 21, 2006.

3. This is a garment factory (name withheld) that I visited in 2007 in a World Bank project. The factory is an investment from a Taiwanese company listed in Hong Kong. The front-line workers are local, but the supervisors are all from Mainland China, largely from the region near Shanghai. The investment was there because of the import quota allowed by the Africa Growth and Opportunities Act (AGOA) in the United States.
4. This is the jargon adopted in manpower planning in many systems.
5. Based on study of seven major multinationals in Hong Kong.
6. According to a report in the local newspaper *Ming Pao Daily*, November 20, 2003.
7. Interview with Managing Director of an investment bank (name withheld) by Hayley Kan and K. M. Cheng, August 17, 2004.
8. Interview with Peter Wong, Senior Partner of Deloitte and Touche in Hong Kong. *Ming Pao Daily*, date unknown.
9. Interview with a graduate of the University of Hong Kong, December 10, 2005.
10. Quoted by Chris Humphries, Director General, City and Guild in his presentation at an international workshop organized by the World Bank Institute, May 15, 2007, Washington, DC.
11. There are reports that in the United States, the average retirement age has come down to 59, against the preferred 65 (Block and Armour, 2006).
12. Charles Handy's writings may serve as a good reminder. See, for example, his collected writings (1996).
13. This is prominently reflected in the "Key Competencies" as is formulated in the OECD: The Definition and Selection of Competencies: Theoretical and Conceptual Foundations Project (DeSeCo).
14. This is best reflected in the wave of theories in the late 1970s that condemn the "human capital" notion. This includes seminal works such as Dore (1976), Collins (1979), and a whole series of writings on "screening theories" which adopt a sociological approach, and "signaling theory" from an economics perspective (see the classical article by Spence, 1973).
15. A vast literature on "human capital" and, at one stage, "manpower planning" and "manpower forecasting" prevailed over educational planning in the 1960s through the mid-1980s. The human capital notion still survives.
16. A succinct yet comprehensive presentation of the theories can be found in National Research Council (2000).
17. This is raised by Senge (2000, p. 42) as one of the tacit assumptions about education in the Industrial Era.
18. See the critical analyses in Gould (1981/1996).
19. Hong Kong had unemployment rates as low as 1.7 percent in the 1980s. It reached a record high of 8 percent at the economic downturn in 2003. It remained at around 6 percent in 2005 and early 2006. Thereafter, it remains at 4 percent regardless of the fluctuations in the economy. At one point, in 2004, youth unemployment reached a record high of 35 percent (Census and Statistics Department, Hong Kong , 2007).
20. In 1989, six leading Institutes of Engineers from the United Kingdom, the United States, Canada, Australia, New Zealand and Ireland came together to agree on benchmarks for mutual recognition of engineering qualifications and professional competence. In 2007, the signatories of the Accord had extended to twelve Institutes, including most of the East Asian jurisdictions: Taiwan, Singapore, Japan, Korea, Hong Kong, and South Africa, and included a few other major countries (Germany, India, Russia, Sri Lanka, Malaysia) as provisional members. See http://www.washingtonaccord.org.

21. This is happening in the Journalism School in Columbia University, United States, as well as with the Journalism undergraduate program at the University of Hong Kong and Shantou University in Mainland China.
22. Announcement by David Blunkett, Minister of Education and Science, February 15, 2000.
23. This is the case in Hong Kong where the newly introduced double degrees attract the most able students. The trend is now spreading in other Asian systems of higher education.
24. Since 1999, in China, for example, there is a move to include integrated papers in higher education entrance examinations, so that students are not limited to either science or arts. There is a similar move in Singapore and Hong Kong to blur the science–arts distinction in secondary schools.
25. This is the major theme of reform in many universities in China. Fudan University, the premier institution in Shanghai, presents the typical case of liberalizing the curriculum, so that students are not required to elect their "major" until the end of the first year, and are allowed to change their choice before the end of the second year. Such arrangements are rather unusual in Asia.
26. The Bologna Process refers to the implementation of the Bologna Declaration of 19 June 1999 which involves six actions in the process to unify higher education within the European Union. The six actions refer to comparability, the system, transferability, mobility, quality assurance and the European dimension of higher education. In terms of the system, the Declaration calls for two cycles: a first cycle geared to the employment market and lasting at least three years, and a second cycle (Master) conditional upon the completion of the first cycle.
27. Tacit knowledge refers to the knowledge that is expected of a professional beyond the technical knowledge of that profession. For example, social awareness, ethical sensitivity and communications capacity are expected of a medical doctor.
28. OECD: The Definition and Selection of Competencies: Theoretical and Conceptual Foundations Project (DeSeCo).
29. Indeed, Howard Gardner has discerned three different cultures about human competence. Among others, he observes that there are cultures where human–nature relations are emphasized, whereas in other cultures human–human relations are basic (Gardner, 1984).
30. In some education systems, the teachers' unions restrict public school teachers' contractual commitments to classroom teaching, sometimes with specified hours.
31. This is the case with the "independent schools" in the United Kingdom (often misleadingly called "public schools," formerly known as "grammar schools"). Such activities fall under "pastoral care" that reminds us of their religious legacy. Many private schools in the United States have the same model.
32. In Chinese education philosophies, in order to prepare a whole person, education comprises three dimensions: moral, intellectual, and physical (in Mainland China), or five dimensions: moral, intellectual, physical, community and aesthetics (in Hong Kong and Taiwan). Each of these dimensions has its own framework and methodology, but moral education always comes at the top. These are part of the culture that was inherited from ancient philosophies, but somehow survived in the modern school system. A typical description of how moral education is practiced in a Chinese school can be found in Lo (2003). Similar philosophies prevail in Japan and Korea.

Morality is almost the sole content of the *Education Decree* made by the
Meiji Emperor in 1898.
33. This is the case, for example, in some Muslim societies.

REFERENCES

Anderson, Chris. 2006. *The Long Tail: Why the Future of Business Is Selling Less
of More.* New York: Hyperion.
Block, Sandra and Stephanie Armour. 2006. "Many American Retire Years Before
They Want To." *USA Today,* July 26.
Census and Statistics Department, Hong Kong. 2007. *Gross Domestic Product
by Economic Activities at Current Price,* May 18. Hong Kong: Hong Kong
Government.
———. 2007. *Quarterly Survey of Employment and Vacancies.* Hong Kong: Hong
Kong Government.
———. 2008. *Hong Kong Monthly Digest of Statistics, March* (Table 2.7). Hong
Kong: Hong Kong Government.
Coordinating Office for the Promotion of Small and Medium Enterprises, Shang-
hai. 2005. *Small and Medium Enterprises: A Development Report.* Hong Kong:
Hong Kong Government.
Collins, Randall. 1979. *The Credential Society.* New York: Academic Press.
Commission on Youth. 2003. *Continuing Development and Employment Oppor-
tunities for Youth.* Hong Kong: Hong Kong Government.
Deal, Terrence E., and Allan A. Kennedy. 1999. *The New Corporate Cultures:
Revitalizing the Workplace After Downsizing, Mergers, and Reengineering.*
New York: Perseus Publishing.
Dore, Ronald. 1976. *The Diploma Disease.* Berkeley: University of California
Press.
Delors, Jacques, et al. 1996. *Learning: The Treasure Within: Report to UNESCO
of the International Commission on Education for the Twenty-first Century.*
Paris: UNESCO.
Gardner, Howard. 1984. "The Development of Competence in Culturally Defined
Domains: A Preliminary Framework." In *Culture Theory: Essays on Mind, Self,
and Emotion,* ed. Richard A. Shweder and Robert A. LeVine, 257–275. Cam-
bridge: Cambridge University Press.
Gardner, Howard. 1999. *Intelligence Reframed: Multiple Intelligences for the 21st
Century.* New York: Basic Books.
Gould, Stephen J. 1981/1996. *The Mismeasure of Man.* New York: W. W. Norton
& Company.
Handy, Charles. 1996. *Beyond Certainty: The Changing World of Organizations.*
Boston: Harvard Business School Press.
Lo, Rita. 2003. *Education for Personal and Social Development: A Case Study
for a Key Secondary School in Shanghai.* PhD thesis, University of Hong
Kong.
National Research Council. 2000. *How People Learn: Brain, Mind, Experience
and School.* Washington, DC: National Academy Press.
Organisation for Economic Co-Operation and Development (OECD). 1998. *Edu-
cation at a Glance: OECD Indicators 1998.* Paris: OECD.
———. 2001. *Education at a Glance: OECD Indicators: Education and Skills.*
Paris: OECD.
———. 2008. *Education at a Glance: OECD Indicators 2008.* Paris: OECD.
Senge, Peter. 2000. *Schools That Learn.* London: Nicholas Brealey.

Spence, Michael. 1973. "Job Market Signaling." *Quarterly Journal of Economics* 87 (3): 355–374.

UNESCO. 2006. World Conference on Arts Education (March 6–8, Lisbon). http://portal.unesco.org/culture/en/ev.php-URL_ID=26967&URL_DO= DO_TOPIC&URL_SECTION=201.html.

U.S. Census Bureau. 2001. *Statistical Abstract of the United States,* Table No. 723. Washington, DC: U.S. Census Bureau.

U.S. Department of Labor, Bureau of Labor Statistics. 2006. "Number of Jobs Held, Labor Market Activity, and Earnings Growth Among the Youngest Baby Boomers: Result from a Longitudinal Survey," *Department of Labor News,* August 25. Washington, DC: U.S. Department of Labor.

Weber, Max. 1947. *The Theory of Social and Economic Organization,* Trans. A. M. Henderson and T. Parsons. New York: Oxford University Press. (Or see a brief version in Max Weber. 1929. "Bureaucracy." In *From Max Weber: Essays in Sociology,* trans. and ed. H. H. Gerth and C. Wright Mills, 1973. New York: Oxford University Press; or collected in *Classics of Organization Theory* [4th Ed., 1996], ed. Jay M. Shafritz and J. Steven Ott, 80–85. Fort Worth: Harcourt Brace).

3 Goals of Universal Primary and Secondary Education in the 21st Century
Reviving the Spirit of Socrates

Kishore Mahbubani

Deeply embedded in the inner recesses of most Western minds is the belief that the twenty-first century will essentially be a continuation of the nineteenth and twentieth centuries. The Eurocentric worldview that has dominated global thinking will continue. Hence, in the world of education, the standard Western toolbox, with minor modification, will continue to serve mankind well. The West believes (with some justification) that this Western toolbox is a gift by the West to the rest of mankind. Hence, the more widely this gift is shared, the better the world will be. The confidence of the Western spirit of enlightenment continues to infuse Western ideas of education.

But the twenty-first century is more likely to be a troubled century. Several new historical forces will come into play. Five hundred years of Western domination of the world, although not Western supremacy, are likely to come to an end. Several other hitherto dormant or passive civilizations will emerge and play a greater role in determining the course of world history. Unfortunately, conflict along civilizational lines is a real possibility. Several early warning signals have surfaced, including 9/11. Huge pools of poverty will remain in many corners of the world. To top it all, the world will shrink even more. All six billion inhabitants of the earth (probably nine billion by 2050) will have to learn to live together in these troubled times in a shrinking village.

With so many new forces of world history being unleashed, it seems naive and even dangerous to proceed on auto-pilot in determining educational goals for mankind in the twenty-first century. The standard Western toolbox of education, which has served both the West and indeed much of mankind, will have to be re-examined to see how it will need to be modified to meet the new needs of mankind. For example, one key goal of education is to both civilize humanity and prevent conflict. The current standard toolbox may not have enough tools to achieve this. But other items in this toolbox, like the science and mathematics components, will probably remain eternally valid and universally applicable. The key goal of this chapter is to stimulate Western educational thinkers to re-examine this valuable Western toolbox that they have generously shared with mankind (and from which I have personally benefited even though I lived on the opposite side of the world).

The answer may well be that context will determine which set of tools to include in the educational toolbox to be delivered in different parts of the world. The standard tools of science and mathematics education may well remain the same. But some items, like literature and history, will have to be culturally and regionally specific. The huge challenge for the twenty-first century will be to weave in some universal elements that will remind children all over the world that they belong to a single common humanity. V. S. Naipaul once suggested, in his celebrated essay on "The Universal Western Civilization," that universal Westernization of the world would achieve this. This historical conceit has now gone. But one key stream of Western civilization, the spirit of Socrates, could well provide some key universal threads to weave humanity together. This is what this chapter will try to advocate.

The first civilization that is likely to emerge to challenge Western intellectual domination of the world could well be the Chinese civilization. The surprise should not be that this is happening. The surprise is that this should be happening so late, when for most of the previous two millennia Chinese civilization has been on par with, if not ahead of, much of the rest of the world. Despite having suffered over 150 years of national trauma since the Opium Wars of the mid-nineteenth century, the Chinese have never lost their cultural confidence. They have studied with great intensity all aspects of Western civilization, especially its science and technology. If it has not already happened, Chinese universities could soon be on par with Western universities in their mastery of science and technology. Chinese also have a huge hunger to learn English but, unlike the Japanese intellectuals at the beginning of the twentieth century, Chinese intellectuals do not believe that they will have to Westernize themselves to succeed.

Hence, as the Chinese economy and society continue to grow and flourish in the twenty-first century (although there will be many bumps on the road along the way), the Chinese will rediscover their deep cultural roots. There will be a huge pride in being Chinese. Already Chinese nationalism has become a major political force in China. Any politician in China who ignores the new Chinese pride does so at his own peril. The real challenge for educationists in China will be to balance this natural tendency to celebrate the huge cultural wealth of Chinese civilization with an equally strong message to Chinese children that they belong to a single common humanity. This challenge is greater in China because it has traditionally been an insular society. China has always perceived itself to be "The Middle Kingdom." Hence, when it is successful, China expects the rest of the world to come to its doorstep. It does not expect to go out and learn about the rest of the world. Indeed, the last Chinese dynasty that was open and cosmopolitan was the Tang Dynasty of the 9th century CE, probably the greatest Chinese dynasty. The question for China's educationists therefore is: How does China revive the cosmopolitan spirit of the Tang Dynasty?

To do so, each Chinese child should be taught that while Chinese history and culture are rich resources, Chinese civilization is but one rich stream among the many rich streams in human civilization. The traditional cultural insularity of China will have to be overcome through the content of the education provided to Chinese children. When Chinese children learn about the many great thinkers in Chinese history, from Confucius to Lao Tse, they should also simultaneously learn about great Western thinkers, especially Socrates. They could also be taught that perhaps one reason why China fell centuries behind the West in development was because of China's huge emphasis on rote learning. The West, by contrast, had bottled the spirit of Socrates in its culture and had consistently promoted a culture of questioning and critical reasoning. Chinese educationists, if they searched hard enough, could surely find some impish Chinese philosophers from earlier days who asked questions as critically as Socrates did. Hence, if critical reasoning and questioning could be woven into the Chinese educational system, the next generation of Chinese is likely to be more cosmopolitan, less nationalistic. It would be a huge contribution to world history if Western and Chinese civilizations could grow and flourish without conflict.

The same spirit of Socrates needs to be infused into another, equally insular civilization: Islamic civilization. Like Chinese civilization, Islamic civilization had its heyday a thousand years ago during the era of the great Caliphates. Like the Tang Dynasty, these Caliphates were open and cosmopolitan. Indeed, these Islamic Caliphates did Western civilization a great favor by preserving the real fruits of Greek and Roman civilizations (after these two great civilizations declined) and then passing back their rich fruits to the West. Despite this enormous contribution that the Islamic world made to human civilization, probably fewer than 5 percent of today's 1.2 billion Muslims are aware of this contribution. (It is equally troubling that few in the West are aware of this contribution.)

Traditional Islamic education has suffered from the same handicap as traditional Chinese education: an emphasis on rote learning. Just as China will have to rise to the challenge of the twenty-first century by introducing a heavier emphasis on questioning and critical reasoning in its educational system, the Islamic world will have to do the same. But the challenge of doing this will be greater in the Islamic world. The prevailing mood in China is one of confidence and pride; the prevailing mood in the Islamic world is one of anger and humiliation. This mood does not provide the most fertile soil for introducing new concepts and ideas, even though the need there is even greater.

One asset here is the rich diversity of the Islamic world. The 1.2 billion Muslims share one religion, but they belong to many different cultures. Each has its own dynamic. Some need more help than others. The Arab world is the heartland of Islam, but it now faces the greatest development

challenges, as documented in the Arab Human Development Reports prepared by the United Nations Development Programme (UNDP) in 2002
and 2003. Today, Finland, with a population of 5.5 million, produces more
(at least by conventional economic valuations of production) than the 280
million people of the Arab world. Only 1.6 percent of the Arab population
has Internet access, compared with 68 percent in the United Kingdom and
79 percent in the United States. I have taken these statistics from a speech
given by Daniel Rose entitled "Fighting Alligators vs. Draining the Swamp"
(2003). In it, he also dispenses the same advice: Reconnect the Arab world
with "the Golden Age of the Abbassid caliphate, when Muslim scientists,
philosophers, artists and educators sparkled in one of the great cultural
flowerings of all time." Mr. Rose adds: "Then Muslims remembered that
the Prophet said 'The ink of scientists is equal to the blood of martyrs'; then
Muslim thinkers were proud of their familiarity with the best of the world's
cultures; then it was taken for granted that science and knowledge belonged
to *all* mankind and that intellectuals' borrowing and lending benefited
everyone. What the Muslim world had once it can have again" (2003).

This vital reconnection between the Islamic world of today and the glorious Islamic era cannot be done by a Western educational toolbox. The
Muslims will have to create one of their own. It will have to include a study
of the best practices of Western science and technology. On the historical
and literary fronts, their textbooks will have to speak about the glorious
era when the Islamic world was open and receptive to the best ideas of the
world. Undoubtedly, as in China, there were many Islamic philosophers
who studied and imbibed the spirit of Socrates. The writing of these Islamic
philosophers should become standard fare in Islamic textbooks so that the
educational habits of questioning and critical reasoning, so vital for any
child in the twenty-first century, are seen to have equally strong Islamic
roots as Western roots.

Introducing these habits of questioning and critical reasoning may be
more difficult in the African context. It is no secret that African societies
are among the most demoralized in the world today. As a prominent African Foreign Minister told me in private, the problem in Africa is that there
is no clear national success story that other Africans can use as a model, in
the way that Japan's early success inspired the Asian people. Personally, I
will never forget a visit I made to a primary school classroom in Liberia in
April 2001. There were more than sixty students per class, with students
pressed tightly together on crowded benches. Liberia was then ravaged by
conflict. I could see hope shining out of these children's eyes. I asked myself
then that if I had to honestly tell these children what lay in store for them,
what hope could I have given them?

This is the challenge every African teacher faces as he walks into a classroom: How does he make the young African children dream great dreams
of the future when the present often looks so foreboding? The answer has
to be that young African children, while they should have access to all the

basic skills of literacy and science and mathematics that are the critical bricks of any educational system, should also be equipped with skills that will equip them to cope with the difficult working environment they will face. To do otherwise would be cruel. An emphasis on practical vocational skills in vocations that will grow in Africa's economies will equip their children to face the future more confidently. Most Africans I speak to are acutely aware that most leading Organisation for Economic Co-operation and Development (OECD) statesmen will make passionate speeches about the need to end poverty in Africa. Yet, as the cotton farmers of West Africa and Uganda have discovered, the cotton subsidies of America will continue to depress global cotton prices and impoverish them. These subsidies will also continue as long as American politicians will have to be elected. Hence, if some deep pools of African poverty are not likely to be reduced soon, how should their children be taught to enable them to cope better with poverty?

At the same time, it is important to remove the blatant prejudices that exist in many minds about Africans. In a 2001 interview with the *Mail & Guardian* of Johannesburg, President Thabo Mbeki of South Africa said:

> Many whites, I wouldn't say all, have a particular stereotype of black people. They would deny it, but it's true. They see black people as lazy, basically dishonest, thieving, corrupt. 'They can't really govern any country. Look at what's happened in the rest of Africa'. That would be the argument (LaFraniere, 2004).

In the current intellectual environment in the West, it is often deemed to be politically incorrect to suggest that the results of educational reform will depend on the cultural or regional context. Fortunately, in one of the first few essays written for the UBASE project, Emily Hannum and Claudia Buchmann (2006) noted:

> A final contributor to contradictory findings, and an important caveat even in areas where consistent results have emerged, is the point that educational impacts are sensitive to context. The human capital perspective implicit in much of the research on educational investments is inherently individualistic, assuming that education will offer the same enabling capacities to individuals regardless of the contexts in which they function. This perspective often fails to acknowledge that within the global economy, within nations, within local communities, and within school systems, social structures shape and constrain the impact of rising education. . . . Reasonable forecasts of the consequences of extending basic and secondary education to the world's most disadvantaged populations need to consider the social structures in which these expansions will occur (pp. 523–524).

The real challenge of promoting universal primary and secondary education in the twenty-first century is that the goals of these educational systems have to be contextually appropriate and must also promote global understanding. It is dangerous to assume that rising educational levels will naturally generate both greater understanding and harmony between different cultures and regions. In the short run, if education only promotes cultural and national chauvinism, the effect of education could be greater global divisiveness and friction. Very little in human history suggests that harmony is a natural condition between different cultures and civilizations.

Since all the different cultures and civilizations (which were once at least separated by geography) will now have to live in close proximity in a shrinking global village, all educational systems must try to figure out how to promote more cross-cultural understanding. One key step that needs to be taken is to introduce greater awareness of all major civilizations in the classroom. Non-European languages have to be taught more widely. Today, in the United States, one million children learn French, a language spoken by eighty million people. By contrast, only 40,000 American children are learning Mandarin, a language spoken by 1.2 billion people. This disproportion reveals the classical problem in educational systems. It takes a long time to develop a consensus on what needs to be taught, and it takes even longer to train the teachers to teach any new subjects. Hence, most of the time, most of the educational systems are teaching directions and contents which were more valid for a previous era of world history. Training enough American teachers to teach Mandarin to one million American children could conceivably take decades, but the impact of a successful and confident China on America will not take decades. One key challenge for all educationists in the twenty-first century is how to promote faster change in educational content and systems.

In the twenty-first century, we are more likely to see the acceleration than the end of history. Little in most educational systems will help prepare most of mankind for the obvious new challenges we face. There is therefore a real urgency to revisit traditional assumptions about the key goals of primary and secondary education systems worldwide. Most of the time the prevailing assumption has been that a wider spread of the conventional Western toolbox of education will do the trick of both preparing humankind for new challenges and preventing conflict as different societies interact more closely with each other. The key purpose of this chapter is to alert educational policymakers that if we enter the twenty-first century on auto-pilot, using existing conventional wisdom, we may be delivering a prescription for both misunderstanding and disharmony. If so, future historians will ask why we did not see so clearly when the twenty-first century began that a new world was clearly being born. If Socrates were alive today, would he be so complacent with conventional wisdom?

REFERENCES

Hannum, Emily, and Claudia Buchmann. 2006. "Global Educational Expansion and Socio-Economic Development: An Assessment of Findings from the Social Sciences." In *Educating All Children: A Global Agenda*, ed. Joel E. Cohen, David E. Bloom, and Martin B. Malin, 495–524. Cambridge, MA: MIT Press.

LaFraniere, Sharon. 2004. "After Reconciliation, Steering South Africa to a Reckoning." *New York Times*, April 27.

Rose, Daniel. 2003. "Fighting Alligators vs. Draining the Swamp." Speech presented at Philanthropy Day 2003, Association of Fundraising Professionals, New York, November 21.

4 What Will Be the Near-Future Goals of Education?

William K. Cummings

While educators and planners propose various reforms, the very slow rate of change of modern education is impressive (Cheng, Chapter 2, this volume). Still, over the past several decades, there have been important shifts in the rhetoric of educational reform, orchestrated especially by transnational entities. Two broad trends are likely to shape the near future of education: (a) the declining influence of the transnational entities that defined the educational agenda of the late twentieth century, and (b) the ongoing information revolution which is eroding confidence in modern education while providing hints of new possibilities on the horizon.

THE CHANGING POLITICAL ECONOMY

Education is a vast industry requiring extensive resources. Hence it depends heavily on the support of national and transnational agencies. Over the last century there were four major stages in the relations of these agencies. The first stage unfolded in the core nations of the modern era: France, Germany, the United Kingdom, the United States, Japan and Russia, as each of these nations carved out its niche in the age of nation-states. Education was harnessed to the goals of fostering the national identity of the core states and the loyalty of their citizens; and in the colonial empires of the core states, education reinforced subjugation. There was no substantial transnational body independent of these great powers.

Following World War II, UNESCO was formed to promote education as a human right and as a resource for the national development of the large group of newly independent states seeking to escape the shackles of colonialism. UNESCO generally advocated, for purposes of efficiency, a centralized educational system focused on promoting national integration.

The UNESCO approach was perhaps overly ambitious and under-funded; it also was insensitive to subnational interests. During the 1980s, it was eclipsed by a new, more decentralized design for education promoted by the international banks, notably the World Bank. Basic literacy and skills (as contrasted with advanced education and knowledge creation/

74 *William K. Cummings*

diffusion/utilization) were strong themes in the WB plan, with increasing attention to the roles of local actors. Schematically, these stages are compared in Table 4.1.

Nations came to view these strategies as inefficient and inconsequential, especially in an era of shrinking national budgets. So, from the early 1990s, donors and nations came to focus on community-based schooling, where local actors might play a greater role in both formulating the goals of education and providing some of the resources for its operations. Additionally, in many developing societies, renewed interest came to be focused on the potential for economic development of creating knowledge indigenously.

Table 4.1 The Auspices of Education

	Multilateral, Centralized	Multilateral, Decentralized	Community-Based
Period of Ascendance	1950–1975	1975–1990	1990–2000
What Assumptions Are Behind Educational Policy	Education is to promote national development	As nation is composed of distinctive ethnic groups, education should be responsive to the majority of the respective regions	Given the constraints governments have faced in reaching out, communities are looked to for educational initiatives
Who Decides on Goals of Education	The centralized state in consultation with donors	The state in consultation with local governments and donors	Local communities
Who Funds	Central governments with donor support	Central and local governments with donor support	Local communities provide a substantial sum, with some outside help
Who Decides Curriculum	The central government	The central government may define structure, with allowance for local content and local language for instruction	The central government may define goals, but local schools decide content and rely on local language for instruction
Who Decides on Educational Personnel	The central government	Local governments following central regulations	Local community possibly in collaboration with sponsor
Who Decides on Admissions	Local officials, based on central regulations	Local officials	School head and community

During this period of increasing recognition of subnational actors, national actors especially in Eastern Europe and Africa came to face new challenges from these actors—often expressed through movements for autonomy and independence. These challenges were often accompanied by rebellious activities including violence and military conflict. These challenges tended to undermine the normal routines of society, including education. The continuity of the 1970s and 1980s came to be followed by increasing examples of discontinuity at the close of the twentieth century.

National educational plans in 1982 identified five generic rationales for government support of education and thirty-four specific outcomes expected from education. In a similar set of plans at the beginning of the twenty-first century, many of the rationales persist (Table 4.2). At the same time, there are several interesting changes:

- The 2001 list has a much greater sense of ambition—e.g., "extend literacy" is now replaced with "eradicate illiteracy."
- The 2001 list is more specific in identifying inequalities that education is asked to address—gender, regional, rural–urban, poverty, and historical injustices.
- The 2001 list highlights a growing interest in technology both as an asset for learning and as a means for social development.
- The 2001 list places a greater stress on values education including democracy, religiosity, and tolerance—but also renews the stress on national unity and the need to counter extremism and terrorism.

Behind these changes is a subtle dynamic. Transnational funding's proportion of educational funding steadily increased through at least the mid-1990s. With it came increasing pressure on nations to accept transnational educational orthodoxies. But there were few clear signs that these orthodoxies were helping nations or their children.

One subtle break with the orthodoxy has been the clamor for more stress on indigenous higher education and research. Rather than remain customers, increasing numbers of new nations feel they can or should be creators and sellers.

A second and potentially more profound break is the revived stress on nation-building. The world has been a scary place for many decades, but the international orthodoxy has largely ignored that reality. With the beginning of the twenty-first century, leaders around the world are coming to recognize that a transnational entity can be depended on neither to guarantee peace nor to provide dependable support for national development efforts. The consequences of this new recognition are as yet unknown. Possible consequences include a war of civilizations, or a retreat to feudalism. Whatever the ultimate outcome, in the near-term era when partners cannot be counted on, nations and subnations tend to enhance their emphasis on autonomy and self-reliance. This change leads to a return to revised nation-building rationales and an increasing stress on the role of education in supporting national defense and security. Goals such as quality and efficiency may be sacrificed by this inward shift.

Table 4.2   Summary of Rationales for Educational Expenditures

Lewin 1982	28 National Reports Published in 2001
Nation-building rationales	**Nation-building rationales**
Develop and consolidate a national identity Promulgate a national language Promulgate a national ideology Promote self-sufficiency and self-reliance Reduce cultural and psychological dependency Strengthen local institutions Develop individual potential fully Localize expatriate manpower Ensure physical well-being and health	Reinforce national unity*** Acquire habits of hygiene and healthcare*** Increased awareness and appreciation of cultural/historical/linguistic identity***** Promote loyalty to national religion* Promote democracy***** Promote indigenous language* Counter extremism and terrorism* Modernize religious schools*
Manpower Development Rationales	**Manpower Development Rationales**
Increase the possession of general skills relevant to the development Increase the possession of skills relevant to the modern sector Provide agricultural development knowledge and skills Increase the prospects for self-employment Extend literacy to increase productivity and innovation Develop non-formal education programs	Produce individuals to contribute towards development***** Establishing strong scientific and technological base** Preparing individuals for world of work**** Match manpower with labor market demands***** Provide labor flexibility and mobility* Promoting economic growth**** Modernize agricultural technology** Eradicate illiteracy*****
Socio Equity Rationales	**Socio Equity Rationales**
Equalize educational opportunities and reduce regional disparities in access Reduce income inequalities Reduce occupational differences between groups assuming from educational imbalances Provide basic education as a human right	Reduce gender inequalities***** Reduce regional inequalities*** Reduce urban/rural inequalities*** Correct historical injustices** Provide free basic education***** Reduce income poverty
Improving Efficiency of Schooling Rationales	**Improving Efficiency of Schooling Rationales**
Reduce dropouts Reduce repetition rates Increase enrollments Improve cost-effectiveness of teacher training Improve efficiency of plant utilization	Decentralize system management***** Transition to transnational (EU) model of education**

(continued)

Table 4.2 (continued)

Lewin 1982	28 National Reports Published in 2001
Improving Quality of Schooling Rationales	**Improving Quality of Schooling Rationales**
Improve educational quality through curriculum development	Update educational content*****
Improve quality through localizing examinations	Remove dogma and ideology**
Improve teacher training	Establish universal minimum requirements*
Improve in-service professional development	Improve teachers' social status*****
Improve resources available to teachers	Launch new teaching technologies*
Enhance planning and research capabilities	Improve infrastructure****
Increase private education standards	Improve teacher training*****
	Decrease student/teacher ratio***
	Technology Rationales
	Keep pace with technological advances****
	Avoid the wrong side of the digital divide*
	Use Internet as education resource***
	Let students learn at own pace as self-learners**
	Develop workers to compete in information age***
	Upgrade technological infrastructure***

Note: Asterisks refer to relative frequency of articulation in Ministry reports with **** indicating very high frequency and no asterisk meaning occasional articulation.

Sources: Lewin, Keith et al., 1982. "Adjusting to the 1980's: Taking Stock of Educational Expenditure." In *Financing Educational Expenditures. IDRC; UNESCO-International Bureau of Education. 2001.* International Conference on Education: National Reports of 2001. Geneva: UNESCO-IBE.

THE POTENTIAL OF THE INFORMATION REVOLUTION

The modern school was an educational innovation that replaced the former tradition of home schooling and self-study. Children were placed in schools some distance from their homes where trained teachers taught them a prescribed curriculum organized in sequential grades. Each new goal and related component of the modern school—the schoolhouse, the curriculum organized in grades and conveyed through textbooks, the trained teacher— while introduced to enhance learning, also added substantial costs. Over the reform-rich twentieth century, there was a succession of innovations in the modern school, such as the increased role for local governments and communities evident in the last decade. Yet, in an age of rising educational costs that are not matched with rising accomplishments, it is inevitable that critics question the value of the goals and components of the modern school, asking if some cannot be modified or even dispensed with. The information revolution opens up many new possibilities.

In the early decades of the modern era, the school was an exciting place for most children—or at least a more attractive option than working in the fields. In today's information society, the school encounters potential competition from many teachers, and often loses. Young people, especially as they reach their teens, frequently express boredom with their schooling. Yet these same young people have dreams of becoming successful adults with interesting careers and a full package of material possessions.

To help children make the transition from youth to adulthood, some societies are beginning to organize internships in workplaces as an alternative to formal schooling. Germany offers a unique program of industry-based vocational schools. This same principle could easily be applied to other occupational areas, such as internships in commercial and industrial corporations, internships in museums and other aesthetic activities such as architectural firms or the music industry, internships in the media and sports and leisure organizations. Societies might propose to offer to every middle-school graduate an opportunity over the next several years to participate in a minimum of three internships. Upon the completion of the internship phase, the young people would have a clearer sense of their occupational aspirations and a stronger determination to commit to the studies appropriate for realizing those aspirations. Boredom might be replaced by purposeful motivation. As these internships would benefit the host sites as much as the youth, the host sites would cover most of the costs—thus relieving the educational sector of many of the expenses currently devoted to high school education.

Teachers' salaries are the major expense of the modern school. Any reduction of the modern school's dependence on teachers is likely to lead to a more affordable school. One vision possible in the cybernetic era is to shift a significant part of the teaching challenge to computer-assisted technology such as the presentation of materials, the facilitation of exercises, the evaluation of student performance, and the analysis of student learning difficulties. Teachers might serve in a new role of coordinating these technical tasks, while intervening to introduce new concepts and to stimulate higher-level thinking. Considerable technology is now being developed to accomplish these various tasks. Ironically, this technology currently has its highest applicability at the tertiary level for adult learners rather than at the primary level where the educational challenge is most pressing. The shift to educational technology also reduces the reliance on school buildings as a site for learning; students can complete most of their learning assignments at home or at a nearby computer center or learning station. Where good instructional technology is in place, teachers' contact hours are reduced and so are educational expenses.

In sum, there are ways to design education that reduce dependence on the modern props of school buildings, the uniform curriculum, textbooks, trained teachers, and one-time national examinations. Focusing on the goals of education as contrasted with the modern means is the key to the elaboration of these possibilities. Educational technology opens up many of these possibilities. Will the twenty-first century, drawing on the power of the cybernetic revolution, launch the third educational revolution?

Part III

Educational Priorities in Poor Countries

5 Quality Education
The Work of Optimists

Beryl Levinger

I have spent four decades thinking about universal primary education. During that time, many of my views have held constant. I have always believed, for example, that education transforms society and that too few girls and members of marginalized or stigmatized groups have access to it. This lack of diversity erodes quality, because it limits education's potential to help students understand how the world really works—both locally and globally. Unfortunately, I also still believe that education often does little to respond to the challenge of preparing individuals in the four performance areas that lie at the heart of quality education: sustaining a livelihood; protecting the environment; being a good family member; and practicing enlightened citizenship. But, in this chapter, I will primarily address how my thinking has evolved—specifically, what has changed in my approach to quality education, and why.

The source of much of this transformation has to do with how I have come to view poverty and the role of education in reducing it. Let's think of just one young girl, whom we'll call Gabi. She lives, as more than a billion people do, on less than $1 a day. Gabi, a ten-year old West African villager, has experienced loss this year; her baby brother died. She frequently labors at least fourteen hours on such grueling tasks as hauling water, searching for firewood, harvesting yams, marketing vegetables grown in the family's small garden, and struggling to care for a younger sibling who is very sick. Often, Gabi herself is tired and hungry; she seldom passes a week without some sort of physical pain or dull ache from an unnamed and untreated illness.

Gabi wanted to study, but the school nearest her home (some five kilometers away) offers only the first three primary grades. The teacher is all too often absent and, when she is present, teaches in a language that no one in Gabi's family can speak. Gabi's parents, who have been engaged in a lifelong struggle for survival, didn't think the sacrifice they would have to make to send Gabi to school was justified. They also doubt that Gabi has the stamina to walk ten kilometers each day for an education. And they're concerned for her safety along a road where violent acts have occasionally been reported. The harsh necessities of Gabi's life have forced her to enter the informal labor force at a very early age.

Gabi doesn't live in poverty. Poverty was *done* to Gabi, because forces well beyond Gabi's control placed her exactly where she is. She's unschooled because little or no suitable schooling was available. She's often sick because adequate health services and clean water aren't available. She's poor because the land her family works is poor, and there are no agricultural extension workers to help them eke out a better living from it. For Gabi, the traditional escape routes from poverty—training, credit, schools, health care, and a facilitative environment conducive to personal betterment—are totally inaccessible. Gabi lives in a canyon that's sealed at the pass.

It's easy to blame Gabi's plight on policy gone awry. Her government should have allocated its resources differently. The debt crisis should have been handled differently. Cash crops should have been introduced differently. Precious land resources should have been managed differently. But, in the final analysis, Gabi is not a centerpiece at some policy-level banquet. Her needs can't be dismissed by mouthing policy platitudes. Even if she's a composite character, she's real.

When we talk about quality education, we must reframe the issue and ask, "What kind of education does *Gabi* need?" What kind of schooling would best equip *her* to confront and change those conditions that keep her and her family ensnared in the poverty trap?

Here's how I would answer these questions. Gabi's education—ideally acquired in a school that is nearby, free, and culturally appropriate—must prepare her to engage in the four most basic tasks of citizens who live in communities where sustainable development is underway: creating a livelihood; protecting the environment; making common cause with others who seek to build a better life; and living in a family that provides appropriate support and nurturance for *all* its members. For Gabi to carry out these tasks she will need the instrumental skills of reading, writing, and basic computation as well as content-driven knowledge in the natural sciences, social studies, health, and nutrition. But Gabi's education must also focus on the realm of values, processes, and attitudes. Three building blocks that form the core of "quality education" lie within this realm.

Building Block #1: metacognitive skills that contribute to the transfer of knowledge and to the solution of novel problems. Gabi's world is changing. Thanks to globalization, the store of economic rewards available to unskilled but hard-working individuals is rapidly dwindling. Attending to life's necessities increasingly entails adaptive thinking. Gabi must become a lifelong learner, and metacognitively oriented instruction is the road map that will bring her to this destination.

Metacognitive instruction addresses the abilities of learners to plan, classify, think divergently, identify assumptions, recognize misleading information, and generate questions. *Metacognition* refers to an individual's ability to think about thinking. It involves being consciously aware of one's role as a problem solver and describes an ability to monitor and control one's mental processing. It is distinct from such other cognitive skills as demonstration of effective memory, the ability to perform defined tasks, or the use of generic strategies for solving new problems (such as outlining a chapter in a textbook in order to bolster comprehension). The individual who exemplifies strong metacognition is one who uses knowledge acquired in one content area (estimation skills in math, for example) to solve a problem in an entirely different area (for example, drawing inferences about the local ecosystem).

In addition to the ability to predict the results of one's own problem-solving actions, basic metacognitive development includes skills that enable individuals to check the results of their own actions, to track their progress toward a solution, and to gauge the reasonableness of their actions and solutions against some larger reality.

Gabi will encounter many never-before-seen problems over the course of her lifetime. Her ability to deal successfully with the unknown is directly linked to the metacognitive competencies she must develop over the course of her schooling.

Building block #2: skills that prepare learners to avail themselves of development opportunities. We need to think of Gabi not just as a potential *beneficiary* of development processes. With the proper schooling, Gabi can also become an agent of change and transformation for others.

In this context, let me introduce the term *participation opportunity*, which represents a potential *productive* interaction in which an individual can engage. Participation opportunities allow Gabi and others to contribute to the development of their nation, community, and family.

Participation opportunities span the course of a person's life cycle and evolve accordingly. Illustratively, they include the chance to go to school; secure a livelihood; influence political or civic affairs; promote family development or protect the environment as well as the opportunity to partake in agricultural extension activities and participate in cultural events. Accessed participation opportunities describe those participation opportunities that individuals actually utilize. As such, they represent a subset of the available participation opportunities found in any particular setting. The notion of accessed participation opportunity is a modern-day analogue to the old saw, "You can lead a horse to water, but you can't make it drink." A citizen may encounter a participation opportunity but choose to ignore it. Or a participation opportunity may be present in the environment unbeknownst to the individual.

The education that Gabi needs will prepare her to recognize available participation opportunities. It will also predispose her to access these opportunities throughout the course of her lifetime. Perhaps most importantly, Gabi's quality education will help her to create participation opportunities for herself, her family, and members of her community. The key to poverty reduction lies in an ever-growing inventory of participation opportunities that are created and accessed by citizens over the course of their lifetimes. That is why the idea of participation opportunity access and creation is so central to the notion of quality education.

Building block #3: processes that add to the store of social capital in the community. Gabi must make common cause with others if she's to create a new future for herself and her family. Her empowerment won't be achieved while flying solo.

Social capital refers to the relations—formal and informal—that bring people together to take action. The oxygen that sustains social capital is trust which, together with a cluster of shared attitudes, values, and rules, lead to a common sense of mutual (or civic) responsibility. Accordingly, Gabi's schooling must model and inspire mutual trust that leads to collaborative effort.

Social capital makes society more than a mere collection of individuals. It is the glue that holds a society's institutions and citizens together. The combination of trust and a willingness to cooperate allows people to form self-help groups and mutual benefit associations. Social capital, therefore, is a resource that facilitates the realization of shared goals in a functional society. It is also an indispensable asset for individuals who want to lift themselves out of poverty through collective action. Indeed, it is social capital that allows individuals to work together to secure fundamental rights—including the right to a quality education—in the face of persistent denial by state actors.

Education can build social capital only when five basic conditions are met: (a) parents and community members come together to play a significant role in all aspects of the educational enterprise; (b) learners create deeply meaningful linkages between what they study in school and the reality of their local community; (c) social interaction is fully integrated into all aspects of learning; (d) teachers model respect for all learners; and (e) the schoolhouse becomes a magnet for *all* children in a community regardless of gender, linguistic background, family income, religion, ethnicity, or physical disabilities.

An enormous literature clearly describes what we need to do to attract underrepresented groups of students to our classrooms. Often, nations that have not made the investments needed to enroll all children plead budgetary constraints.

In recent years, econometricians have developed useful techniques for monetizing the value of social capital stocks. It is now time to forge a new awareness; the costs of *not* engaging every child in schooling may be far higher (considering the value of foregone social capital) than the relatively modest investments needed to achieve universal basic education.

I used to think of education as a self-contained system. The challenge, I thought, was to ensure that each component of this system functioned at the highest possible level. Consequently, I worked alongside many gifted professionals to secure improvements in the basic conditions of teaching and learning. The goal was to improve the system's efficiency. More graduates, fewer drop-outs, less disparity, and greater content mastery would be the hallmarks of these efficiency improvements. Curricular reform, teacher training, advances in educational technology and initiatives aimed at improving children's active learning capacity (e.g., school health and nutrition programs) would comprise the menu of interventions.

But now, with hindsight and perhaps even that touch of wisdom that comes with the passage of time, I see our challenges in a very different light. I now define quality education as the successful transmission of skills, knowledge, attitudes, and behaviors that enable learners to dramatically surpass the full range of obstacles imposed by the circumstances of their birth. Narrow preconceptions about others as well as an inappropriate sense of one's place in the world exemplify limitations of birth that can transcend family income or social class.

The pursuit of quality education is a labor of optimists, for it rests upon a utopian assumption: *it is possible to remove parental status and good fortune as the key determinants of a child's future.* This thinking, wildly hopeful and radical, is what allows me to believe that the story of Gabi and her future children may have a surprise ending.

6 Achieving Education of High Quality in Islamiyya Schools of Nigeria

Bala Ahmed

Universal primary education (UPE) has engaged much attention globally since the Jomtien declaration in 1990, and many countries have launched UPE programs. For instance, in my country, Nigeria, a program was first launched in 1976. Nigerians were very hopeful and confident that the UPE program would be successful. The populace had great confidence and faith in the power of education to raise the living standards of Nigeria's people and to promote the spirit of national consciousness and pride. However, the inability of the government to focus proper attention on the initial program and to commit to it adequate resources led to the program's demise. The program was re-launched as universal basic education (UBE) in 1999.

THE GOALS OF UNIVERSAL EDUCATION AND QUR'ANIC EDUCATION

"Goals" are the expected results at which the knowledge imparted to children aims. In other words, goals refer to those changes that are likely to be effected in children after the teaching-learning process has taken place. Islamic/Qur'anic education has three goals:

Reading ability. The proprietors of most Islamiyya schools train children in both primary and secondary grades to read and understand Arabic texts. The process used is the common method adopted by almost all Qur'anic school teachers. It commences with teaching of the alphabet gradually, until pupils become well acquainted with all the letters and are able to read without someone's assistance.

Writing ability. As children learn how to read correctly they also begin learning to write, with a view to bringing together these two inseparable aspects of learning. Knowing how to write is now one of the goals of universal education in the Qur'anic schools at all levels. Literacy is therefore the focal point of learning.

Good morals and conduct. One of the principal goals of teaching at the primary and secondary levels is to impart to children all the virtues necessary to make them responsible members of the society. Occasionally, one encounters children who have acquired the basic skills in reading and writing but who lack good manners, which makes them seem uneducated. This problem is a major reason for making this goal one of the major goals of universal primary and secondary education.

UNIVERSAL EDUCATION AND THE
GOALS OF ISLAMIYYA SCHOOLS

With the increased support of some international donor agencies and organizations, the goals of universal primary and secondary education have been extended beyond reading, writing, and good morals to include life skills. Consequently, proprietors of most of the Qur'anic schools, especially in the northern part of Nigeria, have changed the traditional Qur'anic schools into Islamiyya schools.

The two types of schools differ in many respects. In this discussion I focus on the goals of the modern Islamiyya schools compared to those of the Qur'anic schools. Many teachers and proprietors of Qur'anic schools have changed their schools to Islamiyya schools by widening the scope of their teaching and learning through the introduction of new methodologies in the curriculum. Teaching has become better organized and more results-oriented. This has led to new educational goals:

Teach in both Arabic and English. Islamiyaa schools, especially those in Bauchi and other parts of northern Nigeria, focus on educating children to communicate in Arabic and English. The two borrowed languages are taught simultaneously, and children communicate well in both English and Arabic by the time they complete their primary education. This was made possible by the introduction of a curriculum to guide teachers.

Train students in record keeping. In the Islamiyya schools, children are expected to learn to record events in both Arabic and English. In the Qur'anic schools, little effort is made to teach children to keep records in the popular style (called the *Ajami*) in the Hausa and Fulani languages. This old method is less effective in comparison to the modern techniques.

Prepare students for professional employment. Islamiyya education is directed toward the creation of job skills. Most of the Islamiyya primary and secondary graduates are employed in various fields such as teaching, the judiciary, agriculture, and other relevant professions.

Impart knowledge of trade and commerce. A final focus of Islamiyya education is knowledge of trade and commerce. When fully incorporated into the curriculum, it is expected to provide youth with ample opportunity for self reliance. The late Shehu Usman Dan Fodio, a writer and Islamic reformer, encouraged his students to be involved in trade and commerce as a means of livelihood.

EDUCATION OF HIGH QUALITY IN ISLAMIYYA SCHOOLS

It is imperative to highlight some of the key elements of an education of high quality. In my experience, the factors that enable effective learning and create positive outcomes include those listed below; they should be taken up by all Islamiyya and Qur'anic schools:

Curricula. Standard curricula across schools are needed. Unless the Islamiyya/Qur'anic schools take up systematic, formal curricula, and unless the development of these curricula are included as a national budgetary priority, an acceptable standard of quality education may not be feasible.

Introduction of examinations. Most Qur'anic schools do not conduct exams to test students' knowledge. It has become imperative to introduce methods of assessing performance weekly, each term, or annually.

Teaching resources. Provision of adequate resources such as desks, chairs, tables, and instructional materials such as text and exercise books is essential for increasing the quality of education.

Avoidance of corporal punishment. The use of corporal punishment to correct deviant behavior is a common practice in most Islamiyya and Qur'anic schools. This method of teaching correct behavior is inappropriate and counterproductive. The practice should be eliminated so that healthy teacher–pupil relationships can develop.

Teacher training seminars and workshops. Teachers should be encouraged to undergo continuing training through special courses, workshops, and seminars to update their knowledge on current teaching practices.

Classrooms. To make the atmosphere more conducive for learning, enough secure and clean classrooms must be provided to cut the menace of sitting in crowded huts and rooms. Governments and parents should organize fund-raising for schools in order to complement the efforts of the proprietors and the teachers, as in most cases these responsibilities are left in the hands of few individuals who cannot keep up with all that schools demand.

Hygienic public facilities. To have proper control of students in Islamiyya school hostels, all sanitary facilities must be readily available within the compound, so that children do not have to leave in search of toilets. UNICEF has made remarkable efforts to provide solutions to the environmental problems faced by Qur'anic and Islamiyya schools through the provision of sanitation and water facilities in many communities.

Hygienic water. Children of primary and secondary Islamiyya schools, especially in the Northern part of Nigeria, often suffer hardships in trying to obtain hygienic water for safe consumption. They are usually exposed to many dangers associated with drinking unhygienic water.

Nutritious food. The learning ability of children is enhanced through adequate and balanced nutrition, as is provided at some modern schools. The children at some Islamiyya and Qur'anic schools must sometimes go out and beg for food. Inevitably, this interferes with the children's access to education. In other cases, they may depend on remnant food and may not be fed sufficiently, or may get enough food but not of the required type.

School uniforms. One may note that at most of the Islamiyya and Qur'anic schools, children go about in ragged clothing. This situation discourages other parents from enrolling their children in such schools.

Bedding and other items. Bedding and other household items such as buckets, kettles, and mats to meet the daily needs of children in the boarding hostels can go a long way in making these children more comfortable and alert to learn.

Remuneration and teacher salaries. Providing remuneration, in cash or in kind, from time to time will motivate teachers at Qur'anic and Islamiyya schools to put forth their best effort in teaching. All human beings appreciate recognition for their work. Placing teachers on salaries is perceived by many to be a major ingredient in increasing the quality of education, as it no doubt makes teachers more devoted to the job and willing to spend more time with the children. Most, if not all, Qur'anic primary and secondary schools teachers are not salaried. Instead, they live at the mercy of a few philanthropists, usually wealthy members of the community who also founded the schools. The payment received by the teachers in this arrangement is usually a pittance.

Supervision. There is an absolute need for a supervisory body vested with the sole responsibility of observing the activities of the schools and especially the children's performances. The aim of this is to ensure that the outlined curriculum is strictly followed, which will enable the authorities to assess schools' performances, progress, and shortcomings.

Timely inspections by parents. Parents must develop the habit of paying frequent supervisory visits to their children at school, and leave behind the age-old practice of abandoning their children until they have graduated. In a similar vein, national and state governments should endeavor to give the support and encouragement necessary to make teachers and students have the sense of belonging to the society.

Formation of formidable Parent-Teacher Associations. Parents and school authorities must work hand in hand to provide an environment conducive to learning. The P.T.A. can be active in ensuring that school facilities are sufficient, for example, by checking to see that there are enough chairs and desks so that children are not sitting on windows, logs, or broken blocks and stones.

Harmonization of school calendars. There is an urgent need to formulate a centralized and effective policy that will harmonize all the Islamiyya schools so that a common calendar and enrollment method can guide schools.

Introduction of vacation. A period of vacation after every three months of school, as is the case with the Western education, affords children the opportunity to have some rest and to return to school refreshed. Breaks, currently a low priority of proprietors and teachers of primary and secondary level Qur'anic schools, should be incorporated into the school year.

RESPONSIBILITY FOR ENSURING THE ACHIEVEMENT OF GOALS

The task of ensuring that the components of a high-quality education listed previously are in place and that the goals of universal education are achieved lies largely in the hands of four groups: authorities, parents, teachers, and communities:

Authorities. The term "authorities" can refer to the government or to the traditional institution in the particular area where a Qur'anic school is situated. The authorities should know best the wants and needs of the people, especially the requirements and goals of education.

Parents. Parents, too, have an important role to play toward the attainment of educational goals. Home is said to be the first school, where children come to know and to learn before being enrolled into nursery or primary Qur'anic schools. As such, parents are truly the instructors at home and therefore shoulder some responsibility for imparting knowledge to their children.

Teachers. Where education levels are low, there may be a general misperception of the role of teachers. Some people believe that teachers carry responsibility solely for the education of the child. I agree that a teacher's greatest responsibility is for directing the education of children. Teachers also achieve success in deciding what knowledge and values should be imparted to the children, and it should be understood that teachers are character builders and behavior molders, as well as reading and writing instructors.

Community organizations. In many settlements one finds a variety of community organizations, religious, tribal, and other groups. Members of these organizations have a role in deciding the goals of education and contributing to the achievement of these goals. They know the yearnings and aspirations of their children, and the areas which, for the betterment of their children and for the society at large, need improvement.

CONCLUSION

Children who receive an education of high quality that meets the goals of universal education will acquire basic knowledge in reading and writing, and will be able to communicate effectively. Once literate, these children can then be among those who fight illiteracy and can make further contributions to society. Their ability to tackle issues that may come their way at any given time will be enhanced. As long as they have acquired the necessary knowledge and skills, these children will be considered responsible members of society. They will have developed good manners and a reasoning capacity.

For these goals to be a reality in Qur'anic schools, the outlined factors must be adhered to, and the knowledge, skills, and attitudes desired must also be identified for the appropriate age groups. Finally, the bodies responsible for overseeing education must work hand in hand with one another to achieve better results.

7 Nurturing Learning Ability
The Goals of Universal Primary and Secondary Education

Camer Vellani

INTRODUCTION

Advocacy for universal access to formal education for children requires definition of its purpose. The purpose may be viewed from various aspects, depending on one's perceptions of need. For example, in this volume, Cheng (Chapter 2) considers preparedness for specific functions in conditions of change and increasing global knowledge; Charfi and Redissi (Chapter 12) focus on acquiring values of tolerance and moderation in the context of human civilization and social and scientific development alongside national and religious identity of the learners.

In this chapter, I have applied generic considerations to identify the purposes of formal education, believing that such an approach could provide a useful guide for definition of learning objectives, relevant curricula, and modes of learning appropriate to cultural beliefs alongside changing socio-economic and political conditions. A crucial aspect of the generic approach is that it considers learning as a continuum, beginning with development of the ability to learn.

The following case history provides an opportunity to reflect on aspects of the purpose of education, from the perspective of an educator in Pakistan. It is a sample of the views held by one young recipient of formal education. Neither the perspectives of the educator nor the views reported in the case history should be construed as necessarily representative of a cross section of opinion in the country.

CASE HISTORY: OUTCOME OF TEN YEARS OF EDUCATION

At the doorstep of a mud-plastered wooden hut some 8,000 feet above sea level on the beautiful pine-forested mountain called Mushkpuri in the Hazara District of the North West Frontier Province of Pakistan, my wife and I met Iqbal, a handsome, bright seventeen-year-old lad who was attending to his bullock. He greeted us warmly. Responding to our curiosity about his life, he affirmed that he had attended school regularly for ten years at a nearby town some three miles up the valley, along the road that skirted the mountainside about seven hundred feet below his home, and possessed the Secondary School Certificate. We were impressed by his determination: walking six miles or more daily in the summer sun and rain would have been difficult enough, but the trudge in the winter snow and ice was unimaginable. He quickly brushed aside our admiration of his achievement and asked, "What use is the Certificate?" Taken aback, my wife commented that at least he could read the newspaper. "What use is that?" He paused and added, "You come from Karachi; you can help me to find a job." "What job would you like?" I asked. "Anything in the forestry," was the instant reply. "But that is a government establishment and the salary will be very low," said I. "Who looks at the salary? Hundreds of thousands of Rupees are made here," he responded. I advised him to submit an application for the job that interested him. With pragmatic wisdom he commented, "Nothing happens without an approach."

Iqbal's candor demonstrated that, by the age of seventeen years, his ability to learn, confidence, forthright communication, and adaptability were well developed. He had learned to read and write but did not give these attributes or any others that might have been acquired at school much importance. He had also learned that the Secondary School Certificate had no value; merit had no meaning; to be employed one had to befriend an influential person; and employment in a government civil service was the desired goal after school. Moreover, skills and ability did not matter; one's livelihood depended not on salary for work required by the employer but on opportunities for extorting bribes, provided by the authority of government regulations.

GENERAL OBJECTIVES OF THE NATIONAL CURRICULUM

The preface to Pakistan's National Curriculum for Classes IX-X (2002, p. 3) states:

> The objectives . . . are framed in the light of the National Education Policy (1998–2010). Purposeful learning competences are suggested in each subject. These aim to provide the learners skills for continuing education, civilized behavior and attitude to become useful and peaceful citizens. The objective is also to provide them with the skills for economic development . . . Attempt is made to make the curriculum more representative and responsive to the Ideology of Pakistan and societal needs.

Iqbal further demonstrated the incongruity of the curricular intent and what he had learnt about the knowledge, attitudes and skills that mattered for survival in his society.

We believe that education bestows many advantages on the recipients, important among them being economic well-being and health as well as peace and synergy that ensue from good citizenship. For these reasons, education is seen as an important element of human development that should be accessible to all. However, since education is an instrument of planned change in behavior, advocacy for universal application provokes misgivings about its purpose; especially when secularism, increasing with growth of knowledge, is seen as an erosive influence on religious and cultural beliefs. Surely, the enormous potential of education to influence behavior is the reason for national, political and religious concern about control of its content and effectiveness.

In respect to the purpose of basic and secondary education, being mindful of the powerful influence of examples in society, as Iqbal illustrated so well, a pragmatic view would focus on the competence required for health, responsible social interaction, lawful economic sustenance of individuals and their dependents, maturation of thought through growth of knowledge and experience, and rational consideration of elements that condition individuals' beliefs, decisions and actions.

LEARNING ABILITY

At the foundation of knowledge and behavior lies the ability to learn, an attribute of the brain that is present at birth and capable of remarkable versatility, enabling learning of a broad range of abstract concepts and physical skills. Establishment of this property occurs progressively through usage very early in childhood, mainly the first three years of life. Memory, another inherent property of the brain, a repository of experience and its associated contexts, serves as an integral component of learning. Development of structural connections within the brain to form networks that support learning and other complex functions are critically dependent upon perception of the environment through all modalities of sensation, driven by curiosity that directs exploration. Sensory perceptions are processed by association with action, past experience and thought to form concepts that represent a level of understanding that is modified with further experience. Establishment of this progressive conceptual development, which also serves the development of language, occurs very early and is very vulnerable to lack of stimulating environments, curtailment of mental and motor activity, and paucity of social interaction, in addition to malnutrition and chronic illness. Since development of the brain is already advanced before birth, it is affected even earlier by the nutritional, chemical and biological environment provided by the mother. Potentially, all of these factors can be influenced favorably by education of parents, care of mothers and appropriate nurture of infant and child.

SENSITIVE PERIODS OF BRAIN DEVELOPMENT

Failure of nutrition and stimulation weakens the ability of a child to attain his or her full genetic potential for mental development (Young, 2002). Evidence for staged development of the brain is provided by the fact that late removal of congenital cataract results in permanent blindness despite intact visual pathways. Clearly, development of neural structures of the brain and their related high-order functional abilities proceeds only in response to visual sensory perception during a critical finite period. A similar sensitive or critical period exists for hearing and learning as well as development of neural and endocrine responses to stress that is facilitated by tactile sensation. These observations underpin the basic concept of sequential, non-repetitive development of the brain (Mustard, 2007).

Further justification for emphasis on early child nurture comes from the cross-sectional study of the growth and development of children from birth to three years in underprivileged communities of rural and urban Sindh done by Avan (2007). The proportion of children with delayed psychomotor development increased nearly threefold in the first three years of life (see Table 7.1). Since psychomotor development reflects development of the brain and nervous system in general, the results indicate that a very large number of children do not attain their genetic potential.

Regression analysis showed independent associations of delayed development with many factors, including malnutrition, source of water, social interaction with parents, health and rural habitat; all potentially modifiable conditions of the child's social environment. Notwithstanding the large number of affected children the fact that psychomotor development of the majority was normal is a reflection of gene expression, due either to better nurture or resilience to deactivation of genes by adverse environmental conditions (Mustard, 2007).

Table 7.1 Psychomotor Development by Age (Avan, 2007)

Age	N	Normal (%)	Delayed (%)
First Year	454	86	14
Second Year	454	78	22
Third Year	336	63	37
Overall	1,244	77	23

Table 7.2   Educational Enrollment in Pakistan (in Millions), 2005–2006

Level	Total (%)	Female	Male
Pre-Primary	7.135 (22)	3.186	3.949
Primary	16.834 (52)	7.288	9.547
Middle	5.262 (16)	2.169	3.093
High (Grade 10)	2.133 (6.5)	0.882	1.251
Higher Sec. (Grade 12)	0.854 (2.5)	0.427	0.426
Degree	0.326 (1)	0.198	0.128
Total	32.544 (100)	14.151	18.394

Source: Ministry of Education. Government of Pakistan. "Education Statistics Table 5 Enrolment by Stage, Gender and Location, 2005–2006." http://www.moe.gov.pk/.

These data suggest that impaired ability to learn could be a determinant of high rates of discontinuation of education, alongside geographic access, quality of education, inability to afford the cost, gender and inaccuracy of official reports. The report of the Ministry of Education, Government of Pakistan for 2005–2006 (reproduced in Table 7.2) shows a precipitous decline in enrollment after primary education, 69% for middle school and 87% for Grade 10.

Development of the brain before and after birth, and the ability to learn well before school age, compels consideration of a holistic view of human development as the frame of reference for assessing the impact of education in schools.

OTHER FACTORS AFFECTING LEARNING

Social competence, learned through interaction, and behavior conditioned by approval and disapproval leads to conformity with the societal norm but masks the limited ability for conceptual learning, resulting in susceptibility to indoctrination and uncritical adoption of peer behavior. Multiple factors modulate an individual's knowledge, which in turn influences adaptation and behavior; prominent among them are moral reasoning, social and economic status, and beliefs derived from religious teaching, tradition and culture. Emotion strongly influences beliefs and behavior but deserves separate consideration because it affects all processes of acquisition and use of knowledge, including memory, perception and development of concepts, social learning, decision and behavior.

PURPOSES OF EDUCATION

Based on the need to nurture the development of learning ability and promote responsible citizenship, the author proposes the following general purposes of formal education for consideration:

1. For basic education: to extend the nurture of learning ability through diverse constructive experiences of perception and thought; to express thought through verbal and written language and images; to experience the application of knowledge and skills; to experience the range and perfection of physical activity; to participate in teamwork; to socialize with confidence; to build self-esteem.
2. For secondary education: to establish one's national and religious identity in a global context; to understand the biological, reproductive, physical and psychological constituents of health; to measure and analyze by applying reason and mathematics; to acquire basic, appropriate knowledge and skills for electronic access to information, lawful engagement in economic productivity, continual learning and survival.
3. For all stages of education: to apply moral reasoning; to acquire a broad range of knowledge about the physical world as a part of the universe; to appreciate life as an unusual phenomenon and understand its history and precarious sustenance in an ecosystem; to appreciate the constancy of human biology and the diversity of civilizations and cultures; to understand the existence of the spiritual constituent of human thought and the diversity of its expression; to express creativity; to acquire attitudes and skills that are relevant to responsible citizenship in one's home, school (representing an institution) and society.

The attitudes and skills include the following: to identify the basic causes of problems as a prerequisite for finding solutions; to evaluate knowledge critically and assess its impact objectively before adopting it; to communicate thought accurately, respectfully and constructively; to learn from experience through thoughtful reflection; to be tolerant of diversity; unwaveringly to be honest, disciplined, and accountable; and to understand the crucial responsibility of parents for child nurture, promotion of health, learning and responsible behavior, anticipating that school children will be parents, in due time.

Many aspects of formal education, particularly the attitudinal, should be complementary to the nurture, behavior and guidance provided to children at home by parents and caregivers.

EDUCATIONAL ASSESSMENT

Consideration of the purposes of education would be incomplete without concern for evaluation of the attainment of educational objectives. Sadly, it is not generally understood that evaluation should facilitate learning; instead, certification and a candidate's scores in examinations are viewed by parents, schools, institutions of higher learning, and the public as the indicators of both an individual's knowledge and effectiveness of education; inevitably, the stakes in assessment are very high for all concerned.

When examinations test mainly information given in prescribed textbooks, in a manner that facilitates learning of standard answers to standard questions, generations of "educated" youth enter the job market and higher education with creditable scores but with neither comprehension of knowledge nor the ability to apply it, and devoid of capacity for reasoning. No significant change in outcomes of education can be expected without reliable assessment of the learners' attainment of curricular objectives. Valid and reliable assessment should be a component of the system that determines the quality of education, alongside a formal review of the educational plan, instructional methods, and the institution's human, learning and physical resources.

CONDITIONS BEYOND THE SCOPE
OF FORMAL EDUCATION

I have emphasized the importance of nurturing the development of learning ability because the attribute is acquired in the early formative period and sets the stage for a child's performance and development through life; it is the basis of adaptation to change in circumstances and the inexorable growth of knowledge; and it provides the basis for rational behavior and productivity. Moreover, the process of development of the brain is dependent on expression of genes that are vulnerable to deactivation in conditions of malnutrition, ill health, unsafe physical environment, paucity of stimulation by the social environment, and aggression. Nevertheless, these deleterious conditions of child nurture can be changed by systematic education and support for parents and caregivers. Evidence for this and the case for investment to support early human development, particularly in disadvantaged communities, has been presented convincingly by Heckman (2006).

Interventions for promotion of early child development, particularly affection, breastfeeding, constructive social interaction and stimulation can be achieved at low cost in underprivileged communities, but they need other multisectoral development of society for sustenance, including nutrition of the mother and child, shelter, safe water and physical environment, health care and opportunity for economic productivity.

Returning to the case history, Iqbal had the ability to learn but little or no evidence of moral reasoning. While the principles acquired suggest weakness of formal education, it must be appreciated that the values and conditions of society have powerful influences on learning derived from experience. For instance, in his world, there were few jobs; it was true that employment generally was not based on merit; and political affiliation did matter for survival.

INFLUENCE OF SOCIETY

It is clear that the behaviors expected as a result of education, such as those outlined in this chapter, cannot be achieved by schooling alone, if they are distant from the norms of society. The government of Pakistan sees its national curriculum as a means of developing a cohesive society based on the country's religious ideology. In the Northern Areas of Pakistan, where the terrain consists of high mountains and valleys that are sparsely inhabited by hardy people adapted to harsh climatic conditions, living is disrupted frequently by landslides and earthquakes, and compounded by violence due to sectarian differences although the inhabitants are Muslims. The Secretary of Education of the Northern Areas expressed his desire for higher education to lead the society to tolerance through respect for pluralism and diversity but recognized that attainment of his ideal "demands improvement of human conditions" and a supportive value system in society.

Change in the human condition requires coordinated effort in multiple sectors of social development. Sadly, sector specificity limits holistic considerations of the multisystem action that is required for societal development. In this regard, emphasis on early child development as an essential goal has the potential of entraining broad considerations of societal development that include provision of public education on parenting, nutrition, environmental safety, health care and economic growth.

Equity, in respect of essential nurture to support human development and acquisition of learning ability, is potentially achievable only at the commencement of life.

CHANGES IN EDUCATION

The Curriculum Wing of the Ministry of Education defines and periodically reviews the national curriculum of Pakistan. The curriculum outlines the objectives, concepts, content, activities and evaluation of subject matter. Separately from development of the curriculum, some twenty-four Examination Boards conduct examinations for certification of Secondary School (SSC, Grade 10) and Higher Secondary (HSC, Grade 12) education. In practice, passing the examinations with the highest possible scores is the goal of education, and expected answers to past questions drive the learning. However, the section of the National Curriculum for Classes IX–X (2002, p. 17) on Assessment and Evaluation states correctly: "The assessment pattern should be in accordance with the needs of curriculum. It should be designed in a way that the students are encouraged for improving skills such as observation, curiosity, creativity, application, etc." Given the disconnection between these complementary functions, meaningful change by evolution of the curriculum however enlightened is unlikely.

In 2002, the Government of Pakistan established the Examination Board of the Aga Khan University (AKU EB) by Presidential Order to provide an alternative examination for SSC and HSC based on the national curriculum. The purpose of the AKU EB is to set an example of reliable, high-quality examinations that will test the acquisition of essential skills of learning and communication as well as comprehension and application of knowledge. The effect of rational assessment, supported by training of teachers and availability of explicit statements of curricular intent, should be evident in the abilities and attitudes of the candidates and their subsequent performance.

The influence of rational educational assessment on the public examination system, to the extent feasible, will not be known with confidence for ten or more years. Such is the latency between an intervention in education and general realization of its effects. Governments and the public, however, recognize only rapid outcomes that are understandable in the simplest terms of specific advantage.

CONCLUSION

Universal access to effective education is a worthy goal, but its attainment is difficult for operational and political reasons. Chief among the former are the paucity of appropriately trained teachers and managers, adequate physical facilities, geographic access and finance. These issues are compounded by the enormous school-age population and public perception of value, especially for girls, in underprivileged communities.

Taking these complexities into consideration, this chapter proposes that the goals of primary and secondary education should focus on the development of generic abilities and attitudes that enable adaptation to changing conditions of life.

The foundation for adaptation is laid during formation of the brain, beginning before birth and continuing apace in infancy and early childhood under the control of genes. The developing brain sets an individual's capacity for health (mental and physical), learning ability and behavior for his or her lifetime. However, expression of the genes that guide development of the brain is vulnerable to deactivation by adverse conditions of malnutrition, illness, and nature of stimulation provided by the social environment. The resulting inability to attain one's full genetic potential persists for life.

The early years of life provide the only opportunity to ensure equity of nurture that supports development of the brain. The education required to achieve this result must reach parents and other caregivers and be applied at home. This activity, focused on development of the child, also requires development of the society for shelter, safe physical environment, and economic productivity that can sustain nutrition and life.

Therefore, perspectives on the purposes of education should be broadened to consider a holistic, interdependent view of human development, encompassing early childhood and development of society. No investment in formal education alone will reverse long-term limitations in learning, health, and behavior that are established in the early stages of life as a result of inadequate child nurture.

REFERENCES

Avan, B. I. 2007. "Early Childhood Development in Pakistan: The Relative Contributions of Neighborhood, Socio-Economic Inequalities and Home Environment to Growth and Psychomotor Development." PhD thesis. Faculty of Medicine, University of London.

Government of Pakistan Ministry of Education Curriculum Wing. March 2002. *National Curriculum Education for Classes IX-X*. Islamabad: Government of Pakistan. http://www.pakistan.gov.pk/divisions/education-division/media/education9.pdf.

Heckman, James J. 2006. "Skill Formation and the Economics of Investing in Disadvantaged Children." *Science* 312 (5782): 1900–1902.

Mustard, J. Fraser. 2007. "Early Child Development and Experience-based Brain Development—The Scientific Underpinnings of the Importance of Early Child Development in a Globalized World." In *Early Child Development: From Measurement to Action—A Priority for Growth and Equity*, ed. Mary E. Young, 35–63. Washington, DC: The World Bank.

Young, Mary E. 2002. "Ensuring a Fair Start for All Children: The Case of Brazil." In *From Early Child Development to Human Development: Investing in our Children's Future*, ed. Mary E. Young, 123–142. Washington, DC: The World Bank.

8 Quality, the Heart of Equity

Vimala Ramachandran

India attained independence in 1947. Mahatma Gandhi had dreamed about a school system that was rooted in the social and cultural context while at the same time ensuring good quality secular education accessible to all children in the country. But as the first government assumed office, education for all was quickly forgotten. We plugged along with the colonial system, partly because there were more pressing economic and political issues to tackle. Mahatma Gandhi's plea for *"Nai Taleem"* (a fresh approach) in education was lost in the din of building a command economy.

It is not that education was neglected. Even at the school level, in addition to regular schools, the government set up a chain of "central schools"—well endowed and competent. But the real attention was reserved for higher education as the ruling elite committed to build quality institutions for professional and technical education. National institutes of technology, science, medicine and management are turning out graduates, who arguably compare with the best in the world. It is no surprise that India has managed to ride the current global information technology wave with confidence. In this rarefied world, excellence and quality are key words.

In 2005, an independent non-governmental organization facilitated a nationwide sample survey on learning outcomes of children. The results were shocking. Close to 35 percent of children in the seven-to-fourteen age group could not read a simple paragraph (Grade 1 level), and almost 60 percent of children could not read a simple story (Grade 2 level). Of children in the seven-to-fourteen age group, 65.5 percent could not tackle simple arithmetic problems, and more worrisome was that 47 percent of children in the eleven-to-fourteen age group could not solve Grade 2 level arithmetic problems (Pratham, 2006). When this survey was repeated in 2006, the overall national reading and arithmetic abilities of children in the age group seven-to-fourteen years had not changed significantly. According to the government, 52.8 percent of children who enter Grade 1 drop out before they reach Grade 8, with children from the most deprived communities and from rural and remote areas constituting an overwhelming majority of dropouts (Government of India, 2006). Education has meant little to these children—they have acquired few skills and little confidence.

For all the official claims, close to half of all children in the appropriate age group receive less than the constitutionally mandated eight years of schooling even if we disregard quality.

How can two entirely different systems coexist in the same space? Is this an area of concern for the government and the larger civil society?

In the early 1950s, education and quality were seen as coterminous, in part because education was a privilege of the few who could afford it. Most children studied in government schools. With modernization and escalated demand for education came pressure for rapid expansion in the public education system. By the mid 1960s, as increasing numbers of children started enrolling in school, the country also witnessed a gradual increase in the number of private-aided schools (private schools that get government funds to pay teacher's salaries and supply children with subsidized textbooks) and unaided schools (private schools that get no government aid). As the 1960s rolled by, people with means moved out of public (government) schools, and a feeling developed that quality was, perhaps, better pursued in private schools. This movement of the economically better-off from government schools to private schools has continued to gain momentum through subsequent decades, resulting in most government schools today becoming the preserve of the poor, those with little voice in society.

With growing pressure to meet globally accepted levels of school enrollment, India joined the great numbers race. Issues of access and quality were analytically separated, and the focus shifted to getting children into schools with the belief that the government could worry about quality later. Statistics acquired an unprecedented status, and we started searching for simple measures like enrollment, transition and completion rates to show progress. Coupled with a no-detention policy that mechanically promoted children from one level to the next if they fulfilled a basic minimum attendance requirement, the system was happy to generate numbers.

This is a warped system! Official statistics told us that all was well with education while our eyes and ears told a different story. India created parallel structures of education, governed by different norms and played by different rules. The education system became more differentiated—that is, between public, aided and private; formal and alternative (non-formal educational centers); and permanent, transitional, and pedestrian coexisting with institutions of excellence. The poorer and the more disadvantaged were pushed into schools with poor facilities, teachers and overall learning environments. This gave rise to a new trend of "hierarchies of access," whereby, paradoxically, the democratization of access to schools was accompanied by a reaffirmation of a child's caste, community and gender in defining which school she or he attended (Ramachandran, 2004). Having pushed the socially excluded into educational ghettos, the government today wants to neutralize the inequalities of the past centuries through affirmative action in the form of reservation of a certain percentage of admissions to specific social groups in higher and technical education institutions.

The economic cake is expanding quickly for some people in India. New opportunities are available to those who have been able to access quality education. There is a clamor for better schools, English education and new technologies. Quality has emerged as the new battleground. Yet we are at a loss to define what we mean by "quality." At the heart of this concern are questions related to the goal of education. Is it to enhance the capabilities of people to negotiate an increasingly unequal, divisive and polarized world from a position of strength? Is it to enable people to reflect critically on their life situation and understand the world they live in to make informed choices? Good quality education, in essence, involves creating a system that enables children to learn to know, learn to do, learn to live with others and appreciate interdependence and diversity, and above all learn to "act with ever greater autonomy, judgment and personal responsibility" (Delors, et al., 1996).

The segregation in education with different social classes enjoying differential access to different kinds of schools cuts at the root and poses a real threat to democracy. As Joel E. Cohen points out:

> Less has been done to address questions about the universality of educational content, which varies across countries and regions. Universal could mean that all children get the same education. Or it could mean that all children get some education, but the content differs by place, type of school, or technology of instruction. Or it could mean that there are universal principles that apply everywhere but that the implementation and specification of these principles in practice depend on the local context. If content differs, there may be some or no common elements for all children. Or it could mean that education is the same for everybody except for those children who are disabled, remote, rural, minority, or otherwise handicapped (p. 10, this volume).

An inability to address the fundamental goals of education does not augur well for democracy. In an increasingly polarized society, caste, religion and language identities are reinforced in politics, and political parties mobilize along caste and community lines—pitting one group against the other to capture votes. Government schools no longer provide a common shared space for children of different backgrounds and communities: children today grow up without getting an opportunity to mix with children from other social groups. While children from middle class and affluent families with greater access to the world media may potentially be exposed to different viewpoints, the majority of poor children attend school where they not only mix with their own kind but also have little access to the media (print and visual). They are thus doubly disadvantaged—by poverty and by poor quality education.

Given the segregation and given that those who can access education of reasonable quality opt for higher status careers, teaching as a career is increasingly becoming a last resort. The last two decades have witnessed a sharp decline in the quality of teachers. The further one moves away from the metropolis and well-endowed schools, the greater the decline in educational level, skills and confidence of teachers. The persisting poverty of the base of the educational pyramid and the declining ability of the system to attract competent teachers reinforce the quality divide.

As we peel away the layers of the education system, more contradictions reveal themselves. Larger governance issues like corruption, rent seeking (especially in teacher appointments, transfers and posting, development of school infrastructure) and a patronage network (where politically networked teachers are able to negotiate posting in schools in urban areas and well-connected rural areas) make an already difficult situation even more resistant to reform; even well-meaning reformers are at a loss about where to begin. Lofty goals are set every few years, the most recent being the nationwide effort to draft a national curriculum framework (National Council for Educational Research and Training, 2005). Yet institutions that are expected to set standards and provide academic leadership at different levels (national, state and district) have been reduced to petty fiefdoms that are least concerned about larger issues, such as the purpose of education. And unfortunately, the larger political debate on education continues to center primarily on writing and re-writing history and peculiar manifestations of affirmative action that only reinforce social divisions and existing inequalities.

The crisis faced by Indian education reflects a global concern. Be it rioting youth of migrant communities in Europe, the exasperated students in South and Southeast Asia, or the palpable unrest in the Americas and Africa—all these are telling something. An education system that emerged in the early industrial period is no longer able to meet the growing aspirations and needs of people across the world. The "best" are happy with the Ivy League, Oxbridge, Sorbonne, the Indian Institutes of Technology and the Indian Institutes of Management, their stepping-stone to money, fame and power. Simultaneously, the media has equalized aspirations and raised hope that education could indeed be the great equalizer. Yet the education that the poor receive adds little real value. The real world is harsh—those on the margins are being pushed further out into the wild.

At the heart of all this is the content of education. Who gets to learn what and how much? What confidence and capabilities does it endow? Who decides what is taught in school? What accountability systems are in place to make sure that children who come to school are taught with love and care, in a non-discriminatory environment and in a manner that enables them to realize their potential? Who ensures that caste, gender, race and community prejudices are not reinforced in school? Is anyone monitoring to see if a level playing field is being created in schools?

All of these questions are about quality—of learning, of environment, of relationships and of experience. Quality is the heart of the struggle for equality and justice. The unwillingness or inability to define what we really mean by quality and institutional mechanisms necessary to realize standards of quality is ultimately a political question. Unfortunately, the communist parties, the social democrats, the centrist liberals and the rightwing ideologues all are on the same side in the education quagmire, together contributing to the growing schism between the rhetoric and reality.

The situation may seem grim. But as we look closer and listen carefully, young people across the world are not in a mood to take this lying down. Maybe there is the silver lining. There is an urgent need to re-imagine education, overhaul the system and link education to life, livelihood, peace and social justice. While striving for equality, the education system should respond to aspirations and opportunities while enhancing choices. A farmer should be able to enhance his or her productivity, weigh the pros and cons of traditional and modern technologies, and make informed choices. Children living in a multicultural environment should have an opportunity to learn about each other while creating bonds of shared experiences—at the same time learning from the catastrophic consequences of racism, parochialism and communalism on humanity. Skilled and unskilled workers should be able to negotiate just wages and resist gender and age inequalities. The education system should have the depth as well as the range to span and bridge the different worlds people live in. A child born into a community that is rooted in a traditional occupation must have the opportunity to move out if he or she so wishes or infuse modern technologies or marketing opportunities into a traditional occupation. This has implications for the education system. We may have to reconstruct education in such a way that it provides multiple points of entry and exit, accommodate the varying paces of learning and enable people to stand tall where they are and reach out to the world with confidence. Young people who do not want to pursue formal schooling after Grade 8 or 10 should have an opportunity to pursue learning in a different stream. Equally, a young person who may have dropped out when he or she was fourteen should be able to pick up the threads at a later stage—if he or she so desires. There is a need to rethink the value of linear progression from primary through higher education.

This overhaul of the system can happen only if people who are committed to an alternative vision have the courage to put an end to the mindless pursuit of numbers (also known misleadingly as "goals") and call the bluff. This is the only way we can strengthen the voices clamoring for meaningful education.

The first step in this direction is to encourage independent teams of people working in education and in civil society organizations to periodically monitor educational outcomes and initiate an informed debate on what and how much are children learning in schools, the overall school environment (especially with respect to non-discrimination, corporal punishment and verbal/emotional abuse) and the academic facilities available to children.

Generating greater public awareness on what really happens inside our schools is essential to ensure reform.

The second important step is to enhance the professional status of teachers and enable them to improve their knowledge and skills through a wide range of academic support programs. This is critical to infuse energy and optimism within the demoralized teaching community.

Finally, it is important to acknowledge that the government alone cannot turn the system around. Deeper engagement of non-state actors in quality improvement could help channel more financial, educational and human resources into the system.

REFERENCES

Delors, Jacques, et al. 1996. *Learning: The Treasure Within: Report to UNESCO of the International Commission on Education for the Twenty-first Century.* Paris: UNESCO Publishing.

Government of India. 2006. Select Educational Statistics, up to September 2005. New Delhi.

National Council for Educational Research and Training. 2005. National Curriculum Framework. New Delhi: NCERT.

Pratham. 2006. *Annual Status of Education Report 2005.* New Delhi: Pratham India Education Initiative.

Ramachandran, Vimala, ed. 2004. *Hierarchies of Access: Gender and Equity in Primary Education.* New Delhi: Sage Publications.

Part IV
Empowering Children through Art and Science

9 The *dia* Program
The Development of Intelligence through Art

Claudia Madrazo

Figure 9.1 Photograph "El Ensueño" by Manuel Álvarez Bravo
© Colette Urbajtel

A group discussion is taking place in a classroom during a *dia* class. This is a glance at one part of the session:

> *Dia teacher:* We've observed the image. You said that the young girl was sad, anxious, concerned, and thoughtful. Now, who can tell us why she would feel that way?
>
> *Juan:* I think her mother won't allow her to go to the party.
>
> *Andrea:* Maybe she doesn't have a pretty dress to wear.
>
> *Daniela:* I think her boyfriend probably broke off with her.
>
> *Carlos:* Or maybe she got bad grades and her mother is going to be mad at her.
>
> *Dia teacher:* Now that we have some ideas of why she feels this way, let's consider what she might do in some of these situations to feel better. If she is sad because her boyfriend broke off with her, what can she do?
>
> *Juan:* She could go see her girlfriends so they can cheer her up.
>
> *Andrea:* Or she can talk with her boyfriend so he'll change his mind.
>
> *Dia teacher:* What an interesting idea, so he'll change his mind. What do you mean by that?
>
> *Andrea:* So he can forgive her for what she did to him.
>
> *Dia teacher:* That's an interesting idea. We'll get back to it. Now, if she is sad because she doesn't have a pretty dress to wear to the party, what could she do?
>
> *Laura:* She could borrow one from a friend.
>
> *Gustavo:* Or she could sew one herself, or ask her mom for help.
>
> *Dia teacher:* Okay. You are providing good options for her to feel better. After talking about how she feels and thinking about what could have caused those feelings, what kind of generalizations could we make?

INTRODUCTION

If today children learn to perceive and to speak with intelligence, heart and sensibility, tomorrow a different story will be told.

The speed with which science, technology, and mass media have developed and expanded over the last sixty years has brought about vast changes in our different cultures and in life's rhythms, among other things. And while this global era of dizzying transformations has prompted many great contributions from and for humanity, it has also engendered a generalized disharmony that is affecting the identities of individuals, the integration of families, the sustainability of communities and, most dramatically, the integrity of planet Earth and its ecological balance.

Considering the relevance of education in preparing future generations, schools and teachers today are required to play a more significant role in the integral education of their students. Educators should become mediators of knowledge who offer meaningful learning experiences that encourage children to learn to think and behave in a sensitive, creative and responsible way.

We are moving into a new era, and every day more and more people agree that we need to expand our view of education and to understand it as more than a process of curriculum learning and acquiring knowledge and skills in the traditional sense of linear transmission and information memorization. Educators should become mediators of integral human development who take into account physical, mental, spiritual[1] and social aspects and seek to help students participate actively in constructing their own knowledge and developing their own potential.

For these reasons, it is of great value to ask ourselves: What kind of individuals do we need to form or to educate in the context of the global era? What are our intentions? A more integrated perspective should seek to form intelligent, self-confident and sensitive men and women capable of making their own responsible decisions and choosing their paths in life, who are both free and at the same time responsible for the roles they play in society; men and women conscious of their attitudes, behaviors, actions, reactions and the consequences of these; men and women who have the ability to use their will and talents in a positive way.

My purpose in this chapter is to present a pedagogical model—created in Mexico—that promotes the integral development of both students and teachers, boosting their "transformation and continuous learning processes" (Madrazo, 2002) so that they can focus with more awareness and intention on developing knowledge, positive attitudes, emotional and intellectual skills for life.[2]

I will begin by providing a summary of the educational context in Mexico over the last several years and then explain what the *dia* program is and how it works. This is followed by a brief description of its history and a presentation of the most relevant challenges I have encountered.

A BRIEF SUMMARY OF THE EDUCATION CONTEXT IN MEXICO

National and international evaluations show that modernization reforms in basic education in Mexico have not been sufficient to positively affect learning in children and youngsters of public schools. According to the Programme for International Student Assessment (PISA) (Díaz Gutiérrez et al., 2007), the achievements of Mexican fifteen-year-old students are seriously low. In reading, a large percentage of students (30 percent) have poor skills for critically evaluating texts, identifying their different parts and are capable of carrying out only basic inference, and logical reasoning. In mathematics, Mexican students score considerably below the world average (380/500) and are not able to recognize and establish problems, express them in mathematical terms or apply operations, understand procedures, interpret or express results. In science, the average performance of the majority of the Mexican students (410/500) reveals that they have only enough knowledge to provide possible explanations in familiar contexts or reach conclusions based on simple research. Their reasoning is direct, and they can only carry out literal interpretations of the results of a scientific investigation or the technological solution of a problem.

These poor results are attributed to several factors: low access to education (presently, only 51 percent of Mexico's fifteen-year-old population attend school); slowness in implementing educational reforms; socioeconomic and cultural conditions in which schools work: extreme poverty and marginality, particularly among the indigenous, rural and marginal urban communities; lack of relevance of some of the educative programs; strong predominance of traditional styles of teaching; and problems in the handling and management of the education system, more specifically weak coordination of actions, evaluations and accountability among the different entities that participate in the education system (Reimers, 2006).

The *dia* program (Development of Intelligence through Art) is a distinctive proposal created by a Mexican organization (La Vaca Independiente, www.lavaca.edu.mx) committed to making a contribution to an increased quality of education by offering an alternative to traditional classroom teachers so that they can change their role and transform themselves into mediators. The function of the mediator of human development is to provide the students with resources and interact with them to help foster their integral development, focusing didactically on the learning process and the construction of knowledge, so that the students become aware of and assume their own learning and transformation processes, allowing them to become free, autonomous and responsible persons.

THE *DIA* PROGRAM: WHAT IT IS AND HOW IT WORKS

Dia is a teaching method that uses visual art as stimuli to trigger perception, thinking and communication processes. It is structured around an open discussion group in which teachers, acting as facilitators, formulate questions and encourage students to observe, think, imagine and express themselves freely and listen to one another while respecting each other's ideas. During these discussions, four areas of skills are developed: affective, communicative, cognitive, and social. All of these are designed to work together for the integral development of the students.

1. *Self-knowledge and affective development.* Emotional security and self-worth to increase the ability to handle and express emotions.

2. *Self-expression and communication.* Activation of expressive and creative potential through communicative and language skills.
3. *Perception and thinking processes.* Construction of cognitive structures that enrich the ability to perceive, think, reflect, understand and discern.
4. *Harmonious social relationships and civic behavior.* Construction of healthy relationships through social skills that create awareness of attitudes and democratic, civic and ethical behaviors.

Dia classes are held once a week in fifty-minute sessions throughout the school term during the six years of elementary education.[3] Each lesson contains two to four images from different cultures and art periods. *Dia* teachers do not need to know about art, since the aim is not to teach art, but to integrate it as a stimulus for education and personal growth.

The *dia* program proposes a model of learning that integrates three elements: the mediator, the students and the visual arts. The mediator, guided by pedagogical principles (Madrazo, 2003), takes advantage of the qualities of the works of art as stimuli to activate a continuous interaction, to improve student's specific skills and to generate construction of knowledge based on a human development curriculum.

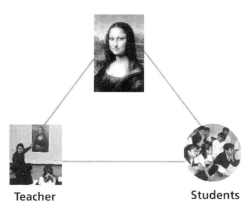

Stimuli/Work of Art

Teacher

Students

Pedagogical principles

Areas of skill

Orientate
Generate
Recover
Motivate
Conclude and Transcend

Cognitive
Communicative
Affective
Social

Figure 9.2   Dia didactic model.

Self-Knowledge and Affective Development

To know ourselves is to become responsible for who we are and our relationship with the world. By generating introspection and self-knowledge, we establish the basis for adequately handling our emotional world.

The expressive nature of art has the power to awaken emotions and feelings, and generate reactions. Based on this intrinsic quality, the *dia* program invites us to identify and name a world of sensations, emotions and moods—which are transformed into skills, attitudes and behavior—so that we begin to understand the reasons for what we feel and learn how to express our inner world, allowing us to relate to other people and ourselves with greater sensitivity and intelligence.

The opportunity to listen to and understand different ways of expressing emotions and feelings allows students and teachers to broaden their repertoire of concepts and ideas. Consequently, they expand their range of possible responses, which in turn provides them with the tools to handle their emotional world more adequately and positively.

The space for free expression provided by *dia* helps students to open up, develop self-confidence and discover themselves through their own words.

A teacher who is open to listening to what his or her students know or feel, the experiences they have lived through, or the knowledge they have acquired, will have more tools to mediate the processes of integral education. Students, once they feel listened to and accepted by the teacher and the group, start to grow more confident.

Self-Expression and Communication

During the *dia* class, children begin to realize that they have a voice. They express their thoughts and show who they truly are,[4] generating original, interesting and valuable ideas. Needing to be understood and appreciated, they seek to articulate and express themselves more accurately and clearly. Moreover, they learn to use their vocabulary more precisely and specifically, developing language skills, which are the grounds for both learning and establishing human relationships.

This dialogue provides teachers and students with valuable opportunities to learn from each other, to converse on the many different subjects that might interest them, and to enjoy a harmonious, secure space.

Perception and Thinking Processes

Perception is the doorway to any mental function (intellectual or affective) and thinking process.

Motivating the students to name, identify, recognize and describe what they see activates their perception and connects them with the world and with the sensations that emerge from it. The process of identifying both the physical and the subjective worlds broadens their conceptual repertoire and thinking categories, allowing them to conceive and construct more relationships. In this encounter, concrete thinking leads the way to abstract thinking. By organizing the perceptual and imaginative experiences, more abstract and complex skills such as comparison, analysis and synthesis, symbolic and metaphorical thinking gradually appear.

A piece of art can be seen as an enigma to be resolved, as well as a question that evokes an answer from us and awakens the spectator's narrative impulse (Arenas, 1997). The encounter between "what is" and "what it looks like," between the objectivity represented by the concrete elements of an image and the subjectivity of its meaning, opens the way to interpretations and offers the students the opportunity to speculate, create stories, reflect, imagine and justify their ideas, based either on logical evidence or on their own experiences and knowledge.

Students enrich the group dialogue by sharing their own experiences, contributing to individual and group understanding and construction of knowledge, a basic process to acquire awareness of their own development.

Harmonious Social Relationships and Civic Behavior

The mediated dialogue created around a work of art with *dia*'s "rules of the game" motivates the students to regulate their behavior, and helps them to acquire specific skills to relate to other people with respect, sensitivity and consideration. This also creates a safe space where children feel confident to express themselves with openness and authenticity, fundamental conditions for self-knowledge and development.

Art can be seen as a mirror of humanity, as it contains everything we have experienced and felt. What we have seen, learnt and imagined; attitudes, behaviors, lifestyles, ways of feeling and thinking. . . . It invites us to see, understand and value not only our customs, myths, habits and behaviors, but also that of other people and cultures, present and past. It opens the doors to respect and tolerance and amplifies our vision and understanding of who we are, as individuals and as a society.

The mediation of its rich content allows us to expand our vision and develop broader criteria to analyze, value and understand our diversity; and to visualize new forms of relationships, attitudes and behaviors which open the possibility to transform our lives.

Discussions and debates are valuable in the measure that they generate participation, affection, tolerance, reflection, action, and because they awaken the students' critical and creative spirit,[5] enhancing ethical and democratic values.

BRIEF HISTORY: HOW THE *DIA* PROGRAM HAS EVOLVED

Convinced of the potential that education has in social and human development, and inspired by the experience of the Visual Thinking Curriculum

(VTC)[6] created by the New York Museum of Modern Art (MoMA) in 1994, La Vaca Independiente[7] created the *dia* program with the aim of bringing art to underprivileged communities and using it to develop critical thinking. Thus it started on a stimulating path of research, implementation and creation.

Origins (1994)

The program began in ten schools in underprivileged communities around Mexico City, focused on twenty groups over the course of three school terms, from fourth to sixth grade, and from ages nine through twelve. The La Vaca Independiente team began working in accordance with the hypothesis that the program could help develop children's abilities to communicate, perceive, interpret and think in a reflective and critical way, so they could learn to respect the ideas of others and develop self-esteem—essential prerequisites for learning, and fundamental tools for everyday life.

We soon began to see results. A few months after the program was implemented, the teachers and students were enjoying the benefits of the sessions. The children were able to follow *dia*'s "rules of the game:" observe images in silence; speak loudly and clearly; raise their hand to participate; listen attentively; respect the ideas of others; and justify thoughts and interpretations on the basis of logical evidence. The space had created a context of respect and security where children felt at ease and happy (and often extremely excited) to communicate and share with their teachers and peers.

Research and Theoretical Enrichment (1998)

After two years of practice we undertook a three-year research project[8] that allowed us to observe the signs of development in the four areas of skills that the *dia* program focuses on (cognitive, communicative, affective and social). We found that the children were thinking in a more systematic and structured way; their vocabulary was increasing progressively; they were using more words and employing them in a more accurate and precise manner; and, furthermore, they felt confident about expressing their own thoughts and feelings and were even including the ideas of others to complement and enrich their own. They had started to build up knowledge based on sharing.

Experience and Pedagogical Construction (1999–2003)

This research was followed by a constructive period of four years. By 1999, we were training and monitoring educators and working in more than one hundred classrooms, from first to sixth grades of elementary school. Most of the teachers appreciated and enjoyed the *dia* class and witnessed a series of benefits that transcended the sessions, influencing other areas of activities and fields of study. The teaching skills they began to develop were helpful in other classes and disciplines as well. Teachers were also able to connect the *dia* class to other curricula to encourage new approaches in learning all kinds of subjects, and some children were even taking the "rules of the game" into their own homes.

After six years of training,[9] practicing, and following up on different *dia* groups in both public and private schools, we realized that much more could be happening with the *dia* program. Teachers were formulating questions and generating a lot of participation from the children, but they were losing golden opportunities to draw on the richness of their students' subjectivity—their experiences, knowledge and ways of looking at the world—so they could recapture and make sense of that information. We reached the conclusion that if teachers had more knowledge, better attitudes and teaching skills, they could concentrate more on the formation of their students' cognitive structures and consequently promote their integral development with more awareness and consistency. The *dia* pedagogical principles were born, *Orientate, Generate, Recover, Motivate* and *Conclude and transcend*; bringing a more systematic approach to the sessions, which brought a more structured and intentional direction to their interactions.

Hence, we began to observe and research not only the students' processes and stages of development in the four proposed areas of skills, but also the teachers' didactic needs. We saw, for example, how difficult it was for them to listen, to perceive with openness and flexibility, to ask the appropriate questions and to seek reciprocity in the answers. They needed to start feeling comfortable and secure—to *flow*—in order to take full advantage of the artwork and activate the students' potential, while simultaneously awakening the inner mediator, so that they could pay attention to their own sensations, doubts and concerns.

A question arose in a case study carried out in an official primary school of the SEP (*Secretaría de Educación Pública*, Ministry of Education): What goes on in a *dia* class? The findings allowed us to evaluate the degree of effectiveness of the actions implemented, to understand the gap between the established norm and the *dia* practice, to clarify and identify improvement areas, to contribute to a theoretical reflection of the program and to document the process so that it could be shared.

The results showed *dia* to be a socio-cultural, dynamic and holistic approach that provides a learning environment where students can develop—in a dynamic and complex way—different analytical-synthetic, dialogistic, self-appraising, empathic and reflexive capacities from the work in the different areas of established skills (cognitive, social, affective and communicative).

The results also provided a typology of the educative communication situation, allowing us to draft a diagnosis of the *dia* class that would help us to reflect on its process and future possibilities.

Consolidation and Growth (2004–)

With these findings we began focusing more and more on the mediation process, and we designed a teaching model based on the continuous interaction of three elements: the students, the mediator and the artwork as a stimulus. We structured the five pedagogical principles: *Orientate, Generate, Recover, Motivate* and *Conclude and transcend*, which help teachers to organize and plan dynamic sessions that demand more complex interactions with their students.

We designed a three-level teacher training program based on the progressive development of theoretical and teaching know-how, skills, abilities and attitudes to exercise mediation: *sensitization, active observation and listening, and meaningful dialogue and group construction of knowledge.* With this method, *dia* has become a practical tool for supporting teachers as they begin a personal and professional transformation process.[10]

RESULTS

The outcome of the *dia* program has been observed at various levels. Concerning teachers, the *dia* program has become a real pedagogical tool. The development of mediation skills, which are reflected not only during the *dia* class, but in all other classes as well, is outstanding. The changes in teachers' attitudes are also notable: they become more open, empathetic, warm and firm. These changes can be seen in the different relationships that they begin to establish with the students and in how their vision of education changes.

With respect to students, they begin to feel more self-confident; their self-esteem develops; their interest in participating increases and they become more active in class. This is a fundamental factor in their development process. They also become more respectful and learn to regulate themselves. As they acquire more vocabulary and language tools, their mental processes tend to become more complex and rich.

In the same way, the students amplify their perception by improving their recognition, identification and change processes. They modify their capacity to interpret and formulate speculations. *Dia* students can improve the quality and nature of their arguments, which they use to validate their ideas. They learn to base their ideas on their own observations and subjective experience. The pupils enter discussions with their classmates and teacher, consider the ideas of others and integrate them into their own point of view.

The students' new cognitive skills allow their thought processes to become more symbolic, abstract and complex, allowing them to establish better differentiations and a greater number of metacognition processes.

WHERE ARE WE?

Since 2006, the *dia* program has collaborated with several international institutions, including the ILCE (Educative Communication Institute of Latin America) and the national and local public education secretaries

(SEP), to carry out a high-impact project that integrates the use of new technology (Enciclomedia[11]), autonomy and management programs (PEC[12]) and the use of art as a vehicle to develop skills (*dia*).

In order to accomplish the goal of applying the *dia* program in fourteen states in Mexico, La Vaca Independiente has directly trained more than 200 local facilitators who will in turn train more than 17,000 teachers and 2,000 monitors. These actions will allow us to reach more than 500,000 children at the basic level, who live in urban, semi-urban, rural and indigenous zones.

The positive results observed with groups of children and teachers have motivated us to implement the *dia* program in other contexts. Since 1999 we have worked with underprivileged groups such as life-term prisoners, children with Down syndrome, indigenous communities, migrant workers and homeless children. In these spaces, new questions emerge along with new possibilities for mediating through art.

Currently, one of the most important challenges of the *dia* program is the teacher's formation as mediator. Changing educators' mind sets, their paradigms about what children can achieve and what they can do to help them activate their potentials, is a real challenge. Through *dia* activities for professional and personal development, we have realized that there are many teachers ready to make this shift. However, the challenge of scaling a teacher program like *dia* is undoubtedly a big one. Mexico has a teachers' union with almost one million members. Integrating new pedagogical tools implies working hand in hand with the system, not only in updating programs for practicing teachers but also in preparing the curricula for the new ones.

If we as educators can transform paradigms, share experiences and further our own development process, tomorrow another story will be told.

NOTES

1. Spirituality understood not in the religious sense, but as the human need to find inner peace and transcendence.
2. According to Feuerstein et al.'s (1997) theory of modifiability, human beings can modify the structure of their intellectual functioning in order to adapt to life's varying situations.
3. Currently, materials for preschool and secondary school are being developed.
4. In the words of the Minister of Education in Nuevo Leon Mexico, José Martinez: "In public schools, the average time students have to express their own ideas, unrelated to the curricula, is between three and five minutes per year" (The Effect of the *dia* Program on Students: Research Results (conference), May 6, 2002, hosted by Subsecretaria de Servicios Educativos para el Distrito Federal and La Vaca Independiente S.A. de C.V. at Centro Nacional de las Artes).
5. Related to Deweynan's experiential and reflexive perspective; see Díaz Barriga (2006).

6. See the *Visual Thinking Curriculum* (VTC) created in the 1980s by the education department of the New York Museum of Modern Art (MoMA).
7. La Vaca Independiente, founded by Claudia Madrazo in 1992, is a laboratory of creative ideas formed by a group of interdisciplinary professionals committed to the development and stimulation of human sensitivity, intelligence and communication. It achieves its objectives through art.
8. Undertaken by Centro Educacional Tanesque A. C., a non-profit organization created in 1979, devoted to educational research and child psychotherapy. The research project worked with control and research groups, applying a series of pre-test and post-test instruments to measure and observe changes in linguistic, cognitive, social and affective skills.
9. By the year 2004, we had trained more than 13,000 teachers in Mexico at the national level, extending the benefits of the program to approximately 285,000 children.
10. From 2002 to 2008, 30,000 teachers have been trained in over fourteen states in Mexico. Many of them are now carrying out the *dia* class. We have observed that the impact and reach of the program is determined to a large degree by the level of commitment of the local government.
11. Multimedia program for fifth and sixth grades of elementary school, launched by SEP and ILCE.
12. Programa Escuelas de Calidad, created by SEP in 2002.

REFERENCES

Arenas, Amelia, Abigail Housen, and Philip Yenawine. *Visual Thinking Curriculum—Year Two*. The Museum of Modern Art, NY. Working paper. 1993
Díaz Barriga, Frida. 2006. *Enseñanza situada: Vínculo entre la escuela y la vida*. Mexico City, Mexico: McGraw Hill.
Díaz Gutiérrez, María A., Gustavo F. Vasquez, and Felipe M. Rizo. 2007. *PISA 2006 en Mexico*. Mexico: Instituto Nacional para la Evaluación de la Educación. http://www.inee.edu.mx/images/stories/documentos_pdf/Publicaciones/PISA2006/pisa2006-w.pdf.
Feuerstein, R., J. Mayor Sánchez, J. M. Martínez Beltrán, M. Krechewsky, D. Tzuriel, H. C. Haywood. 1997. *¿Es modificable la inteligencia?* Madrid: Bruño.
Madrazo, Claudia. 2003. *Lenguaje para conocer. Guía de trabajo*. Mexico: La Vaca Independiente.
Madrazo, Claudia. 2002. *Sensibilización. Guía Didáctica*. Mexico: La Vaca Independiente.
Reimers, Fernando. 2006. *Aprender más y mejor. Políticas, programas y oportunidades de aprendizaje en educación básica en México*. Mexico: SEP, FCE, ILCE, Harvard Graduate School of Education.

10 Educational Goals
Art, Science, Love, and the Importance of Binocular Vision

Joel E. Cohen

I became concerned with the goals of education through my work in demography and population biology. In my 1995 book, *How Many People Can the Earth Support?,* I observed that panaceas proposed by others for solving demographic, environmental, economic, and cultural (including political) problems fell into three categories: bigger pie, fewer forks, and better manners. "A bigger pie" means amplifying human productive capacities through better technology, including reduced material throughput in production. "Fewer forks" means reducing human demands through voluntary reductions in fertility and consumption. "Better manners" means reducing violence, inequity, corruption, perverse subsidies, and economically and socially irrational barriers to movements of goods, money, and people.

In 1998, I conjectured that giving all children in the world a basic and secondary education of high quality might contribute simultaneously to a bigger pie, fewer forks, and better manners. But whether ten to twelve years of education of high quality for all children would effectively support these three approaches depends on what that education aims to accomplish. Education that does not aim to inspire and enable innovation through instruction in science and technology would not promote a bigger pie. Education that does not give young people an understanding of the operation and maintenance of their own bodies could not promote fewer forks. Education that aims to prepare young men for the workforce but neglects young women, that does not develop empathy, or that fails to encourage respect and affection for people with different points of view, could not promote better manners. Education that does not encourage children and young adults to value the imaginative search for rational, nonviolent, broadly inclusive approaches to solving demographic, environmental, economic, and cultural problems risks diminishing, distorting, or misdirecting the potential benefits of a bigger pie, fewer forks, and better manners.

Thus the goals of education matter crucially. My tentative thoughts here about the goals of universal primary and secondary education are intended in part to be provocative rather than definitive.[1]

For whom are these goals intended? I have visited classrooms of privileged private and public schools in the United States and Singapore and

Australia, as well as poor schools in Burkina Faso and Cambodia and India, among other places. For many children in poor countries, the immediate goals of education are a rudimentary ability to read, write, and do elementary arithmetic. Sometimes the major goal is rote mastery of sacred texts. But even the way these rudimentary skills are taught can serve larger educational goals. The goals I propose in this chapter are intended for children and young adults in both poor and rich countries. The weighting of priorities must depend on the resources available for education.

SKILLS, KNOWLEDGE, ATTITUDES, AND VALUES

The Organisation for Economic Cooperation and Development and others (Salganik and Provasnik, Chapter 20, this volume) propose that competence rests on skills, knowledge (presumably factual knowledge), attitudes, and values. I use these categories to propose several goals for education.

Skills include the ability to read with understanding, write with clarity, and speak with confidence. This proposal raises the questions: In which language(s) should students learn to read, write, and speak? Who decides which language(s) to use, and how is the decision reached?

Joel Spring (2000) suggested that "all people have the right to an education that teaches [both] their mother tongue [and] the dominant or official language of the nation" (p. 33). The intent of this proposal is to give people "an understanding of their own [culture] and their relation to it [as well as] an understanding of the effect of the world culture and economy on their own culture and economy" (p. 37). When Mauritius, a tiny island nation where fifteen languages are spoken, became a nation, it was necessary to choose a language of instruction for the schools. Although the commonest language is Kreol, a seldom written form of French Creole, the chosen state language was English, an ethnically neutral language that gave all students easy access to the world's economy.

I find Spring's suggestion attractive. I also suggest that children whose native tongue is one of the world-dominant languages, such as English or Chinese, should be required to master at least one other language, preferably not closely related to their native tongue. Speaking two (or more) languages teaches that there are ways of seeing the world and conventions in speaking of the world other than those of the culture into which one happens to be born.

Another necessary skill for basic and secondary education is numeracy, which is the ability to read, understand, and compute quantitative information as required in daily life. In a study of the literacy of United States college students, the American Institutes of Research defined quantitative literacy as "The knowledge and skills required to . . . identify and perform computations, either alone or sequentially, using numbers embedded in printed materials. Quantitative examples include balancing a checkbook, figuring out a tip, completing an order form, or determining the amount of interest on a loan from an advertisement" (Baer, Cook, and Baldi, 2006, p. 4). This definition is equivalent to numeracy. According to this study, 20 percent of U.S. college students completing four-year degrees and 30 percent of students earning two-year degrees "have only basic quantitative literacy skills, meaning they are unable to estimate if their car has enough gasoline to get to the next gas station or calculate the total cost of ordering office supplies."[2]

I sent an announcement of this study to a professional mathematician and to a professional mathematics educator. Both responded that the problem lies in the inadequate quantitative education offered in primary and secondary schools. The inadequacy arises, they suggested, from an emphasis on reading at the expense of numeration on the part of parents before children get to school, from low expectations of mathematical performance by parents, teachers, schools, and society at large (how many times have you heard someone say, often with pride, "Oh, I was never good in math in school"?), and from inadequate training, supervision, and continuing education of teachers of mathematics in elementary and secondary schools. Not all societies (notably, not the Chinese) have such low expectations and achievements of quantitative literacy. To be innumerate today, to lack quantitative literacy as defined by the American Institutes of Research, is to be half blind, or more than half. No society and no individual can afford to be without numeracy.

Equally necessary are social skills. One social skill is finding peaceful ways to manage and resolve conflicts within and between social groups. Different cultures have totally different ideas about how to do that. Some decide by compromise, others use consensus, some take a majority vote, others appeal to tradition. All are successful in different contexts, and all unfortunately fail in the face of certain conflicts. Other necessary social skills are the ability to analyze and make choices about personal life and work, the ability to be productive, and the ability to find satisfaction in personal life and work.

Knowledge includes knowledge of self, which can be attained through the natural sciences (How does my body work?), the social sciences (Where do I fit in? What traditions and institutions do I inherit?), and the arts and humanities (What is the purpose of my life? What is my responsibility in shaping the direction of my life? What is beauty, and why is it important to me and others?). Knowledge also includes knowledge of others: family, the local community, other communities and cities, the nation, other countries and cultures, and humankind. It includes knowledge of nonhuman entities, including other living species and nonliving components of Earth. It includes knowledge of other times and the sources and limitations of our understanding of past and future. I return to the arts and sciences later in this chapter.

Attitudes permit people to recognize conflicts of competing values without being disabled by those conflicts and to find a personal balance (changing with time) among the competing values. For example, innovation sometimes conflicts with continuity (How much do we change, and how much do we continue in the norms of the past?); between initiative and obedience (Do I obey the rules even if I think they are harmful, senseless, or counterproductive? How much do I try to get them changed?); between competitiveness and cooperation (How do I respect my own interests while I respect the interests of others and seek collaboration for mutual benefit?); and between skepticism and respect (How do I respect what others have to say, while still asking for the evidence behind it?).

Education also instills values. What those values ought to be is intensely controverted. Bok advocates for "minimalist values most easily recognized across societal and other boundaries: the most basic forms of the positive duties of care and reciprocity; of constraints on violence, deceit, and betrayal; and of norms for procedures and standards of justice" (1995, p. 41). I would advocate that education ought to instill these values, and that each community and each culture needs to discuss publicly the values it wishes to add to Bok's minimal set.

The goals I have sketched here take for granted an adequately nourished learner in good health in a safe environment. In too much of the world, these assumptions are invalid. If universal education contributes as hoped to a bigger pie, fewer forks, and better manners, future generations' learners will enjoy adequate nourishment and good health in a safe environment, and then the educational goals I propose could be relevant to all learners.

ARTS AND SCIENCES

Elliot Eisner wrote:

> One of the generally neglected resources that promote the development of the whole child is the arts. The arts make it possible in vivid ways to eliminate a distinction between cognition and emotion. For example, creating images requires, on the one hand, a feel for the expressive character of the image and, on the other, forms of thinking that use feelings to make rational choices along the way. In this relationship between feeling and thinking, the two dimensions become unified in a single, inseparable process. Artistic forms of cognition in all kinds of activity, including scientific activities, represent the most complete form of integration that humans are likely to achieve. Schools can promote such opportunities by ensuring that the arts are included in the curriculum and that they have the kind of pedagogical support that enables students to take advantage of their educational possibilities (2005, p. 18).

Eisner listed "ten lessons the arts teach":

1. The arts teach children to make good judgments about qualitative relationships;
2. The arts teach children that problems can have more than one solution and that questions can have more than one answer;
3. The arts celebrate multiple perspectives;
4. The arts teach children that in complex forms of problem solving purposes are seldom fixed;
5. The arts make vivid the fact that neither words in their literal form nor numbers exhaust what we can know;
6. The arts teach students that small differences can have large effects;
7. The arts teach students to think through and within a material;
8. The arts help children learn to say what cannot be said;
9. The arts enable us to have experience we can have from no other source; and
10. The arts' position in the school curriculum symbolizes to the young what adults believe is important. (2002, pp. 70–92)

As a working scientist with a lifelong active interest in music and poetry and an appreciation for other arts, I find compelling Eisner's argument for the broad benefits of education in the arts for all students. A similar argument for education in the sciences seems to me equally valid, though rarely made. However, it seems likely that the benefits of education in the arts and sciences can be attained only when the teaching of each is significantly better than is often available in primary and secondary schools now.

Eisner's ten lessons look like this if arts are replaced by sciences:

1. The sciences teach children to make good judgments about both qualitative and quantitative relationships. In every science, qualitative judgments are required to decide which factors merit inclusion in an experiment, calculation, or theory.
2. Contrary to what is widely believed, the sciences (including mathematics) can teach children that problems can have more than one solution and that questions can have more than one answer. For example, the Pythagorean theorem, widely taught in high school geometry classes, has hundreds of different proofs, and new ones are still being discovered though the theorem is thousands of years old. Multiple proofs shed light on different aspects of a single result. Moreover, alternatives to the Pythagorean theorem hold on surfaces (like a sphere or a saddle) that are not flat.
3. The sciences celebrate multiple perspectives; molecular biology, genetics, cell biology, physiology, epidemiology, clinical medicine, and environmental sciences all make different important contributions to the health of individuals and populations.

4. The sciences teach children that in complex forms of problem solving purposes are seldom fixed; accidental discovery (for example, of penicillin) is a hallmark of an alert scientific investigator.

5. The sciences vividly demonstrate that neither words in their literal form nor numbers exhaust what we can know; scientists regularly admit having no provable answers to many questions of scientific interest and human concern, despite having intuitions about them.

6. The sciences teach students that small differences can have large effects; this lesson is central to the mathematics and sciences of nonlinear and chaotic behaviors.

7. The sciences teach students to think through and within a material; the physicist Richard Feynman was famous for practicing and teaching the art of animating and putting himself into the mathematical and physical systems he was theorizing about. If you want to understand mountains, think like a mountain.

8. The sciences help children learn to say what cannot be said; high school algebra permits students to say what words are inadequate to say (try solving a quadratic equation with nothing but words). The most creative mathematics captures concepts never before reduced to symbols.

9. The sciences enable us to have experiences we can have from no other source; perhaps the only thrill greater than the thrill of thoroughly understanding how something works, even if the discovery is someone else's, is the thrill of discovering or proving something that no other human has known before. Moreover, the instruments of science (microscopes, telescopes, computers) make possible experiences no other sources can provide.

10. The sciences' position in the school curriculum symbolizes to the young what adults believe is important; if the sciences are taught well and generously supported, students understand that adults value facts, rational understanding, and the sustained effort and high creativity required to master science and make it grow.

In addition to these ten lessons, an experience of science as it is practiced teaches much more. I distinguish science as practiced (which looks outward from the sphere of the known to the surrounding space of the unknown) from science as often taught in schools (focused on the known). Science as practiced gives training in the exciting and productive tension between solitary creativity and collaborative creativity. It gives a sense of participating in a cumulative human enterprise that is much larger than oneself. It gives a sense of the universality of the human impulse to understand experience, regardless of the origin, language, creed, or other characteristics of the scientist. It gives an opportunity to work with people of enormously different backgrounds and to feel part of the human family, a privileged part with a shared language and shared concepts.

The content of science has civic implications as well. For example, scientific education about human uses of resources both living (forests, fisheries, farms) and non-living (energy, water, land, atmosphere) can make clear how my local actions today affect other people in other places and future times as well as here and now. Environmental education based on sound physics, chemistry, and biology displays the mutual dependence of people, other species, and natural systems around the globe and opens a path to greater dialogue and cooperation across national, linguistic, and cultural boundaries. Science applied to forensic identification can improve the quality of criminal justice and raise awareness of the fallibility of human judgments.

Science as practiced requires lucid, persuasive, and engaging communication; work that is not reported to one's scientific peers is not scientific work. Science as practiced requires honesty; fraud and cheating are suicidal. Science as practiced requires and teaches humility; around the edges of every success loom the unknown, the inscrutable, the recalcitrant, and questions still unanswered. Science as practiced teaches modesty. For each of the numberless complex skills required to do science, always somebody else can perform that skill better, and despite the riches of human talent, nature is cleverer in posing riddles than humans are in answering them. Science as practiced requires and teaches enormously hard work and sometimes rewards it. An experience of science as practiced teaches the importance of deriving satisfaction from the work itself, from knowing that one has pushed oneself to the limits of one's ability.

Aside from the very important technological and economic benefits of scientific education (and technological education, which I include here with scientific education), these cultural and personal benefits of scientific education seem to me to justify the goal of giving every child an experience of science as practiced. Giving every student this opportunity will require teachers who can teach the sciences with love, excitement, and accurate understanding.

LOVE

Love has a fundamental relation to education. Jacques Delors (1996, p. 12) wrote that education is "an expression of affection for children and young people, whom we need to welcome into society, unreservedly offering them the place that is theirs by right therein. . . ." The word "love" occurs in six chapters in this volume. Charfi and Redissi (Chapter 12) write: "The state has no business worrying about the salvation of souls. Still, it should teach such virtues as loyalty, generosity, courage, love of neighbor, peace, and good works. Without a respect for such virtues, social life is given over to evil" (p. 155). Suárez-Orozco (Chapter 15) writes: "Children growing up today will need to develop the skills to learn, work, love, and live with others, which are increasingly likely to be of very different racial, religious, linguistic, and cultural backgrounds. Globalization will place a great premium on transcultural understandings. New forms of transcultural empathy and perspective-taking will be at a premium for survival and success in the twenty-first century" (p. 208). I want to explain why love should be recognized as a key ingredient in the preparation of children for basic and secondary education, in the processes of education, and in the long-term outcomes of education.

Before a child ever gets to a school or begins other formal education, he or she is normally born into a family. The child's parent, parents, or caretaker (I will use "parents" as an abbreviation) either love the child or do not, and usually the child responds by loving the parents or not, and loving himself or herself or not. Whether or not the child loves and is loved by the parents, the parents are the child's first teacher(s). It seems inevitable that a child should associate his or her learning from parents, which happens no matter what, with the love that binds him to the parents or the lack of love that estranges him from them. When a child begins basic education in a school, teachers may be the first adults other than parents and relatives with responsibility for care of the child. In the fortunate case where the child and parents were bound by love, the child is prepared to transfer to the teacher the emotional bonding associated with learning. In the unfortunate case where the child did not associate learning with parental love, the child and schoolteacher face the hurdle of changing the emotional sign associated with learning from negative to positive. A role of love in basic education is to associate learning with the most positive of all emotional experiences, the giving and receiving of love.

A child who comes from a home with siblings learns from them as well as from his parents and establishes some mix of love and rivalry. The child may be fortunate if parents and siblings establish a practice of love among siblings, and unfortunate if not. When the child enters school, he or she is also equipped to associate with learning from his peers at school whatever mix of love and rivalry that child associates with learning from siblings at home. A task of the teacher and school is to assure a positive sign to the learning between peers for those not fortunate enough to have brought a positive sign to peer learning. This task is crucial for children where relations with siblings were negative, and will be increasingly important if demographic trends toward reduced fertility increasingly make single-child families more frequent than larger ones.

For children who unfortunately did not establish the habit of loving themselves as a result of the gift of parental love, primary and secondary schools can implant the habit of self-love through explicit positive input from teachers and peers. Without the habit of self-love, love for others is crippled at the starting gate.

The role of love in education can be treated scientifically. In a comprehensive review of the science of early childhood development (Shonkoff and Phillips, 2000), the first recommendation is:

Resources on a par with those focused on literacy and numerical skills should be devoted to translating the knowledge base on young children's emotional, regulatory, and social development into effective strategies for fostering: (1) the development of curiosity, self-direction, and persistence in learning situations; (2) the ability to cooperate, demonstrate caring, and resolve conflict with peers; and (3) the capacity to experience the enhanced motivation associated with feeling competent and loved. Such strategies and their widespread diffusion into the early childhood field must encompass young children both with and without special needs. Successful action on this recommendation will require the long-term, collaborative investment of government, professional organizations, private philanthropy, and voluntary associations (p. 6).

Moreover:

Parents and other regular caregivers in children's lives are "active ingredients" of environmental influence during the early childhood period. Children grow and thrive in the context of close and dependable relationships that provide love and nurturance, security, responsive interaction, and encouragement for exploration. Without at least one such relationship, development is disrupted and the consequences can be severe and longlasting. If provided or restored, however, a sensitive caregiving relationship can foster remarkable recovery. The time is long overdue for society to recognize the significance of out-of-home relationships for young children, to esteem those who care for them when their parents are not available, and to compensate them adequately as a means of supporting stability and quality in these relationships for all children, regardless of their family's income and irrespective of their developmental needs. Early experiences clearly affect the development of the brain. Yet the recent focus on "zero to three" as a critical or particularly sensitive period is highly problematic, not because this isn't an important period for the developing brain, but simply because the disproportionate attention to the period from birth to 3 years begins too late and ends too soon (p. 7).

The words "love," "beloved," "loved," "lovable," and "loving" appear throughout this scientific document.

Adam Smith (1759) premised his great book, *The Theory of Moral Sentiments,* on the happiness and well-being people derive from the happiness and well-being of others. He began his first chapter, "Of Sympathy," thus:

How selfish soever man may be supposed, there are evidently some principles in his nature, which interest him in the fortune of others, and render their happiness necessary to him, though he derives nothing from it except the pleasure of seeing it. Of this kind is pity or compassion, the emotion which we feel for the misery of others, when we either see it, or are made to conceive it in a very lively manner. . . . As we have no immediate experience of what other men feel, we can form no idea of the manner in which they are affected, but by conceiving what we ourselves should feel in the like situation.

Adam Smith's sympathy, today called empathy, is a form of loving others as oneself. A neurophysiological basis for empathy was discovered in the function of nervous tissue called "mirror cells" (Iacoboni et al., 2005; Rizzolatti et al., 1995).

In basic education, a crucial goal is to teach a love of learning initially through love of teachers and fellow students from whom one learns. In secondary education, love between teachers and students and between students and students remains an essential catalyst of learning, but increasingly teachers model for students a love of advanced subjects of learning, including the living and nonliving natural world, the worlds of art and imagination, the larger society, other cultures, peoples, times and places, and abstract structures of pure thought. One young woman, recalling a teacher important in her own and her friends' secondary education, wrote: ". . . the teachers most of us remember fondly are those that seem instinctively able to transfer their students' affection for them into academic engagement" (Karnasiewicz, 2006). To the extent that secondary school teachers can foster love of the subjects of secondary education, they establish the motivation and habits of loving learning throughout life.

Another role of love at the secondary level of education is to enlarge the scope of the learner's self-love to envision and create a life of multiple meanings, engagements, and satisfactions. The learner's love earlier focused on family and teachers should be, at the secondary level, indirectly guided by the personal examples of teachers and parents to love of learning about all aspects of the world. The form of love changes from early crushes on teachers and fellow students to an acceptance of the worth and dignity of other people who may be very different in appearance and habits. That acceptance is a form of love. It provides the foundation for civility in a diverse society and for civility among diverse national and global communities; among civic, religious, linguistic, and gender communities; and among past, present, and future communities. The adequate receipt, development, and practice of love can help to extend the values (which ought to be universal) "of nurturing and of internal curbs on violence, deceit and betrayal" (Bok, 2002, p. 287) from familial, tribal, or national boundaries to the entire human species initially, and then eventually to other species. Love is one of education's key ingredients and products.

My claims about the role of love in education are empirically testable and have practical consequences for educating teachers (Annabel J. Cohen, personal communication, November 1, 2006). The question for empirical research is: What should teachers do to show that they care about each student (and about their subject matter, at higher levels of education), and if they do this, will students learn more and better? Randomized controlled studies could be designed to identify how teachers should behave to show their care for each student and for their subject, and whether students will learn better as a result. If such trials show that students learn best when they love their teachers and their teachers love their subject, then educators should be taught how to encourage their students to love them and their subject.

THE IMPORTANCE OF BINOCULAR VISION

Binocular vision means having two eyes view the same scene from slightly displaced positions. Binocular vision makes it possible for the brain to create a perception of depth. I think educational analogs of binocular vision should be used much more broadly.

For example, earlier in this chapter I recommended the mastery of at least two languages (one's native language and at least one global language) and active knowledge of at least two ways of imagining, knowing, and representing the world (art and science). Mastery of two or more languages is the linguistic analog of having the stereoscopic vision that two eyes give. First-hand experience with art and science is a conceptual analog of binocular vision. Dual viewpoints give the world a depth not possible with only one point of view.

The desirable educational possibilities of binocular vision do not end there. The arts are plural, not singular. Knowing music, poetry and painting, as examples, gives a deeper vision of the creative possibilities of the human mind than knowing only one of them. Knowing the music of India, China, Africa, and Western Europe gives a richer perspective on the possibilities of human musical imagination than knowing any one of them alone.

Binocular vision in music, as in other areas, can be turned to favorable civic ends. For example, Cape Verde is a former colony of Portugal in West Africa, and Portugal's largest immigrant group originates in Cape Verde. When Portuguese children aged nine to ten studied and learned popular songs of Cape Verde along with popular songs of Portugal, their level of stereotyping of dark-skinned people was significantly reduced relative to their level of stereotyping prior to the program; their level of stereotyping was also significantly less than that of a randomized control group of children who studied and learned only Portuguese popular songs (Sousa, Neto, and Mullet, 2005). Annabel J. Cohen, a psychologist of music at the University of Prince Edward Island, has suggested investigating whether teaching children the music of children in other countries considered enemies of their own countries would make those students less likely to view people in the other countries with hostility (personal communication, October 6, 2006).

Like the arts in this respect as in so many others, the sciences are plural, not singular. Having a working understanding of some part of mathematics and some part of an empirical science gives two radically different points of view on the roles of reason and experience and the differing meanings of truth in different sciences. In higher education, knowing two academic disciplines immunizes against the parochialism of either one and creates awareness of the multiplicity of academic specialties and parochialisms.

Religious education can benefit from the analog of binocular vision as well. In high school, by good fortune I was forced against my will to take a course on the world's major religions. Like each of my classmates, I was obliged to write an extensive expository paper on any religion other than my own. I developed an admiration for the strengths of the religion I selected for my paper and an awareness of its limitations. This exercise gave me an enlarged perspective on my own and other religions. That perspective has remained a valuable part of my vision of the world.

Similar benefits could have accrued had I been required in primary or secondary school to study the history of regions other than western Europe and northern America. While it is impossible for basic and secondary education to provide a detailed comparative perspective on every area of human interest, basic and secondary education can provide children with enough, progressively more sophisticated examples of a comparative perspective that seeking binocular vision becomes a habit.

The educational importance of binocular vision precedes and extends beyond formal education. Important learning goes on at home long before a child begins formal education. Binocular vision at home is also desirable. Having more than one adult caretaker and model provides an infant and growing child more than one model for responding to the world, brings the child multiple sets of experiences, perspectives, and alternatives to the extremes of any single personality. Encouraging the child to love both family and school, and later encouraging the adult to love family and work—emotional analogs of binocular vision—provide balance and depth in life.

I commend as a goal of education inculcating by repeated example the knowledge that, where there is one way to do a thing or view a thing, there is probably also another. Where one value is important, another value is likely to be important as well. A first step toward leading a life of choices is to have the habit of recognizing that choices exist.

ACKNOWLEDGMENTS

This chapter benefited from the constructive comments of Sissela Bok, Annabel J. Cohen, Walter Feinberg, Claudia Madrazo, Martin Malin,

Fernando Reimers, and Rosanna Warren. I thank Annabel J. Cohen for giving me the paper of Sousa, Neto, and Mullet (2005). I thank the late William T. Golden and family for hospitality during this work.

NOTES

1. I make three disclaimers. First, I make no claim to either originality or comprehensiveness. Second, I do not claim to have documented in any systematic fashion the sources where these thoughts may have originated or may have been anticipated independently. Third, I do not attribute these suggestions to my colleagues in the UBASE project, the American Academy of Arts and Sciences, or the funders of the UBASE project. These are personal suggestions.
2. http://www.air.org/news/default.aspx#pew (accessed February 2, 2006).

REFERENCES

Baer, Justin D., Andrea L. Cook, and Stéphane Baldi. 2006. *The Literacy of America's College Students*. Washington, DC: American Institutes for Research. http://www.air.org/news/documents/The%20Literacy%20of%20Americas%20College%20Students_final%20report.pdf.
Bok, Sissela. 1995. *Common Values*. Columbia, MO: University of Missouri Press.
Bok, Sissela. 2002. Rethinking Common Values. In *Worlds in Collision: Terror and the Future of Global Order,* ed. Ken Booth and Tim Dunne. London: Palgrave Macmillan.
Cohen, Joel E. 1995. *How Many People Can the Earth Support?* New York: W. W. Norton.
Delors, Jacques, et al. 1996. *Learning: The Treasure Within: Report to UNESCO of the International Commission on Education for the Twenty-First Century: Highlights.* Paris : UNESCO. http://www.unesco.org/delors/delors_e.pdf
Eisner, Elliot W. 2002. "The Arts and the Creation of Mind." In *What the Arts Teach and How It Shows*, 70–92. New Haven: Yale University Press. http://www.naea-reston.org/tenlessons.html (accessed June 4, 2006).
Eisner, Elliot W. 2005. "Back to Whole." *Educational Leadership* 63 (1): 14–18.
Iacoboni, Marco, Istvan Molnar-Szakacs, Vittorio Gallese, Giovanni Buccino, John C. Mazziotta, et al. 2005. "Grasping the Intentions of Others with One's Own Mirror Neuron System." *PLoS Biol* 3 (3): e79.
Karnasiewicz, Sarah. 2006. "Classroom Confidential." *Salon.com.* http://www.salon.com/mwt/feature/2006/04/27/teacher_student/print.html (accessed May 22, 2006).
Organisation for Economic Co-operation and Development. 2005. "Executive Summary." *The Definition and Selection of Key Competencies.* https://www.pisa.oecd.org/dataoecd/47/61/35070367.pdf.
Rizzolatti, Giacomo, Luciano Fadiga, Vittorio Gallese, and Leonardo Fogassi. 1996. "Premotor Cortex and the Recognition of Motor Actions." *Cognitive Brain Research* 3 (2): 131–141.
Shonkoff, Jack P., and Deborah A. Phillips, eds. 2000. *From Neurons to Neighborhoods: The Science of Early Childhood Development.* Washington, DC: National Academy Press.

Smith, Adam. 1759. *The Theory of Moral Sentiments*. London: Adam Smith Institute. http://www.adamsmith.org/smith/tms/tms-p1-s1-c1.htm.

Sousa, Maria D. R., Felix Neto, and Etienne Mullet. 2005. "Can Music Change Ethnic Attitudes Among Children?" *Psychology of Music* 33 (3): 304–316. http://pom.sagepub.com/cgi/content/refs/33/3/304

Spring, Joel. 2000. *The Universal Right to Education: Justification, Definition, and Guidelines*. Mahwah, NJ: Lawrence Erlbaum Associates.

Part V

The Special Role of Skepticism as Universal Educational Goal

11 What Does "Universal" Education Mean?

James Carroll

Universality is spoken of as a virtue, and the quest for it is usually talked of as, well, *universally* positive. That may be true now as never before. The fulfillment of the social, economic, and political promises of a shrunken, "globalized" world requires the major effort toward an agreed program of intellectual development applying across nations, cultures, and class-es—a purpose embodied in the ideal of "universal basic and secondary education." Economic vitality, political equity, and social progress are all understood as flowing from, indeed depending on, the worldwide growth of literacy, cooperative skills, critical thinking, and moral reasoning that the UBASE project aims to foster.

In the past, ideals of universality have not been perceived by all concerned as virtuous. Indeed, they have been exposed as extensions of parochial assumptions, imposed by and for power. But in the twenty-first century new conditions of communication, technology, governance, and mobility are understood as making the idea of a global commonality, to the benefit of every society instead of a few, of all peoples instead of elites, the core of a realizable and desirable program. The contemporary notion of "universality" is embodied in the United Nations' Universal Declaration of Human Rights, which calls for "a common standard of achievement for all peoples and all nations." Who can dispute the idea that every human being deserves certain basic protections, and that no local culture, tradition, or religion—no matter how transcendent its claims—can be used to justify violations of those protections? The rights of minorities must be honored, but not when the practices of minority groups conflict with "universally" defined human rights. Slavery is not allowed. The denigration of women is not allowed. The exploitation of children is not allowed.

But such "universals" cloak the difficulties adhering in the movement from general norms to specific applications. Is a migrant worker whose low wages lead to imprisoning indebtedness a kind of slave? Is sexual lewdness focused on the female body a matter of liberation or denigration? Is the "hurried" child of the American suburb exploited?

"What went wrong with Islam?" was a question famously asked by a leading Western scholar (Bernard Lewis) after 9/11. "What went wrong with Europe?" was a question put in response by an Islamic scholar (Seyyed Hossein Nasr). The contrasting worldviews of post-Enlightenment Europe and, say, post-Colonial Islam make very clear that foundational definitions of human value remain in dispute. That all people living in all societies can affirm any shared basic notions of fulfilled, moral, creative human existence is called into question by the so-called "clash of civilizations," a phrase which, coined by the man who asked the first question referred to previously, itself betrays a set of cultural assumptions. Ethical norms, often unexamined or unadmitted, undergird every argument. No one pronouncing on the "clash of civilizations" is neutral in that putative "clash."

A certain wariness about making claims for "universality," humbly rooted in knowledge of past abuses of such claims, does not necessarily preclude the construction of a global program of education. Thoughtful reflection on the complexities of such an idea must be part of that program, that's all. As a kind of warning of what can happen without such awareness, it may help to consider some of the most powerful precedents to the UBASE initiative's universalizing impulse, which were the massive education programs that went hand in glove (or hand on sword) with urgent, and often wildly successful, projects of religious proselytizing.

In the Christian tradition, Jesus is remembered (Matthew 28:17–19) as having given his followers a last command, just before ascending to heaven. Because the words are attached to the moment of his final disappearance, they have always rung in the Christian ear with transcendent authority. The declaration assumes an absolute universality, and points to the educational mandate—missionizing—that inevitably follows from it. "All authority in heaven and on earth has been given to me," Jesus said. "Go, therefore, make disciples of all nations; baptize them in the name of the Father, and of the Son, and of the Holy Spirit. And teach them to observe all the commands I gave you."

This command to "teach" draws attention to the less-than-obvious fact that not all programs of "universal" education are alike, and indeed one thing that sets them apart is the way they understand universality. Here, too, a nuanced reading of the experience of the Christian tradition is instructive. While it is true that the proselytizing impulse of the Jesus movement led to an astoundingly rapid spread of Christian devotion—"Church membership"—in the Mediterranean world, the "commands" that were learned in this early "educational" program were not nearly so univocal as is commonly assumed today. Hard and fast distinctions between the synagogue and the church, to take one example, were not consistently observed in the first three centuries after Christ. The "command" Jesus gave was not necessarily to leave the "old" religion for the "new." Neither was the even more fundamental distinction between the monotheism of Christianity and Judaism and the polytheism of the Roman Empire nearly so sharp as is imagined now—as the Trinitarian formula attributed to Jesus by Matthew indicates, on one side, and as the then-emerging primacy of the Roman sun god indicates, on the other. The command to honor the "one" God was not necessarily what we imagine it was.

In recalling the words attributed to Jesus in Matthew (a text dating to about 90 CE), one should also recall that those words meant something very different after the emperor Constantine, more than two hundred years later, turned the project of Christian "teaching" into a method of expanding his control over the far-flung Roman Empire. His "universalizing" of the faith (imposing a univocal creed, making heresy a capital crime, absolutizing the difference between synagogue and church) served a political purpose.

The word "monotheism" is a clue to the necessary distinction between two meanings of "universal." The work monotheism does as a noun is like the work "universal" does as an adjective. The biblical tradition from which Rabbinic Judaism, Christianity, and Islam derive was unlike other religions of the ancient world in asserting that its God was "One"; that its God, that is, was the *only* God, was everybody's God, whether they knew it or not. Genesis is unique among ancient creation myths in that it accounts for the creation not of the tribe's world, or even of humankind's world—but of the very cosmos. This God is the *universal* God, and claims made in this God's name are believed to be universally authoritative. This is why the three monotheistic religions are themselves absolute religions, and why, not incidentally, so-called "holy war" has regularly found a place in the accepted practice of these religions. Absolute claims come to be enforced absolutely.

That is why getting the "universal" right in "Universal Basic and Secondary Education" matters so much. Does the "one" implied in "universal," or in "monotheism," for that matter, have a numerical character—meaning "one," as in, "We're number one!"—or does it have a moral character—meaning, as the U.S. motto has it, "Out of many, one." If the latter, then the unity being celebrated is not the lonely singleness of a digit, but the communal solidarity of a group. "Universal," in this second meaning, is inclusive, rather than exclusive. An essential pluralism is implied in such a notion of universality, a ready acknowledgment that, however absolute is the claim being made, there is more than one way to understand its meaning.

"Universal" truth may be understood as referring to a truth that applies across time, place, and culture, but time, place, and culture shape every perception and every expression of such truth. Therefore, any given— "one"—statement of truth must be offered and taken in awareness of truth's inevitable contingency. Therefore, truth, to use another essentially numerical word deriving from "one," is not univocal. If it were, then education would quite simply amount to the student's conforming his or her mind to the truth as stated by the teacher (whether speaking for the established religion, the state power, or merely the conventional wisdom). There is an elusive character, that is, even to something regarded as "universal" truth, and education begins and ends with respect for that elusiveness, which means a teacher's goal is not the student's mind conforming, but its engaging.

There is, of course, a profound cultural assumption embedded in this idea of the essential elusiveness of truth, and in the pedagogy that follows from it. That assumption is itself a matter of fierce debate across the societies in which the UBASE project aims to operate. One way to articulate that assumption is to contrast static ontology with a philosophical view that gives emphasis to process; is "being" primary, or is "becoming?" The difference here shapes thinking in such diverse arguments as that between "creation science" (which sees reality as having been established once, in an originating act of creation) and evolution (which sees reality as unfolding), or that between opponents of abortion (who may see human life as beginning at conception) and advocates of "choice," who may see the growth of fetal life into fully human as gradual. Each side in such disputes will stake its claim to "universality."

But what divides these contestants, perhaps most fundamentally, is that an understanding of "universality" that is inclusive, not exclusive, assumes the contingency of truth and affirms the "process" character of reality. The consequent necessity of pluralism must leave room for the point of view that denies all of this. Universal education, to be truly universal, must have a built-in acknowledgment that the ideal of universality, in addition to being humane and politically germane, is also problematic. Such an approach to education would be consistently self-critical, aware of the implications of power, and permanently alert for a Gnostic imposition by those who know on those who do not—all the pitfalls that have turned previous efforts at "universal" education into exercises, however nobly defined, of imperial triumphalism. And of course the teaching of such intellectual humility amounts, finally, to the most important act of universal education of all.

12 Teaching Tolerance and Open-Minded Approaches to Understanding Sacred Texts

Mohamed Charfi and Hamadi Redissi

Educational institutions occupy a pivotal place in the social system, linking childhood and adulthood, the domestic and the political, the private and the public. In modern democratic states, the education offered by public schools promotes the values of liberty and equality without ratifying the moral convictions held by any specific religious group. In many modern Arab countries, by contrast, the state is not neutral and neither is the education it offers its citizens. Instead of simply promoting the values of liberty and equality, the public schools also endorse the moral authority of Islam.

Most Arab states (through the influence of dominant elites and individuals) uphold an outdated and conservative vision of the role of religion in educational institutions. As a result of their educational policies, such states generate chronic cognitive dissonance among students, who are exposed to the secular ideals promoted by many political leaders as well as the religious doctrines promulgated by their Islamic teachers. An ambivalent and divided citizenry becomes a chronic source of potential political crisis at home, and of terrorism abroad.

Under the circumstances, a reform of basic education is absolutely urgent in order to modernize Arab states. The goal is to stop schools from aggravating the contradictions between moral communities and liberalizing regimes, and between historical religion and civil religion. Public schools in Arab states need to instill, instead, the value of tolerance and the skills needed to read sacred texts with an open mind. The Tunisian example shows that reform is possible—on the condition that a political will for reform can be cultivated by the leaders of Arab and Muslim states.

Since at least September 11, 2001, a great deal has been written on the Islamic educational system, including excellent analyses of the damage caused by madrasas, but little has been written on how to reform this system. This chapter is not offered as a work of neutral scholarly research, but as a contribution to the reformation of the teaching of Islam in public schools, a reform that is yet to be realized. Inspired by the Tunisian experience of reform as implemented by Mohamed Charfi while Minister of Education, it addresses, in a secular and liberal *engagement*, the main question posed to any Islamic educational system today: Should public schools teach Islam? If so, how should Islam be taught? And what should be taught? The chapter is prescriptive in tone, offering genuine technical solutions, never offered before, aimed at balancing Islamic tradition and civil religion.

ARAB COUNTRIES BETWEEN TRADITION AND MODERNITY

Since the nineteenth century, when the Muslims entered the Modern Age, recurrent efforts have been made to reconcile Islam, revised and reinterpreted, to modern conceptions of law and the state. These efforts have oscillated between attempts to impose a stringent secularism (as in Egypt under Nasser and Iran under the Shah) and equally strenuous efforts to protect the political authority traditionally exercised by religious institutions (as in Saudi Arabia and in Iran after the Revolution). One consequence of these oscillations is that many Arab and Muslim states today are neither totally traditional nor wholly secular, but rather marked by "a distorted duality" (Sharabi, 1988, Fr. Trans., 1996, pp. 23–28) or a "fundamental breach" (Shayegan, 1989, pp. 65–79), which has ultimately produced "composite formulae, if not failures" (Badie, 1986, p. 177).

The Political Context

All Arab countries have constitutions except Saudi Arabia and Libya. The former has a law decreed by the king (who has legislative power) in 1926 that governs public power and a 1958 regulation about the functioning of the council of ministers, both recently confirmed by a 1992 "fundamental charter." In Libya, a 1977 resolution of the "General Congress of the People" takes the place of a constitution.

Regarding the constitutional relationship between religion and state, Islamic states are classified in four categories: eleven have declared themselves to be Islamic states, twenty-two have declared Islam as the state religion, eleven have declared themselves to be secular states, and eleven have no constitutional declaration (Stahnke and Blitt, 2005). The constitutions of most Arab states rather grant an important place to the Islamic sacred law (*sharîa*), even as they adopt, at least formally, some principles of secularism.

In the first place, either the state religion is Islam or else the *sharîa* is the principal source of legislation. In many cases, constitutions simply state that Islam is the religion of the state.[1] In other cases, the state proclaims itself as Islamic.[2]

An avowedly Islamic state such as Saudi Arabia is supposed to apply the *sharîa*. By contrast, in a country like Tunisia, where the state religion is Islam, there is no such expectation. This is because Islam is not the same as the *sharîa*. It is larger and susceptible to diverse interpretations, not to mention the fact that the state reserves the right to proclaim norms that do not conform to the letter of the *sharîa*.

In many countries that uphold Islam as a state religion, the law as a result does not necessarily conform to the *sharîa*. This is true for penal legislation in most Arab countries. In such countries, judges, in the absence of an express disposition dictating recourse to the *sharîa*, uphold the laws passed by the representatives of the people (Charfi, 1987).

Unfortunately, in countries where the state has proclaimed itself Islamic, the constitution often stipulates that all laws must be in conformity with the letter of the *sharîa*. The clearest example is Saudi Arabia. The law of 1926 governing public powers states in article 6 that "legal norms should be in conformity with the Book of God, with the *sunna* [tradition] of the Prophet, and with the conduct of companions and the first pious generations." More recently, in 1992, the kingdom decreed a "fundamental charter" proclaiming that "the constitution is the book of God and the *sunna* of the Prophet."[3] Other constitutions indicate in varying fashions that the *sharîa* itself is a "principal [or major] source" of legislation.[4] Apart from the Koran, Libya does not recognize the three other sources of the *sharîa* (the tradition of the Prophet, consensus, and the analogical reasoning of legal scholars). "The Holy Koran is the law" is the sole principle governing the country (the second clause of the 1977 resolution).

In many Arab states, accession to high office is conditional upon the candidate's belonging to the Islamic religion. In cases where the constitution does not expressly stipulate it, this condition can be deduced from the general statement of the Islamic character of the State. Only the 1926 Lebanese constitution and the 1992 one of Djibouti are silent on the religion of both the state and the head of state.

Different Arab states regulate religious beliefs and practices in different ways. Some charge a Religious Ministry with overseeing worship, while others appoint a *Mufti,* a functionary with religious competence, who is charged with furnishing religious *responsa* (consultations), or supervising a house of *ifta* (consultation). Some states have simply taken over the hiring of preachers and of prayer *imams*, the financing of charitable associations and institutions of religious education, and the massive construction of mosques. Throughout the Arab world, states sanction the use of the Islamic calendar alongside the universal calendar; guarantee the commemoration of religious festivals; and organize competitions of a religious character (Koranic litanies). They also insure that public places close during the month of fasting, prohibit the sale of alcoholic beverages during this same month, and prescribe the broadcasting of the Friday prayer on state radio and television.

At the same time, the constitutions of many Arab states do accept the organic and functional separation of powers and the separation between governmental and administrative authorities. Three constitutions declare in their preambles the state's adherence to international treaties on the rights of man.[5] Still, it is often stipulated that the conditions for the exercise of these liberties should not threaten public order, national interest, and morality.

Most Arab Muslim countries with the exception of some Gulf States hold periodic elections. Even if these elections rarely have real democratic value because they are not organized in an honest, transparent, and regular fashion (due to the existence of a single party or a dominant party supported by the administration), the formal existence of a parliament that supposedly represents the people means that legislative power has been, officially and actually, removed from the *ulema* (or clerics), and entrusted to representatives of the people.

The State and Education

While the other countries of the world prepare their children to enter a complex and heterogeneous society, most Muslim countries continue to prepare young people for a life of religious purity. Unfortunately there are few exhaustive studies on the status of religion in Arab public schools. Numerical data are skimpy, monographs on particular countries uneven, and analyses of the content of school textbooks fragmentary. We know little about average years of schooling, rates of literacy, or the disparities in education between rich and poor, men and women.

Three Arab Muslim universities have survived since the Middle Ages: Zeitouna in Tunisia, Al Azhar in Egypt, and Qarawiyin in Morocco. Various reforms of these universities were initiated in the nineteenth century, but they all failed. More recently, these same universities have formed secularized and modern subsidiaries that teach the natural sciences and humanities in a way that is still imbued with religion.

Most modern Arab schools make the teaching of Islam a central part of their curriculum. It is hard to say how many hours of teaching are devoted to Islam, due to the fact that it is taught in all disciplines. Moreover, one has to take into account the para-scholastic influence of the *Kouteb* (private Koranic pre-schools) and of private Koranic schools that are operating in practically all Islamic countries from Afghanistan to Morocco. Several studies of public education (Nucho, 1993; Rugh, 2002; Salloum, 1995) suggest that the number of hours devoted purely to religious instruction is high from the first to the twelfth year of education: "In Bahrain, Egypt, Jordan and Kuwait, for example, an average of about 10% of total class hours is devoted to it each year. In Saudi Arabia it consumes 32% of class time for grades 1 to 3, 30% in grades 7 to 9, and then 15% or more for grades 10 to 12. The figures for Qatar are 17–20% in grades 1–6, 14% in grades 7–10, then 8–11% in grades 11–12" (Rugh, 2002, p. 404).

Much of this teaching turns out to be *contrary* to human rights. The civil war between Muslims and non-Muslims in Sudan that has dragged on for many years probably explains (without justifying) the lengthy passages on *jihad* in the schoolbooks of that country, where one finds an apology for this violence alongside the frequent reminder of the legal rules concerning it.[6] Egyptian books speak of tolerance but add that Islam is the only true religion.[7] The legal principle of "enjoining what is right and forbidding what is wrong" [3:104][8] is used to explain that struggling against evil can go on in both word and action, thus indirectly inciting justification of the violence that Islamists commit against the state and persons[9], which has been criticized (Abu Zayd, 1992, p. 104).

In still other Arab textbooks, women always have a position inferior to men. Mother is in the kitchen while father is in the library.[10] This situation is not only a social fact but also a religious rule. A Yemeni schoolbook pushes the duty to obey even farther, stressing a rule invented by the *fiqh* (Islamic law) that a woman's submission to God is unacceptable if it is not accompanied by submission to her husband; a woman's prayer is even inadmissible when her husband is discontented with her.[11] Similarly, Moroccan school textbooks, modeled on those of other Muslim countries, teach all the corporal punishments ordered in the *sharîa*, from whipping to stoning (supported by justifications for them).[12] They also assert[13] that freedom is permitted only on condition that the *sharîa* is not questioned, and as long as reason and the critical spirit are not employed for the criticism of the *sharîa* rules.[14] In most Arab countries, an apologetic presentation of the history of Islam is found not only in religious classes but also in language instruction. For example, a Moroccan book called *Rules of the Arabic Language*[15] exalts the Caliph Harûn al-Rashid to the status of a "just and virtuous prince"—whereas the reality is much more nuanced, to say the least.

As a whole, most textbooks are meant to encourage students to live in an "Islamic ambiance." For example, the Moroccan book of Arabic readings used in the sixth year of primary school, supposedly a language and not a religious book, takes as themes for the opening lessons: 1. Koranic verses; 2. Prophet's *hadiths* (sayings); 3. "I am Muslim"; 4. Islam and consultation; 5. Koranic verses; 6. the most worthy faster, etc.[16] A Morrocan survey of 865 young boys and girls from the urban middle class confirms the impact of such readings: 69 percent assert believing in magic, 75.8 percent in superstition, and 79 percent trust only family; for the most part they think that "Islam enjoins freedom, justice, fraternity and equality" while "capitalism cultivates hate, exploitation and segregation"; and in a communist system, people "are deprived from freedom and live in horror and repression" (Bourqia et al., 2000).

Under pressure from traditionalists, each Arab country has witnessed a manipulation of the education system. As a result, throughout the Arab world, many elements of education are incompatible with human rights and the liberal values of the modern democratic state.

TOWARD A REFORM OF EDUCATION IN ARAB COUNTRIES

To prepare students better to assume the duties of citizenship in a world that every day becomes more cosmopolitan, a certain number of reforms seem to us essential.

Forging Communal Ties in an Age of Globalization

What are the markers and emblems of an Arab and Islamic identity that are compatible with the rights and duties of democratic citizenship? And by what process of identification does the student feel Arab and Muslim?

It is extremely difficult to answer these questions. Even if one had a correct answer, one might truly hesitate, when it comes to education, between revealing the truth to students and inculcating the founding myths of the community. There is surely an age at which education deconstructs the myths and helps historical truth to triumph. But, at what age? Plato in the *Republic* concedes that one should teach children the city's fables and myths, after which one initiates them into true discourse. For us, the ideal would be to gradually educate them in the relativity of things: teach them that identity is far from stable, static, and permanent, but rather is fragile, fluctuating, and transient.

Unfortunately, for the whole Muslim world and especially for the Arab world, this way of seeing things poses problems. For obvious political reasons, pan-Islamic and pan-Arab identities have been diffused in schools as if such identities were indisputable, permanent, trans-historic, and transnational. This creates a grave tension between truth and history, identity and change, national and transnational identities. Three issues loom large in Arab schools today: how to teach students about their identities as Muslims, as Arabs, and as Arab-speaking language users.

Islamic Unity

While it is true that one can find more or less common markers of Islamic identity, it is no less true that Islamic unity is a chimera. It is manifestly illusory to hope someday to reunite within the same political entity countries as different and alien to each other as, for example, Afghanistan and Senegal, both part of the Organization of Islamic Conference, an international organization created in 1972 (Rabat-Morroco), founded on the criterion of one single condition, that is, allegiance to Islam that gathers together fifty-seven countries otherwise divided by ethnicity, language, and culture. A diversity that precludes transnational identity also affects the principle of trans-historic identity. The expression "*Umma,*" community of believers, which once referred to the small number of the faithful around the Prophet in Medina (622 CE), can today no longer have a relevant political implication. In medieval times, this *Umma*, supposedly represented by the Caliphate at Damascus (661–750) and then Baghdad (750–1258), willingly compromised with dynasties and autonomous regional powers, starting in the ninth century in the Middle East, the Maghreb, and Andalusia. These powers emancipated themselves, either de facto and by the sword, or *de jure* and through tacit agreement, from the control of the central caliphate. This fact has been historically recognized. In the eleventh century, Mawerdi proposed a distinction between "the emirate of conquest" (*imarat al-istila*) and "the emirate of attribution" (*imarat al-istikfa*), precisely to differentiate provinces that had freed themselves through violence from those that had been freed through a gentlemen's agreement between the caliph and a warlord (Mawerdi, 1982, pp. 59–70). Now that nation-states are constituted on the basis of territorial contiguity, there remains only faith to unite Muslims, as it does Jews, Christians, and the followers of other, non-monotheistic religions, all spread among internationally sovereign countries.

In truth, Islam is a religion and not truly an identity, since many countries are Muslim without sharing a single identity—unless you reduce cultural and national identity to religion as identified by immutable traits. In short, it is absolutely necessary to teach students that Islam is neither a homeland nor a national identity and that it has changed over history.

Arab Unity

Something similar applies to the idea of Arab unity. With the creation of the *Ba'ath* Party in 1941 by a group of revolutionaries gathered around Michel Aflaq, and again with Nasser's accession to power in Egypt on a pan-Arab platform in 1952, Arab unity became a key political goal in many parts of the Arab world. But unity has proved elusive. Ba'athism and Nasserism failed to forge an alliance in the late 1950s, and the Ba'ath states of Iraq and Syria became bitter regional rivals. The Gulf War of 1991 revealed Arab unity to be a fiction, an ideology that has masked the reality of authoritarian power founded on *raison d'etat*.

In fact, the Arab world is made up of sovereign nations, some completely constituted, others in the process of formation. These nations have separate interests. Under the circumstances, even the most enthusiastic partisans of Arab unity have to admit that such a goal is remote.

In other words, it is necessary to teach students that the really imperative goal is multiform Arab cooperation and the modernization of nation-states whose independent existence is no longer subject to dispute.

Does this mean that one must banish the teaching of Arab identity from Arab schools? Surely not. Teachers cannot erase the feeling of belonging to a wider ethnic community. What education should do is suggest to the student by means of concrete examples how culture is constructed and how its meaning varies throughout history.

The history of classical Islam is from this viewpoint rich in lessons. Its "medieval identity," a source of pride, is the result of the mixing of various influences: Persian literature, Greek wisdom, the transmission of the divine word, and the translation of the Ancients that Muslims owed to the Jews and the Christians. Medieval authors like Tawhidi and Miskawayh eulogized this mixing. In an unequaled humanist vein, they sought in it what the Greeks called "the excellent man" and what classical Arabs called "the perfect man" (*al-insan ak-kamil*).

Language

In all Arab countries, teaching is done essentially in Arabic and, secondarily, depending on the country and the discipline, in English or in French. Some countries do this out of necessity, in order to have access to the sciences, and others by cultural choice, so as to know foreign cultures. In fact, language is more than a tool; it is a means of knowing oneself and others.

Nevertheless, language being somehow linked with identity, the question of the place of Arabic is often charged with passion, especially because in certain Arab countries, mathematics, physics, and the natural sciences are taught in a foreign language. Some complain of the marginalization of Arabic, and others fear that if scientific disciplines are taught in Arabic, it will lower the level of teaching. In order to remove some heat from the debate, one must definitively assert the privileged place of Arabic as a national language and recognize the important place of foreign languages as a fundamental means of knowing the world. Happily, apart from "fundamentalists" of a single language (whether Arabic or foreign), the consensus on this point is established.

Between Islamic Tradition and Civil Religion

The teaching of religion poses real problems. First, should one teach Islam at school, or proclaim the neutrality of the state in this respect and leave to parents' discretion the issue of whether to teach their children themselves or send them to private religious schools? Second, if the public schools choose to teach Islam, how should they go about doing so? The answer to the first question is sociological, and to the second it is intellectual or philosophical.

Should public schools teach Islam?

Our preference would be for the public school to desist from teaching the precepts and dogmas of Islam. But this solution seems to suit societies that have accomplished the historical process of secularization. Such societies have passed from the "mechanical solidarity" derived from similitude to the "organic solidarity" derived from the division of labor (Durkheim, 1994), or from a "community" defined by solidarity to a "society" defined by competing interests (Weber, 1995, p. 65).

Most Arab societies, unfortunately, have not completed the historical process of secularization. They are "societies of the Book," still in transition.

Two extreme cases demonstrate the difficult relation between public education and religious education: Turkey and the Indian school of *Dar Uloom* of Deoband.[17]

In choosing to enshrine secularism in the constitution and empowering the military to safeguard it, Turkey has ceded the teaching of religion to private schools. Between 1982 and 1992, 5,000 Koranic schools were created in Turkey, as opposed to 270 secular ones. On the recommendation of the Council of Security, entrusted with watching over Turkey's secular constitution, the teaching of religion became obligatory in public schools (Jéro, 2002). The result: Turkey has been caught up in the Islamization of a portion of the elite formed in these schools, helping to create support for the *Party of Justice and Development* of Recept Tayyip Erdogan, which won the legislative elections of November 2002.

The school of Deoband meanwhile contributed to the advent of the Taliban (Rashid, 2001, pp. 196–206). After Indian independence, private religious schools were left untouched by the secular state. When Pakistan separated from India in 1947, Abdul Haq, a former student of Deoband, founded a school of similar religious tendencies near Peshawar on the border of Afghanistan. This is where the Taliban would learn the most retrograde Islam—which they would apply in Afghanistan.

As a result, the 100,000 private *madrasa* (religious schools) that exist in modern day India have become subject to suspicion. And in Pakistan, after having been integrated in the formal educational system in 1980/1981, some 20,000 religious *madrasa*, supported by public money coming through zakat funds set up by the government in 1980 (about 10 percent of the alms collected by public agencies are devoted to religious education) are becoming subject to scrutiny. After September 11th, General Musharraf called for a new reform, in order to increase control over the clergy as a part of the war against terrorism (Malik, 2002, pp. 20–21). Whether or not the state takes charge of religious education, in practice both pre-school institutions (the family) and post-school ones (the social milieu, custom, religious parties, private schools) have a tendency to compensate for any weakness of the secularized state. This is what happens in the immigrant Muslim communities in the West: although they go to public schools, the children of the second generation are deeply attached to their traditional religion as interpreted by non-professionals or traditionalist jurists or ulemas.

Hence our answer to the first question: it is prudent and reasonable for Arab states to take charge of religious education; indeed, experience shows that it is dangerous and counter-productive for the public school to abandon religious education to other social actors.

How should Islam be taught?

Within the religious domain we propose making the following distinctions: worship, dogmas, virtues, and social relations. This fourfold distinction is governed by two principles: the principle of respect that liberalism owes to *all* religions and the principle of tolerance applied to the reading of Scripture. In effect, liberalism is not "indifferent." Inasmuch as it accepts cultural, religious, and metaphysical pluralism and the diversity of interpretations, so it promotes a liberal approach to understanding Scripture.

This is what Hobbes, Spinoza, Locke, and Kant accomplished in the West. And this is what certain Muslim intellectuals (of whom we will speak in a later section of this chapter) are trying to do in the Arab world today. Liberalism "modified" for an Islamic context allows reconciliation between the universal claims of liberalism and the culture of Islam, between the requirements of modernity and the teaching of Islamic tradition.

Worship

As concerns worship, Islam rests on five pillars: the profession of faith, prayer, fasting, mandatory alms, and pilgrimage to Mecca. These are "personal duties," private obligations (*fardh 'yan*) that every Muslim should render, *ut singuli*, as a sign of obedience, strictly in relation to God. It would be normal to continue teaching them in classic fashion.

Dogma

The same is true of the metaphysical aspects and questions of dogma (belief in God, his kingdom, purgatory, eternal bliss. . .). Public education is charged with teaching them in a traditional way, while advancing (as we shall see) an external and historical critique as well as promoting liberal exegeses of Scripture.

We propose, however, that both worship and dogma be taught tolerantly, according to the principles of Lockean liberalism. In effect, on both issues (*cultus* and *credenda*), Locke demanded "absolute tolerance." A Magistrate cannot force subjects either to worship or to believe (Locke, 1992, p. 105 et seq.). A related idea expressed by John Rawls in *Political Liberalism* is that political liberalism is also philosophical, and therefore it extends tolerance into philosophical and metaphysical debates. To safeguard such tolerance, worship should be regarded as a private matter, in the sense that the state is not accountable for the performance of these duties; in addition, the state, while protecting the right of believers to worship, will not punish those who neither believe nor worship.

Unfortunately, the liberal principle of "unconditional and unlimited tolerance" is hard to apply in practice in most Arab countries, due to the popularity of Islam, and the various sociological pressures that result from being a "society of the Book." The state is often torn between liberalism and popular religious demands. For example, it faces hard choices about closing public places during Ramadan, and about forbidding the consumption of alcohol.

At this level, the choice in Islamic countries is not between "absolute tolerance" and "zero tolerance" but between two other modes: "conditional tolerance" and "the primacy of public good over tolerance." Conditional tolerance, according to Locke, is extended to beliefs and practices that do not threaten security and the public good. But while certain beliefs and practices may be left to the discretion of citizens, others should not. For example, a right to polygamy (which Locke considered should benefit from conditional tolerance) is incompatible with a conception of public good governed by sexual equality. This should also be the case in Islamic countries. Specifically, in this case "public interest must prevail over tolerance." (In fact, apart from Turkey and Tunisia, most Arab states still allow polygamy.)

Virtues

The same considerations should guide the domain of moral virtues. The state has no business worrying about the salvation of souls. Still, it should teach such virtues as loyalty, generosity, courage, love of neighbor, peace, and good works. Without a respect for such virtues, social life is given over to evil. Thus it is desirable to teach Arab values, what tradition calls the "chivalric virtues" (*makarem al-akhlaq*) such as honor, respect for promises made, courage, pride, hospitality, etc., and which the great Orientalist Goldziher has compared to Jewish Noachim law, and to the Latin *vertus* (Goldziher, 1976, I, pp. 11–14). The public schools should also teach the humanist values of Islam: magnanimity, love, compassion, mutual aid, and peace (Boisard, 1979).

The moral duty to "enjoin what is right and forbid what is wrong" has to be managed with prudence. Although this duty is of Koranic origin (3:104), it is according to tradition a collective duty (*fardh kifaya*). This means that the individual is absolved of it as long as the community represented by the public authority accomplishes it instead. If the duty to forbid what is wrong is taught, then the schools run the risk of pushing young people to conclude that a perceived failure of the public authority to uphold this duty obliges them to render justice themselves, or else proclaim themselves communitarian judges.

Different challenges are posed by the teaching of two other collective duties in Islamic tradition: the duty to seek knowledge, and the duty of *jihad*.

The first is established by the Koran (7:185, 69:2) and confirmed by the tradition of the Prophet's enjoining of scientific research. Teachers can easily show how the community fulfills the duty to know through public schooling. At the same time, the duty to seek knowledge has become individual and universal in modern societies. Here Arab educators may cite the first pages of the *Decisive Treatise* of Averroés (1126–1198) in which the philosopher, after having established that "Revelation declares obligatory the examination of beings," deduces that this examination is best made through the "demonstrative syllogism" of philosophy, the science of sciences in his day (Averroés, 1996, § 3–5).

When it comes to *jihad*, teachers should show how its lexical root signifies "to make an effort." *Jihad* is not holy war but rather, on a personal level, an effort to combat one's natural penchants and inclinations. In fact, textual interpretation can show that the "great *jihad*" is the struggle to master oneself and that only the "small *jihad*" refers to war (Abu Zahra, 1962;

Hamidullah, 1968). The pacific spirit of *jihad* properly understood should extend to knowledge of others, and teaching should foster peace and fraternity among peoples of all countries. The educator should insist on the fact that war has been banned in modern international relations, and the Islamic states, being members of the United Nations, uphold the right only to legitimate defense in the case of aggression. An assigned reading of the Charter of the United Nations would show that recourse to war is forbidden.

Finally, in the last years of public schooling, educators should show how Koranic virtues belong to the order of belief, and not to the order of knowledge. The difference is based on the fact that beliefs cannot be proved except through rhetoric; belief rests on faith, not facts. Knowing presupposes true understanding according to the protocols of science. The teacher would reassure the students, though, by insisting that the existence of God and the immortality of the soul are beliefs that are necessary for the realization of the sovereign good as the goal of the moral life. They are, as Kant said, "postulates of reason," plausible hypotheses, but grounded only in moral duty, which in turn is based on the autonomy of practical reason, which at the level of action imperatively prescribes what is to be done or not done, notably to act in such a way that we are all free (Kant, 1985, IV & V).

Social Relations

Arab educators should approach social relations according to the principle of freedom. On this theme, we have one of the rare cases in which classical Islam is perfectly in accord with liberalism. Islam promotes contractual freedom of property, of buying and selling, and of movement; it possesses legal mechanisms that guarantee the security of economic and commercial transactions.

It would be fortunate if public education stressed freedom of enterprise, and showed that social relations (unlike religious duties) are subject to evolution. For example, while a rate of interest was forbidden in the classical age, the requirements of modern life render necessary recourse to a banking system based on a notion of investment, dividends, and interest.

In summary, we propose that both worship and dogmas be taught according to tradition, but combined with principles that promote tolerance; that the virtues, despite their religious roots, be taught as public duties under the aegis of the state's authority; and, finally, that social relations obey the principle of freedom consecrated by classical Islam and modern liberalism. We also suggest that teachers present religion as a matter of faith at the outset, deferring a critical exposition until later years, so as not to disorient young children who need time to form their personal ideas of faith.

Reconciling Religion with Human Rights

How can we reconcile the need to teach religion with the fact that society is founded largely on the principles of abstract and secular humanism, or on convention and a social pact freely consented to by free and equal social partners? If liberalism has been adapted to Islam, it is because of the new interpretations of the Koran offered by a variety of Arab reformers (Charfi, 2001; Redissi, 2004).

Among the founders of modern Islam, authors such as the Egyptians R. Rifaat Tahtaoui (1801–1873), Qacem Amin (1863–1908), Mohamed Abduh (1849–1905), Ali Abderrazak (1888–1966), and Taha Hussein (died 1973) and the Tunisians Kherredine (1810–1879), Ibn Dhiaf (1803–1877), and Tahar Haddad (died 1935) ought to find a significant place in schoolbooks.[18] The work of the Moderns in Islam raises three questions for us that are at the heart of the re-reading of Scripture: (a) religious tolerance; (b) secularization; and (c) sexual equality. These issues should accompany a reform of education in (d) human rights.

Tolerance

In classical Islam, the world was divided into three realms: that of Islam (the world of *sharîa* and justice), that of war (the impious world of anomie), and that of reconciliation (the world of non-aggression). Inside the Islamic world Islamic law prevailed, but the *dhimmis*, those protected by Islamic law,[19] could keep their beliefs and their jurisdiction. They benefited from protection conditional upon payment of a personal poll tax (Qur'an 9:29).

In the modern age, equality was established in principle between Muslims and non-Muslims: equality before the law, equality with respect to taxes, and equality with respect to military service. This was a major achievement of the Turkish reforms of 1839 (Khatt Sherif) and 1858 (Khatt Humayum) and the Fundamental Pact ('Ahd al-Amen) in Tunisia (1857).

Three principles should be conveyed in teaching: belief is a private matter; prophecy is not a warrant for domination; and compulsion cannot produce religious belief. There are textual and historical precedents for all of these principles in Islam. The Koranic verses that personalize belief, make it a private matter, are as follows: "O ye who believe! Ye have charge of your own souls. He who erreth cannot injure you if we are rightly guided" (5:105); "Whosoever goeth right, it is only for (the good of) his own soul that he goeth right, and whosoever erreth, erreth only to its hurt. No laden soul can bear another's load" (17:15). Other verses affirm that the Prophet cannot force people to believe; at the most, he has the duty to warn them: "Remind them, for thou art but a remembrancer, Thou art not at all a warder over them" (88:21–22). Such a constraint arises from the absolute divine will: "If the Lord willed, all who are in the earth would have believed together. Wouldst thou (Muhammad) compel men until they are believers? It is not for any soul to believe save by the permission of Allah" (10:99–101). Still other Koranic verses suggest the limits of coercion in matters of faith: "There is no compulsion in religion" (2:256); regarding those who think otherwise, "reason with them in the better way" (16:125).

Secularization

The classical theory of power in Islam was that of the Caliphate, also called *imamat* (guidance). It was founded on the idea that the caliph, which etymologically means successor, "deputized for prophetics in the safeguarding of religion and the administration of earthly interests" (Mawerdi, 1982, p. 5). The Caliph (or Prince) applied the *sharîa* but possessed all earthly power. Then, in the nineteenth century, the question arose of whether power ought to be secularized. Reformers set themselves the task of showing that Islam did not confuse the temporal and the spiritual and that it was able to adapt to the modern age. Tunisians like Ibn Dhiaf and Kherredine did so in a way that today could be criticized, but at the time was very suitable. The former, author of the *Fundamental Pact* (1857), in his *Chronicle of the Kings of Tunis* (1873) classified political regimes into three categories: "republican power," "despotic power," and "power limited by the law." Neither the first nor second corresponds to Islam, which is as much against the power of the masses as against despotism. Only a monarchic power tempered by the law wins the adherence of Ibn Dhiaf ([1873] 1963, vol. 1, pp. 6–77). Kherredine, prime minister and great reformer, in his *Essays on the Reforms Necessary for Muslim States* ([1867] 1987), pleads for the need to borrow modern institutions from Westerners. He says, in effect, that borrowing is wisdom (*hikma*). The possible objections are the same as those used today by adversaries of the modernization of education: the opposition between modern institutions and the principle of religious law, the ignorance and incapacity of the masses to assimilate them (Kherredine, [1867] 1987, 133 ff). "Any enlightened man," he says, "can see that these objections have no foundation" (pp. 135–136). Reforms are "compatible with the provisions of our sharia, religious law" since the ideas of liberty and justice are "the fundamental basis of our religious Law" (pp. 88, 93). In support of this proposition, a panoply of proofs is solicited: the *hadith* (sayings of the Prophet), texts from jurisconsults, the historical experience of good caliphs and virtuous princes.

In Egypt, similar work was done by Abduh and refined by Ali Abdherazak. In a series of famous articles published in 1898 and later compiled under the title *Al-Islam, dîn al-'ilm wa al-madaniyya* (*Islam, Religion of Science and Modern Civilization*), Abduh makes a division between faith and politics. Belief in God and in his unity, he says, can only be acquired through "rational proof," which arises from the "natural order" (*al-tabîa*). Islam, he thinks, has never known a fusion of the temporal and the spiritual. Islamic Law has conferred upon the Caliph the management of human affairs, nothing more. Power, if you will, is *ab initio* civil. But how can one articulate the relation between power and religion, the affairs of this world and those of the next?

Abduh enunciates a few principles:

- The use of reason to obtain belief; here reason is an instrument (*was-sila*) and a proof (*hujja*).
- The primacy of reason over the letter of the Koran. This means that in cases of incompatibility between reason and the tradition recorded by the doctors of the Law (*naql*), the former takes precedence.
- The refusal of the *takfir* (accusation of nonbelief). Abduh enunciates the principle that if proffered speech is liable to lead to unbelief in a hundred possible cases and to be taken in a single instance in a sense compatible with Islam, then one should prefer the single case in question over the hundred inquisitory interpretations.
- The "overturning" (*qalb*) of religious power, which means that Islam "has destroyed" (*hadama*) this type of power for the sake of a direct relation between God and his creatures without an intermediary.
- Tolerance: If Christianity is a religion of tolerance according to St. Matthew's Gospel (5:39–40), Islam equally enjoins magnanimity (*samâaha*), amnesty (*'afwu*), and friendship (*mawadda*) with people of other religions and a rejection of excess (*ghuluw*) in religious matters (Abduh, 1978, vol. 3, pp. 243–350).

Abduh's innovative interpretation was radicalized in 1926 by his disciple Ali Abd al-Raziq, who argued that political power is part of social relations and not of dogma. Mohammed was a prophet like Moses and Jesus, and not a political leader; the theory of the caliphate is not Koranic; and finally, the Koran does not prescribe any particular form of government, and so Muslims are free today to choose the system of government that suits the modern age (Abd al-Raziq, [1926] 1994). This thesis would be refined and developed by others (Charfi, 1996, p. 28; Filaly-Ansary, 1997, pp. 110–148; Charfi, 1998, pp. 157–202, Redissi, 1998, pp. 93–123).

It is of the highest importance to explain to the young that the Koran imposes no determined form of political organization; the Caliphate is a human institution that the first Muslims adopted precisely in the absence of clear and irrefutable Koranic indications about the nature of power. And it is necessary to explain to them that power in the classical age was authoritarian and that today nothing prevents power from being organized according to democratic norms.

Sexual Equality

In the classical age, inequality between women and men was a normative social fact. Women were considered inferior in physical state and also as "lacking in reason and religion." The legal code included a host of discriminatory provisions benefiting men, some of Koranic origin and others customary: a right to polygamy, the man's right to repudiate a marriage unilaterally, a ban on a Muslim woman marrying a non-Muslim man, wedding ceremonies performed in the woman's name by her guardian, the primacy of the husband in the home and in practically all matters relating to it, and the veiling of women in public.

In the nineteenth century, Arab reformers began quietly to criticize such discrimination against women. The Egyptian Tahtawi (1801–1873) wrote a large book titled *Al-morshed al-amin li al al-banat wal banin* (*Guide for the Education of Girls and Boys*) in which he pleaded, among other things, for the right of girls to receive a basic education (Tahtawi, 1972, vol. 2, pp. 271–767). Thirty years later, Qacem Amin (1863–1908), a spokesman for women's liberation, went farther in two books, *Al-mara'a al-jadida* (*The New Woman*) and *Tahrir al-maraa* (*Liberation of Women*), recognizing a woman's right to unveil herself and to go to work (Amin, 1976).

A decisive stage was reached by the Tunisian Tahar al-Haddad (died 1935), whose book *Imraatuna fi al-sharia wa al-mujtama'* (*Our Women, Legislation and Society*, 1929) went farthest in the direction of emancipating women. Haddad argued not only for the liberation of women (Haddad, 1978, pp. 149–240) but also for their legal promotion (Haddad, 1978, pp. 21–147). On the social level, he defended an education system that was general, practical, moral, emotional, and physical, as well as the right to work and the suppression of the veil. He vigorously criticized premature marriage of young girls and unions arranged by parents, and the general masculine domination that he imputed to ignorance, to underdevelopment, and to custom. On the legal level, and based on an audacious interpretation of Koranic verses, he grounded the conjugal tie upon the couple's free choice (and not on parental guidance) based on love (not the sexual instinct). He attacked the unilateral right of the husband to repudiate his wife, which he proposed to correct by legal divorce. Finally, he attacked the taboo of polygamy by pointing to the Koranic verse saying that a man can never be equitable among his four legal wives (4:129). Based on this statement in the Koran, the first leader of the independent state of Tunisia, Bourguiba (1903–1999), promulgated in 1956 the Code of Personal Status, which criminalized polygamy, fixed a minimum age for marriage, instituted free consent in marriage and divorce, abolished repudiation, and replaced it with equal right to legal divorce.

With the exception of Turkey and Tunisia, almost all Arab and Islamic countries remain attached to the application of traditional norms. This includes Egypt, despite the intellectual precedents that we have noted. On this matter as many others, the intellectual bases and the work of interpretation do in fact exist for a moral reform of Islamic society—only the political will is lacking.

If the latter were manifested and the theoretical support made available, it could be translated into the school by providing obligatory schooling of girls and boys mixed together in classrooms, and also by teaching equality of the sexes.

Education in Human Rights

One of the school's duties is to prepare children to integrate into society through education for citizenship according to the norms of the modern, liberal, and secular state. From this perspective, civic education is an essential subject that should be made completely independent of religious education.

Students should be made familiar with the rules of how a modern state functions: local and regional administration, separation of powers, an independent judicial system, relations between executive and legislative branches, and the principles and voting methods of elections. Students should also be taught the values on which democratic states are founded: the fundamental principle of equality and nondiscrimination among human beings and in particular between men and women, the principal individual and collective freedoms, the rights and duties of a citizen. Finally, civic education should stress the idea of historicity, that is to say, the evolution of ideas and institutions across different historical eras and in different regions of the world.

Thus the pupil would discover that the only legitimacy worthy of the name is democratic and that the history of humanity is, in a certain manner and as a whole, the history of an evolution from pre-modern forms (primitive, authoritarian, theocratic, etc.) to democracy: in other words, the shift from an absolute power that asserts its ownership of truth to a power that leaves the absolute to each person's conscience and governs in realms of the relative where contestation is permitted, pluralism is practicable, and pacific alternance is possible.

And so humanity arrived (on December 10, 1948) at the Universal Declaration of Human Rights, a text that should be read, explicated, and commented upon in all schools. This was the case in the reform of education that took place in Tunisia where each year, on this date, schoolteachers explain to students the principles and value of this founding text.

This "direct" teaching of the principles of democracy and human rights should be accompanied by the "indirect" teaching of these principles. It is fundamental that the choice of texts for all subjects in the humanities be oriented in this direction—since no choice in any subject matter can pretend to innocence. The choice of written and visual materials to illustrate books designed for children in primary schools is important. For example, images of boys and girls playing together or of the father and mother performing the same tasks, both noble and banal, habituate students to the idea of women's emancipation and sexual equality. By contrast, the image of an educated and active father and of an ignorant mother confined to housework normalizes a masculine, patriarchal, and misogynistic society.

This pedagogy about equality of the sexes is necessary not only in the curriculum and textbooks: life inside the teaching establishment should be based on coeducation. In the Arab world these days most schools are single sex. It is imperative to put an end to this segregation so as to suppress any inferiority or superiority complex by reason of sex and in order to foster healthy and natural relations between the girls and boys of today, the women and men of tomorrow.

But all this does not mean that the teaching establishment should become ideological. The liberal school cannot permit this. Quite the contrary, in the promotion of the ideas of liberty, equality, democracy, and human rights, the school should present all theories, all doctrines, in harmony with the principle of pluralism that characterizes liberalism. This diversity will teach the young to recognize themselves in some ideas and to relativize others; it will help them to acquire the critical spirit and will foster in each the formation of his or her personality.

Conditions for the Application of Reform

An ambitious reform such as the one advocated here presupposes that certain conditions of effectiveness will be filled. We regard three conditions as especially important: the proper teaching of modern science; the proper training of teachers; and promoting a broader culture of critical pluralism.

Although the matter does not seem to relate directly to religion and human rights, the teaching of science matters a great deal in Islamic countries because most Islamists boast of having scientific training, to the point that they are nicknamed "PhDs with beards." Now, everything depends on how the sciences are taught. A good reform of the education system should aim to overhaul not only the humanities but also change methods of teaching the "exact sciences" so that the young truly understand the nature of physical, chemical, and biological phenomena. Theories that are often considered taboo, such as the Big Bang or human evolution, should be broached and explained.

A school of knowledge is also a school of criticism in which the student will discover that scholars have progressed by trial and error, by posing hypotheses and having doubts, and that scientific truths are often provisional and need to be completed or rectified. In short, the history of scientific truth is strewn with errors and challenges, which does not mean one should contest or reject the possibility of scientific truth, as do certain skeptics.

In general, narrow specialization should be avoided: even if he has learned to solve mathematical equations or use a computer, the Arab scientist today usually has only a summary general culture at best. Only a common syllabus that is as extensive and as little differentiated as possible can avoid the premature specialization that results in training citizens who are expert in the sciences and ignorant in the humanities. Specialization in secondary schools should take place only two years before the baccalaureate, to allow engineers, doctors, and researchers to acquire an appropriate understanding of a general culture that is common to all.

In addition, reform can succeed only if the teachers fully participate in it. In France since the end of the nineteenth century, teachers have been the "Republic's hussars." Because of circumstances of pure historical chance, the Third Republic was installed in 1875 only provisionally, since the population still supported the monarchy. Thanks to the schools, though, in the space of a generation the republican spirit replaced the monarchist spirit among the population. Thanks to the cohesion among the body of teachers and their involvement in a democratic school that was secularized and open to all, the public school went hand in hand with universal suffrage (J. Ozouf, 1993; J. Ozouf & M. Ozouf, 1992). Luc Ferry, the current minister of national education in France, has stated that "there is no democracy except through the school, in other words, democracy grows out of a pedagogy that is democratic" (Ferry and Renaut, 1985, vol. 3, p. 170).

In Arab and Islamic countries, teachers lack uniform training: some have a traditional Muslim training and others a modern Western education; some are monolingual and others bilingual; some have been trained at home, others abroad. As a result, some teachers favor reforms and others do not. Experience shows that the viewpoint supported by the authorities will orient the schools, which means that radical reform will not succeed unless the teachers are aware that an educational policy corresponds to the state's clearly expressed will, especially at the top. Hence the imperative need for states (which are infrequently unitary, but are often led and influenced by diverse elites) to opt publicly for a policy of modernization through the classroom and for them to apply it with the highest vigilance and the greatest vigor, and without the least hesitation.

Finally, while a reform of education policy is important for all Arab and Islamic countries, so is a reform of the broader culture. It is up to intellectuals and artists to do this. Unfortunately, since Arab states dominate the media, government officials also have to assume some responsibility. In many Arab countries, Arabic and Islamic media are only deepening the idealization and sacralization of tradition instead of promoting critical pluralism. Even the private television networks (Al-Jazira, ANN) that were welcomed in the beginning have tended to idealize Islamic tradition. We now know that the policy of promoting Islam in order to cut the ground from under the feet of Islamists has in fact always backfired and served the latter. Cultural policy should be oriented toward wholly free creation, widespread support for intellectuals and artists, and ever greater openness toward universal culture.

THE EXPERIENCE OF REFORM OF CIVIC AND RELIGIOUS EDUCATION IN TUNISIA (1989–1994)

The reform of the educational system in Tunisia introduced by the law of July 28, 1991 was conceived in the spirit we have just sketched, both in its content and in its practical application. The Tunisian case thus merits careful study.

For didactic reasons, we will first offer a history of reform efforts in Tunisia since the nineteenth century.

The First Reforms

At the beginning of the nineteenth century, Tunisia was entering its fourth century of economic and social stagnation. As European nations began to modernize, a new awareness arose of the need to reform Tunisian society. The first reforms were initiated under the reign of the two monarchs Ahmed Bey (1837–1855) and Mohamed Sadok Bey (1859–1882) (Brown, 1974).

In 1840 Bey founded Bardo, a military academy on the Western model that taught cadets foreign languages and the exact sciences. He built a cannon and gunpowder foundry. And new factories appeared: one to manufacture cloth, another to produce leather, a mill for flour powered by a steam engine, and a refinery for oil (1844–1845). A national bank was created in 1847, one of the first in the Arab world. In conjunction with these initiatives, a rationalization of taxation took place, notably with the institution of direct taxes, a lessening in export taxes, the suppression of taxes on certain products (oil, arable land), and certain others collected by regional tax collectors (governors, sheikhs). The Waqfs (religious endowments) were centralized in 1874.

On the legal and political plane, Courts were reorganized and a new penal code implemented. Slavery was abolished between 1842 and 1846. The *'Ahd al-aman,* a sort of declaration of the rights inspired by the Turkish Tanzimat (1839 and 1853), was decreed in 1857; this was followed by a new constitution that limited the power of the monarchy for the first time in the Arab world (1861, suspended in 1864).

These reforms corresponded to the spirit of the times. In particular, the penal code was remarkably modern. For example, article 203 enumerated the range of punishments: the death penalty, forced labor, prison, banishment, and fines—no more corporal punishment. Article 204 stated: "It is forbidden to pronounce punishments other than those permitted in the preceding article and that could involve physical suffering." Apostasy, not covered in the code, was therefore not punishable either. Article 281 legalized the sale of alcoholic beverages, which was to be sanctioned only if they were sold outside specially authorized points of sale. A Prud'homme tribunal charged with arbitrating work conflicts was created (1877). As in Turkey, two educated modernists and men of state played a crucial role in this period, Prime Minister Kehrredine (1810–1877) and Ahmed Ben Dhiaf (1803–1877) (Van Krieken, 1976).

Finally, in the realm of culture, a renaissance occurred, notably with the birth in 1860 of an official press and the first newspaper, *Al râid-attûnisi* (*Tunisian Guide*). Even more important was the creation in 1875 of Sadiki, a new secondary school. Offering a modern curriculum of classes in the exact sciences, modern languages, and world history, the *lycée* in the years that followed would produce many of the nation's political and cultural leaders (Sraïb, 1995).

While Sadiki attracted many of Tunisia's best and brightest, religious teaching remained unchanged. The country had 1,250 *meddebs* (traditional teachers) in *kouttebs* (private Koranic schools) where only boys were taught the alphabet, elements of Arab grammar, and the Koran. No modern university existed yet. The traditional Islamic university, the Zeitouna, consisted of some 30 to 40 *cheikhs,* religious educators who dispensed both secondary and higher education to nearly a thousand students a year at the end of the nineteenth century. But the level of absenteeism was high and teaching non-obligatory, so that barely three hundred students a year graduated by passing the examination (Ben Achour, 1991, pp. 105–110). Once they had their diplomas, the graduates of Zeitouna tended to become judges in religious courts, notaries, or *imams* in mosques.

The Zeitouna curriculum did not include the exact sciences, mathematics, or engineering. It revolved instead around the study of Islam as a religion and the study of history and law in conformity with traditional interpretations. Teachers expected students to memorize facts and ideas without rational discussion of their premises. Rationalist Muslim theologians like the *mutazilites,* enlightened Arab philosophers like Averroes, and Arab historians of world civilization like Ibn Khaldun were mentioned only to be criticized for their heresies. The pre-Islamic history of Tunisia was ignored, as was the wider history of the world. Except for questions of personal status (marriage, divorce, and inheritance) that related to the expertise of future judges in religious courts, Zeitounian education was disconnected from time and space and scarcely corresponded either to the requirements of modern times or to the evolution of moral standards.

Efforts to reform the traditional religious curriculum invariably failed, because such efforts were opposed by the *ulemas.* At the same time, the popularity of the new Sadiki College produced an elite that was increasingly polarized. On one hand, a growing number of political and intellectual leaders held liberal values and a nationalist political orientation; on the other hand, a substantial number of jurists and clerics who upheld a traditional—and illiberal—understanding of Islam and disdained any direct involvement in politics.

The modernizers directed the development of the nation, successively creating the "Young Tunisians" movement (1911), then the Destour party (Constitution, 1920), and finally the Neo-Destour party (1934), which demanded and led the way to independence. The traditionalists meanwhile controlled the magistracy, and accused the modernizers of Francophony and of idolizing the infidels.

The history of Tunisian society in the final decades before independence may thus be schematically described as a struggle between an urban, secular, modern, and politically active elite (the Sadikians) and a traditional religious and conservative elite that was politically incapable of assuming a constructive leadership role (the Zeitounians).

Independence

Once independence was achieved in 1956, the leaders of the national movement set about trying to modernize the country. We know that the outcome of any modernization depends on the key agents who lead the process of change (Huntington, 1968). In Tunisia, the leaders were secularized intellectuals and civil servants, unlike the scriptural elite in Morocco and the revolutionary elite in Algeria (Henry-Moore, 1970).

After independence, the Sadikians assumed responsibility for foreign affairs, the army, the police, the national guard, agriculture, industry, public works, communications, and public health. Lacking political and technical competence, the Zeitounians were relegated to subsidiary functions. Marginalized, they became restive. In response, the new government hired Zeitounians in large numbers to staff courts and schools. The judges and teachers were expected to ratify the reforms of the modernizers; in fact, they became a chronic source of opposition to such reforms.

In the first months of independence, the government instituted a new legal code. It criminalized polygamy, instituted civil marriage, fixed a minimum age for marriage, legalized adoption, sanctioned divorce, and outlawed spousal repudiation. Judges with a traditional education were asked to apply this new code. They did so—but whenever there was room for interpretation, they applied traditional Muslim norms. As a result, family law in Tunisia to this day suffers from a contradiction between a modern legal code and its traditional interpretation by judges trained in the traditional way. Matters are further complicated by the growing power in lower courts of judges trained in secular law faculties.

After independence, education became obligatory, free, and coeducational for both sexes from the age of six. Public education generally followed the example of the Sadiki curriculum. Arabic was taught alongside French in primary schools, and English in secondary schools. Classes in the exact sciences were introduced. The various humanities curricula (philosophy, history, geography, civics, and religious studies) were fixed according to modern standards. Yet, at the same time, Zeitounian graduates were recruited to teach Islam, Arab history, and the Arabic language. As a result, schooling in Tunisia to this day suffers from a chronic tension between the modern parts of the curriculum, which are taught by secularists, and the more traditional components of education, which are generally taught by religiously trained teachers in as traditional a spirit as possible.

Crisis and Reaction

The end of the 1960s witnessed instability in the education sector, following a crisis in Tunisia's political life. The reasons for the turmoil cannot be fully recounted here, but they included the institutionalization of a single party (1963), the cult of personality around the head of state, Bourguiba, and the authoritarian imposition of socialism (1963) (Camau, 1998).

The secular and progressive intelligentsia organized itself into a movement called "Perspectives" after the title of its clandestine paper published between 1962 and 1968, before a portion of its leadership became taken with ideas of the extreme Left and adhered to the international Maoism then in vogue in Europe. In response, the regime committed a double error. The political mistake was that it resorted to harsh measures to rebuff the demand for the democratization of political life (arrests, mass trials, heavy prison sentences, torture). The second mistake was cultural: to counterbalance the vogue for far Leftist ideas among the young, a decision was taken at the highest level to "re-Islamicize" education.

The Islamists in the 1970s were a small group of traditionalists who had already been socialized in an Islamicized public school but were sufficiently opportunistic to avoid attacking the regime head-on by contesting the cult of personality or by challenging the single party and economic policies. At the moment when democratic opposition was repressed, starting in 1972, the Islamicists and their associates became authorized to spread their ideas in their own newspapers such as *Al-Maarifa* (Knowledge), *Jawhar al-Islam* (Essence of Islam) and *Al-Mujtama* (Society). Gradually, a tacit alliance (sometimes explicit) was forged between the traditionalists and the men in power: pan-Arabists, reactionaries, and clumsy politicians. The social gamble was to make Tunisia into a politically authoritarian country in their hands, and a culturally conservative country in the hands of the Islamists.

The latter infiltrated the structures of public education. By successive strokes, they radicalized still more the Islamization of the school curriculum. In return, the Islamized school multiplied the recruitment of militants. Finally, the Islamicists, from a simple Association for the Safeguarding of the Koran in 1971, enthusiastic about the Iranian revolution they had welcomed, were transformed into a political party, the Islamic Tendency Movement in 1979.

Between 1970 and 1975, several Islamizing reforms affected the education system. First, there was an impromptu decision at the beginning of the 1970s to teach in Arabic the subjects of philosophy and history, which until then had been taught in French. No doubt such a decision was legitimate, but taken in haste and politically motivated to counter the Marxist Left. It meant that all the foreign visiting professors were fired; thus, bilingual teachers with modern training were marginalized or quit teaching because they were required to teach their courses in Arabic within the space of a few weeks. They were replaced by less qualified teachers (with secondary school diplomas or the *bac* plus one year), who were either former Zeitounians or graduates of universities in Egypt, Iraq, and Syria. Both of these groups were sympathetic to pan-Arab and Islamicist ideologies.

These changes would have consequences for the respective status of philosophy, civic education, and religious education—three separate disciplines in Tunisia. Until 1970, philosophy was a principal subject and was taught in French alongside Islamic philosophy. After 1970, Islamic philosophy absorbed general philosophy and took on aspects of an anti-modern and anti-liberal medieval theology. The religious education that had been marginalized was now valued again. For political reasons—to mobilize the traditionalists against the liberals on the eve of a congress of the single party, Monastir II, in 1974—the High Council of National Education gathered urgently to decide on doubling classroom time for Islamic education. Teachers of religious education were also charged with providing courses in civic education, although it was a subject totally foreign to their specialty—and this would in turn augment their influence over the youth. The schedule of religious education was de facto tripled.

Finally, the content of the curriculum was sharply revised. Language textbooks used religious examples to illustrate grammatical rules. In the teaching of philosophy, non-Muslim philosophers were flatly ignored or else caricatured in a sentence, and dismissed as miscreants (e.g., Bertrand Russell) or Zionists (Jean-Paul Sartre). Students were even instructed to avoid reading their books.[20]

The two rival systems of communism and capitalism were criticized in favor of the "best economic and social system," namely Islam. Muslim philosophers, who were known as Universalist and to be enlightened, were marginalized in favor of the theosophical school of Ghazali (died 1111), whose members had violently criticized "pure" philosophers such as Farabi (872–950) and Averroes (1126–1198). In the teaching of French and English, the reading of classics by Montesquieu, Voltaire, Rousseau, and Locke disappeared in favor of an instrumental approach to language, according to which a foreign language is simply a tool for mastering the sciences. The discipline of civic education, emptied of its substance, was transformed into a second course of religious education, its content purged of all reference to human rights, the rule of law, or democracy.

Consequently, young Tunisians schooled in this period scarcely knew about Hannibal, were ignorant of the works and even existence of the Tunisian Saint Augustine, and considered as foreign any history prior to the Islamic conquest. The latter was presented in a triumphalist and emotional manner to the point that, for example, the glorious resistance of the Berber leader Kahena and his troops to the Arab invasion were, if not kept quiet, then at least presented in an almost shameful manner. For the later period, the history of Tunisia itself was swallowed up in that of the Islamic empire. The whole reform movement of the nineteenth century was ignored.

In the teaching of values, the revival of traditionalism in the curriculum proved even more catastrophic. Corporal punishments reappeared in textbooks that went so far as to declare that anyone who denies one of the pillars of Islam, the obligation to say prayers, is an apostate.[21] The equality between the sexes instituted by the legal code was ignored, and children were taught that the husband has the right to repudiate his spouse without legal divorce, and that he may if necessary administer a punishment to her,[22] in defiance of the law that penally sanctions the perpetrator of such an infraction. The republic was unfavorably compared with caliphate. Democracy was criticized as a Western doctrine foreign to Arab civilization[23] and a form of government hostile to Islamic religion.[24] In international relations, the duty of jihad was taught alongside the right to reduce prisoners of war to slavery.[25]

In short, the schools of Tunisia functioned between 1970 and 1989 as a breeding ground for radical Islamists.

Reform (1989–1994)

On October 1, 1989, the Minister of National Education, Mohamed Charfi, presented the outlines of a frankly modernizing reform of education.[26] The Islamists accused the minister of wanting to "dry up the springs" of Islamism. A fierce public debate ensued—though ultimately the reformers prevailed.

The reform as a whole was meant to harmonize the relation between the state, society, and education. It divided education into two cycles: the first, basic, lasting nine years, and the second lasting four. It instituted a common core curriculum lasting two years, in hopes of avoiding a polarization of graduates, premature specialization, and the production of "PhDs with beards," scientists competent in research but reactionaries on a cultural level.

An education law of July 29, 1991, ratified the new plan. In the remainder of this chapter, we discuss three key aspects of the reform, and how it has changed the teaching of identity, modernity, and citizenship.

Identity

The first article of the education law affirmed the goal of "consolidating awareness of the Tunisian national identity and of belonging to Maghrebin, Arabic, and Islamic civilization." This is not a denial of the cosmopolitan spirit. No educational system can ignore the insertion of the young into a natural community. But the nature of this community is hardly self-evident. Thus, the reform developed knowledge of the first thousand years of Tunisian history, especially the Carthaginian and Roman heritage (Hannibal, St. Augustine, Apuleius). A visit to the National Museum was required to familiarize students with the idea that the nation is rooted in several civilizations.

In matters of religion and law, the reform sought to prepare students "for a life that leaves no place for any form of discrimination or segregation based on sex, social origin, race, or religion" (art.1, al. 3). It aimed to incul-cate instead "values of tolerance and moderation" (art. 1, al. 6). At the same time, both metaphysical questions (the existence of God, prophecy) and worship or religious duties (the five pillars of Islam) were to be taught in classical fashion, "adapted" to the subject of religious education in the first years of primary school.

In later years, students were to be introduced to the idea of religious toleration. For example, lesson 3–4 of the seventh-year basic text for reli-gious education stresses the common values of the monotheistic religions. A table in the text compares the injunctions of the Koran with the Ten Commandments, and a genealogical tree illustrates the narrative of the kinship between Moses, Jesus, and Muhammed through their common ancestor, Abraham—and hence the common origin of Judaism, Christi-anity, and Islam. Students also become aware of the spirit of reform that has animated Islam in Tunisia and elsewhere in the Arab world since the nineteenth century.

Finally, both Muslim and Western modernists are part of the civics cur-riculum. Their approaches are explained to allow students to reconcile the writers' ideals and their own reality. For example, the textbook of the eighth year is devoted to religious thought. It is divided into four parts; the first deals with historical foundations of religious thought. The second treats renewal and reform through the writings of contemporary reformers (the Egyptians R. R. Tahtawi and M. Abduh, the Yemenite A. b. A. Shoukani, the Syrian Kawakbi, the Moroccans A. Fassi and M. A. Lahbabi, the Algerian A. Ben Badis, the Tunisians Kherredine, A. Ibn Dhiaf, General Hussein, T. Ben Achour, etc.). The third part deals with "Islam and Christianity" through the seminal text by Abduh, which we have mentioned as criticizing religious fanaticism (Abduh, 1978). And the fourth part explicates some Koranic rules based on verses: speak with moderation, verify sources of information, search for peace, man is a social being by nature, faith is conviction and rational examination and action. Currently, of 135 authors studied in religious educa-tion, 111 are contemporary, 6 date from the nineteenth century, and 18 are ancient.[27] The timetable of religious education is 1.5 hours per week, which is much less than in other Arab countries.

In addition, the theological university of Zeitouna has been reformed. A 1995 decree fixed its goal as realizing a balance between belonging to Islamic civilization and the requirements of life (arts. 1–4). Its courses have been revised so that the future theologian also masters "the different branches of modern knowledge that allow him to accede directly to the products of the universal spirit" (art. 4).

Modernity

The education law of July 29, 1991, balances teaching about belonging to spe-cific communities with "openness to modernity and to human civilization" (art. 1). The new curriculum also insured there would be no more dissociation of scientific training from the broadening of minds. It insisted on the notion of parity: students should be equally educated "in the sciences" and "in moral, cognitive, affective, and practical" matters (art. 8). Specialization was to be delayed. Along with Arabic, the official language (art. 4), the student was required to learn French starting in the third primary year (for nine years), French and English in the eighth year of the same school, and had an option to take a third language (German, Spanish, or Italian).

Openness to universal civilization presupposes a knowledge of world history, geography, and philosophy. The curriculum re-established the traditional balance in the study of philosophy, dividing it into themes as follows: what philosophy is, the body, language, consciousness and unconsciousness, instincts and institutions, visions of the world. This curriculum was integrated with the science and math baccalaureate, where stress was put on scientific rationality and the social sciences. Each philosophical theme was to be illustrated by the main schools of philosophy from Greece to the modern day. For example, under the heading of instincts and institutions, there is one text of Islamic thought (from the sociologist Ibn Khaldûn) among nineteen selections, and under "visions of the world", three texts among twenty-eight (Ghazali, Farabi, and the writer Abdelkebir Khatibi).

Citizenship

A self that is simultaneously situated and open-minded should be cosmopolitan in the Kantian sense of the word. Here the reform aimed to foster an interest in political and human rights. The teaching of civics was dissociated from religious education (of which it had been part) and given autonomy in the faculty of letters and social sciences, in hopes of encouraging some students to become teachers of civics themselves. The new curriculum included the following elements: administration, separation of powers, elections, equality and nondiscrimination between sexes and peoples, individual and collective freedoms, rights and duties of citizenship including fiscal ones, the individual, civil society, popular sovereignty, modern political regimes, the history of political regimes, etc. The intention is clear: to show that history is a gradual evolution from theocracy to democracy and from authoritarianism to pluralism.

CONCLUSION

The Tunisian example proves that a constructive reform of education is possible in the Arab world, at least under the right circumstances.

In Tunisia in 1989, reform was supported by the state at the highest level and by a majority of the population. It was implemented only after wide consultation among relevant stakeholders. Its application was administered by a broadly constituted commission, itself divided into commissions grouping together the principal partners. The result was impressive: more than two hundred textbooks were published, and a 1,200-page decree defined the curricula subject by subject for each of the thirteen years of education (nine basic and four secondary), dated March 29, 1993.

The reform was to be evaluated regularly, and this job was given to the Institute of Educational Sciences, a body entrusted with ethical oversight and given financial autonomy. The first full assessment took place in June 2002, when students who had entered the school system in 1989, the date of the reform, would be graduating and entering university. But it is too early to make a definitive assessment.

In years to come it will be practically impossible to modify the content of the reform or to betray its spirit without creating a major political and cultural crisis in Tunisia.Of course, since 1994 (when Charfi resigned as Minister), successive education ministers have each tried to roll back aspects of the reform, but without success.

A new education law was adopted in 2002, but its goals were purely formal and political. What is essential in the reforms—aspects relating to philosophy, civic and religious education—has been preserved.

On the whole, one can affirm that Tunisia presents a model of how to school young Arabs in a Muslim culture that is simultaneously modern and cosmopolitan.

ACKNOWLEDGMENT

This chapter was translated by Susan Emanuel in January 2003.

NOTES

1. Jordan: 1952 constitution (art. 2); Tunisia: 1959 constitution (art. 1); Iraq: 1968 constitution (art. 4); Algeria: 1996 constitution (art. 2); Morocco: 1996 constitution (art. 6); Mauritania: 1991 constitution (art. 5).
2. Bahrain: 1973 constitution (art. 2); Preamble to the Moroccan constitution; Mauritania (art. 1).
3. Fundamental Charter of March 1, 1992 (art. 7).
4. Kuwait: 1962 constitution (art. 2: one of the principal sources); United Arab Emirates: 1971 constitution of union (art. 7); Egypt: 1971 constitution (art. 2 as revised in 1980); Qatar: 1970 constitution (art. 1); Syria: 1973 constitution (art. 3: Islamic law is the principal source); Oman: 1996 constitution (art. 2); Yemen: 1994 constitution (art. 3: of all legislation); Iraq: 2004 constitution (art. 7A). This is also the case in a non-Arab country, Iran: 1979 constitution (art. 2: divine sovereignty).
5. Djibouti, Morocco, and Mauritania.
6. See in particular, *Islamic Education, 3rd year, middle level*, pp. 8, 15, 37, 40, and *5th year*, p. 83, etc.
7. *Islamic Education, 2nd year, middle level*, p. 40.
8. Trans. note: This is the Everyman translation of the Koran by Marmaduke Pickthall; the French translation is "to command the good and avoid the

evil"—rather different in connotations. Translation of the Koran by A. Yusuf Ali (1983). Maryland, Amana Corp. "What is right includes right conduct and what is wrong is broader than indecency." The legal principle belonging to Islamic law, but grounded on the Koran, reports only a part of the verse which is however much longer (3:104) as a personal or a collective duty.

9. Institut Arabe des Droits de L' Homme (IADH), Report on Egypt, p. 39.
10. *Egyptian reader, 1st primary year*, pp. 28, 30.
11. *Islamic Education, 3ʳᵈ year, middle level*, p. 37.
12. *Islamic Education, 2ⁿᵈ secondary year*, 1996 edition, p. 85 ff.
13. *Islamic Education, 9ᵗʰ primary year*, 1996 edition, p. 65.
14. Moroccan book, *Islamic Thought and Philosophy*, 1996.
15. *Basic education, 8ᵗʰ year*, p. 175.
16. One could fill dozens of pages with examples of this kind from the Moroccan *Language Lessons* (in Arabic) from the fifth year of basic education, a grammar book that gives a rule and follows it with a text that illustrates it. The themes of these illustrations are not chosen at random. One finds on page 3 the suffering of the first Muslims persecuted in Mecca, on page 38 Mecca, on page 41 the necessity of being a good Muslim, page 59 the conduct of Omar the Second Caliph, page 78 Muslims of science throughout history, page 84 the Prophet's conduct, page 85 Muslim Andalusia, page 91 Baghdad in the era of the Abbassids, page 103 a prayer, page 136 Ramadan, page 139 Mulsims obeying the Koran, and on page 140 the Prophet.
17. A private religious school created in 1867 in northern India in the state of Uttar Pradesh by the holy man Muhammed Qacim Nanautawi, ten years after the closing of the schools by the British in 1857.
18. Among the contemporaries, one might cite as examples Mohamed Talbi and Abdelmajid Charfi in Tunisia, and Nasr Hamed Abu Zayd and Ashmawy in Egypt and Filaly-Ansary in Morocco.
19. Dhimmi means in Arabic "under protection." Protection and autonomy were granted upon the payment of a poll tax by the "people of the Book" (Qur'an 9:29), that is, Jews and Christians; however, this status was extended by Islamic Law to Sabeens, Samaritans, and Zoroastrians who were considered to have a "quasi-Book."
20. *The whole Islamic education book, sixth year of secondary*, published in 1988.
21. Op. cit., p. 170.
22. *Book of Islamic Education, fourth year of secondary*, 1988 ed.
23. *Book of Islamic Education, fifth year of secondary*, 1988 ed., p. 39. Previous editions contained the same developments on different pages.
24. Op. cit., p. 73.
25. Op. cit., pp. 124–139.
26. See Jonathan Randall, "Tunisia Attuned Education to Islam and to Democracy," *The Washington Post*, September 7, 1995.
27. As demonstrated in a thesis defended by Michel Guillaud at the Pontifical Institute of Arabic and Islamic Studies in Rome in 1995, dealing with religious education in Tunisia.

REFERENCES

Abd al-Raziq, Ali. [1926] 1994. *L'Islam et les fondements du pouvoir*. Trans. and notes Abdou Filaly-Ansary. Paris: La découverte.

Abduh, Mohamed. 1978. *Vol. 3* of *Œuvres complètes*. Beyrouth: Al-muassasa al-arabiya li al-dirassat wa al-nashr.

Abou Zayd, N. H. 1992. *Naqd al-khitab al-dîni* [Critics of religious discourse]. Cairo: Sina.

Abu Zahra, Mohamed. 1962. *La conception de la guerre en Islam*. Cairo: Conseil Supérieur des Affaires Islamiques.

Amin, Qacem. 1976. *Œuvres complètes*. 2 vols. Beyrouth: Al-muassasa al-arabiya li al-dirassat wa al-nashr.

Averroès. 1996. *Discours décisif*. Trans. Marc Geoffroy, Intro. by Alain de Libera. Paris: Garnier-Flammarion.

Badie, Bertrand. 1986. *Les deux États. Pouvoir et société en Occident et en terre d'Islam*. Paris: Fayard.

Ben Achour, M. El Aziz. 1991. *Jami' azzitouna* [La Mosquée Zitouna]. Tunis: Cérès.

Boisard, Marcel A. 1979. *L'humanisme de l'Islam*. Paris: Albin Michel.

Bourqia, Rahma, et al., eds. 2000. *Les jeunes et les valeurs religieuses*. Casablanca: Eddif.

Brown, L. Carl. 1974. *The Tunisia of Ahmed Bey, 1837–1855*. Princeton, NJ: Princeton University Press [Princeton Studies on The Near East].

Camau, Michel. 1998. *La Tunisie*. Paris: PUF/que sais-je?

Charfi, Abdelmajid. 1996. "La sécularisation dans les sociétés arabo-musulmanes modernes." In *Pluralisme et modernité*, Publications du GRIC (Groupe de Recherches islamo-chrétien). Paris: Bayard-Centurion.

Charfi, Mohamed. 1987. *L'influence de la religion sur le droit international privé des pays musulmans*, vol. 23. Cours au Recueil des Cours de l'Académie de Droit International (RCADI). Leiden, The Netherlands: Martinus Nijhoff.

Charfi, Magid. 1998. *Tajdid al-fikr al-dini* (Renouveler la pensée religieuse). Maroc: LeFennec.

Charfi, Mohamed. 1998. *Islam et liberté*. Paris: Albin Michel.

Charfi, Mohamed. 2001. "Religion, Droits de l'homme et Éducation." *Islamo-christiana* 27: 23–36.

Charfi, Mohamed. 2002. "Reaching the Next Muslim Generation." *New York Times*, March 12.

Durkheim, Émile. 1994. *De la division du travail social* (1893). Paris: PUF/Quadrige.

Filaly-Ansary, Abdou. 1997. *L'Islam est-il hostile à la laïcité?* Casablanca: Le Fennec.

Ferry, Luc, and Alain Renaut. 1985. *Philosophie politique*. III. Paris: PUF.

Goldziher, Ignas. 1976. *Muslim Studies*, vol. 1. London: Georges Allen & Unwin Ltd.

Haddad, Tahar. 1978. *Notre femme, la législation islamique et la société* [Our Women, Legislation and Society]. Première édit. 1929. Tunis: MTE.

Hamidullah, Muhammed. 1968. *Muslim Conduct of State*. Lahore: Ashraf.

Henry-Moore, Clement. 1970. *Politics in North Africa: Algeria, Morocco and Tunisia*. Boston: Little Brown.

Huntington, Samuel P. 1968. *Political Order in Changing Societies*. New Haven, CT: Yale University Press.

Ibn Dhiaf, Ahmed. [1873] 1963. *Ithaf ahl azzaman bi akhbar tunis wa ahd al-aman*. (Chronique des Rois de Tunis et du Pacte Fondamental), 6 vols. Tunis: MTE.

Jéro, Mario 2002. "The Pressing Shadow of the Army." *Le Monde, Dossier*. December 15/16.

Kant, Immanuel. 1985. *Critique de la raison pratique*. Paris: Gallimard.

Kherredine. [1867]1987. *Essai sur les réformes nécessaires aux États musulmans* [Essays on the Reforms Necessary for Muslim States]. Trans. Magali Morsy. Paris: Edisud.

Locke, John. [1686] 1992. *Lettre sur la tolérance*. Trans. Jean Le Clerc. Paris: Garnier-Flammarion.

Malik, Jamal. 2002. "Traditional Islamic Learning and Reform in Pakistan." *ISIM Newsletter* No. 10, July. Leiden, The Netherlands: International Institute for the Study of Islam in the Modern World.

Mawerdi, Abul-Hassen. 1982. *Les statuts gouvernementaux* (11th C.). Beyrouth: Les éditions arabes et islamiques.

Nucho, Leslie S., ed. 1993. Vol. 1 of *Education in the Arab World*. Washington, DC: AMIDEAST.

Ozouf, Jacques. 1993. *Nous les maîtres d'écoles*. Paris: Folio/Histoire.

Ozouf, Jacques, and Mona Ozouf. 1992. *La république des instituteurs*. Paris: Gallimard-le Seuil.

Rashid, Ahmed. 2001. *Taliban: Militant Islam, Oil and Fundamentalism in Central Asia*. New Haven, CT: Yale University Press.

Redissi, Hamadi. 1998. *Les Politiques en Islam: Le Prophète, le Roi et le Savant*. Paris: L'Harmattan.

Redissi, Hamadi. 2004. *L'exception islamique*. Paris, Seuil.

Rugh, William A. 2002. "Arab Education: Tradition, Growth and Reform." *Middle East Journal* 56 (3): 396–414.

Salloum Hamid I. 1995. *Education in Saudi Arabia*. Beltsville, MD: Amana Publications.

Sharabi, Hisham. 1988. *Neopatriarchy, A Theory of Distorted Change in the Arab World*. Oxford: Oxford University Press; Trans. Yves Thoraval (1996) as *Le néopatriacat*. Paris: Mercure de France.

Shayegan, Daruysh. 1989. *Le regard mutilé*. Paris: Albin Michel.

Sraïb, Nourredine. 1995. *Le Collège Sadiki de Tunis, 1875–1956: Enseignement et Nationalisme*. Tunis: Alif.

Stahnke, Tad, and Robert C. Blitt. 2005. "The Religion-State Relationship and the Right to Freedom of Religion or Belief: A Comparative Textual Analysis of the Constitutions of Predominantely Muslim Countries." *Georgetown Journal of International Law* 36: 947.

Tahtawi, Riffaat. 1972. *Œuvres complètes*. 3 vols. Beyrouth: Al-muassasa al-arabiya li al-dirassat wa al-nashr.

Van Krieken, Gerard S. 1976. *Khayr al-dîn et La Tunisie*. Leiden, The Netherlands: E. J. Brill.

Weber, Max. 1995. Vol. 1. of *Économie et société*. Paris: Plon/Pocket.

13 Educating All the People for Democratic Governance
A U.S. Perspective

Deborah Meier

The language we commonly use in everyday conversation, newspaper editorials and political speeches to explain the value of a K–12 education (or for that matter a college education) has important repercussions. The most popular off-the-cuff explanation—which we offer kids, their teachers and the public—is that it prepares kids for jobs that America needs filled and enables them to earn money for their own prosperity. We say it in a variety of ways, but the needs of the economy on one hand and the need for a job on the other are far and away the defining explanation for the money we spend publicly on schools. Underlying the first explanation is the assumption that a better educated citizenry is needed to meet the needs of The Economy. Underlying the second explanation is the close correlation between students' future income and the number of years of schooling. I don't intend to argue here why both are shaky propositions nor why the current definition of success—improved test scores—makes them shakier still.

The trouble is that if the first proposition—the needs of The Economy—is shaky enough, the second argument, whether true or not, is a questionable public need. The assumption is that more schooling leads to better jobs for individuals; but if a lot of young people get better educated it does not follow that the number of them with better jobs will change, nor that the demographics of who has those better jobs will change. The notion of "closing the gap" even in test scores, much less the gap in who is where on the ladder of success, is sufficiently absurd, above all at a time of increasing inequalities in all the other indicators of life success.

So the purposes of schooling—those long, long twelve to fourteen years we now see as basic, much less the additional four that are really essential for obtaining a decent job—remain murky. Try explaining it year after year to bored, restless, confused kids who haven't the foggiest idea what all this "academia" is about. And for those who do not naturally or easily do well in this schooling game, the temptation to dismiss it as "white" or "effete" and "unmanly" is hardly surprising.

The argument that the Academic Disciplines are closely connected to what employers are looking for from most of their employees is hard to defend. Try it. Explain why the history of Western or global civilization is what will prepare you for a good job; or why calculus is likely to play a future in your job picture, much less Shakespeare or Toni Morrison. No, it's not necessary to defend everything as "relevant," but the job of defending academic education gets hard when (a) it's hard to defend anything as relevant, and (b) the subject matter is not intrinsically interesting, a response to natural human curiosity.

So why educate? Why not focus, as we once did, on a short basic schooling (ending in about sixth grade) followed by a modern form of job training that combines both experience in the working world and training that relates to job skills?

The best I can do is fall back on thinking about why the "ruling class" (everyone these days) needs something else to be well educated. What is it that is sufficiently unnatural but also sufficiently critical to pass on to the next generation? What forms of thinking, and caring, about past, present and future are essential to nourish and extend the values we believe in as a society? Stuff that can't be assumed to be passed on naturally in the course of "just living," nor that can be learned easily, by rote. This was the startling idea that John Dewey so forcefully put forth nearly a century ago. Yes, every potential voter needs the education that was once reserved for the ruling classes, except that in saying this we need to rethink what the ruling class of today needs! Classic education was not intended to develop the habits needed for democracy, but at best for democracy's elite. While the two overlap, they may not be the same.

Surely the idea of "academia" has no natural strong attraction to the average citizen; it is more likely to denote dry and obscure, jargony and boring, and intentionally impractical. It is thought of as "hard" but not therefore more valuable. It's a rite of passage that some take to like ducks to water and others find humiliating and onerous. The latter have spent decades making themselves comfortable by putting down the effete academics, nerds, oddball scholars so that in fact even those running for the highest office in the land underplay their academic histories, "dumb down" their vocabulary, and dismiss their schooling success (assuming they had any). Only hero athletes sometimes also brag about their scholarly success, as though only then is it not misunderstood as a sign of weakness.

The task is to reverse this view, so that people see school as a tool for enlarging the intellectual and by extension the social and moral life of our citizens, as, above all, the place where everything must be justified by how it prepares people to be decision makers in the larger society, how it allows them to join the debate on the future of their community, state, nation and planet—in short, how the having of ideas, big and small, relates to social power. That most of these habits may be useful in the job market is at best a lucky coincidence. If it fails the latter test, then we need to insist that K–12 schooling is not the place to make it up.

This approach lies at the heart of the work of the Coalition of Essential Schools, the Padaeia plan, and other similar reform efforts. It has been given a back seat for a century. Only on occasion has it caught even a serious portion of the public's interest. But for me the important conclusion of nearly forty years of work in America's urban centers is that nothing less will work. Other reforms will seem faster, easier, cheaper and thus "more realistic," but that is only because they avoid the problem facing our society and the here-and-now needs of growing kids.

Such goals need to permeate not merely formal schooling, but all the ways in which we consciously contribute to develop in our young strong democratic habits of heart and mind—appropriate intellectual skepticism and informed empathy for others unlike ourselves. It enters into the ways we engage in sports, the arts, or "hanging out." It is formed by the media the young are introduced to or discover on their own. It is formed by the ways in which we organize time so that the young are not isolated from the adult world into tight peer packs, or separated by class, race and talents from even each other at an early age.

Educational institutions—formal and informal—intended to elevate democratic culture must be places in which democratic habits of mind and heart are at the core of life, where equity is not an add-on but at the heart of democracy. As Churchill once reminded us, the idea that ordinary people must be in a position to make important life decisions for society is an absurd idea—as I am reminded day after day in school and out—until one considers the alternative. What is utopian is to imagine that it is easier to pretend that schools can solve the problems of the economy which in turn will solve the problems of democracy, or that edicts from above can turn schools into serious places of work and study, or that putting more money into schooling will turn poor kids into rich ones (which doesn't mean it's a bad idea), or that money alone will attract the best and brightest to teach in our least academically successful schools. To imagine that a cheap mass-produced test can capture how well educational institutions elevate democratic culture is surely even more utopian. Not even smaller class sizes or smaller schools will by themselves produce anything much different.

I am arguing for a task for several generations: to use schools as models of the kind of intellectual life we are seeking for all citizens in a democracy; to provide adults and kids with a host of experiences, 365 days a year, in making appropriate judgments about matters of importance to them. Every cent we spend in schools needs to be justified on the basis of its capacity to contribute to such a transformation. Every cent must be seen as expanding the way adults and kids see and understand what the life of the mind could be like—to use fancy jargon. You cannot become a baseball fan if you don't have an opportunity to see it played well; and if one is not even a fan one cannot imagine engaging in the hours and hours of practice needed to go from novice to expert. It is no less true of the use of our minds to tackle intellectually interesting tasks, such as uncovering the mysteries of the world. Schools are hardly designed to make for many fans. Few of us have even had the chance to be part of communities devoted to such purposes, much less to get good at them. Few of us have had the opportunity to imagine that such activity could be fun, or that people "like me" would want to and be able to aspire to membership in such a setting.

As long as we look for answers by withdrawing important intellectual tasks—tasks that require high levels of both knowledge and reasoning power—from our schools we dumb them down, and in the process deprive teachers, students and their families of an important opportunity to taste what the power of the mind can do. If the power of the mind can't be of use in the settings in which young people spend so many precious years, how might we hope to convince them it's worth all the effort we expect of them?

But am I not being unrealistic in imagining a world in which teachers would jump at such opportunities to take responsibility for their own practices and the ideas that lie behind them? Or in imagining that parents would seek schools devoted to such ideas? I'm hardly that foolish. Parents and teachers too are the products of our schools, and we cannot jump over our history and produce schools that run counter to a century of malpractice. That's why, at best, it's a task of a generation or more. We must start with those most ready to take the leap, and encourage others to follow. What we cannot do is use the difficulty as an excuse for putting off beginning—and meanwhile moving in the opposite direction!

The litmus test of each and every reform is whether it provides more, not fewer, opportunities for the adults who surround kids to be taken seriously, to exercise judgment, to show off knowledge in public settings and to bear witness to the problems of democratic decision making. The litmus test of good reforms is whether they encourage respect for the power of one's own and other people's ideas. Rather than make it easy to follow the path of least resistance, and least accountability, we need to confront accountability by making people want to be held accountable because they want to carry out their ideas. That means, of course, venturing to have ideas, to debate them, to play them out in life, to reflect on them, to change one's mind and to try again.

Yes, good schools for democracy are, as Dewey once again reminded us, always an experiment. So is life. The "scientific" mindset he so admired is precisely of this nature: a setting in which people can collectively explore the impact of their practices and—this is critical—make changes in them. This mindset needs exercising in every aspect of the life of our youth, whether in putting on a play, playing soccer, building a house, or studying calculus or Plato. We are at the moment moving fast in the opposite direction; and the schools designed during the exciting past thirty years to produce powerful citizens for a complex 21st century are thus suffering. It's not a technical failure—that can be overcome by teacher training alone—but a cultural failure, a choice made—explicitly or otherwise—to use schools for other ends. Alas, the current direction of our schools will neither alter the rank order of Americans (so that more poor people come out on top) nor save our economy. But it will continue to dumb down our politics so that it becomes easier and easier for the best of us to design the future "for" but not "by" and "with" the people. I've tasted the difference, not only in the schools I've designed, but in the many more I've visited that have carried out this mission in quite different ways. It is do-able, if we have the will to put democracy first.

Part VI
Educating Global Citizens

14 Educating for Global Competency

Fernando Reimers

When it comes to education, to paraphrase computer scientist Alan Kay, the best way to prepare students for the future is to equip them to invent it. The educational paradox of the beginning of the twenty-first century lies in the disconnect between the superb institutional capacity of schools and their underperformance in preparing students to invent a future that appropriately addresses the global challenges and opportunities shared with their fellow world citizens. Whether these are the challenges of collectively improving the living conditions of the global poor and destitute, of achieving sustainable forms of human environmental interaction, of finding fair and sustainable forms of global trade, of addressing health epidemics, or of creating the conditions for lasting peace and security, few schools around the world today are equipping students with the skills and habits of mind necessary to collaborate with others, across national boundaries, in inventing and implementing lasting solutions to these challenges. These are, without a doubt, complex issues, and their resolution can involve multiple options, some of which are controversial. Preparing students to deal with such complexity and controversies is at the heart of global education. Such preparation is absent today in most schools around the world.

This is paradoxical, because we live at a time of extraordinary educational institutional capacity. The vast majority of the world's children today have the opportunity to begin an education and to complete several years in these relatively recent inventions we call schools. For much of the world, that is for the developing world, this transformation from societies where most people were unschooled to effective mass education was achieved over the last century, and accelerated since the approval of the Universal Declaration of Human Rights, with its focus on education as a fundamental human right, and the creation of the United Nations more than sixty years ago.

When I describe schools as effective I refer to the fact that all nations have created a legal framework and a set of institutions that ensure that most children begin school and spend in them several years in the early stages of their lives. The extraordinary organizational capacity refers to this goal of including the intended beneficiaries of education. With regard to the goal of teaching students what schools intend to teach them, there is much greater heterogeneity in the effectiveness of schools within nations and among nations. But the real paradox comes from focusing on the effectiveness of schools on yet a third goal: the goal of preparing students for the social and economic contexts in which they will have to invent their lives. With regard to this goal of relevance, particularly relevance to live in a world ever more integrated, most schools fail. Addressing this paradox requires repurposing mass education.

Making global education a serious priority for schools around the world, with a focus on the development of global competency, necessitates a narrative that describes this purpose, conceptualizes it, and suggests how to achieve it, so that different social actors can collaborate in the improvement of the global efficacy of schools. This chapter offers such conceptualization.

THE TRI-DIMENSIONAL NATURE OF GLOBAL COMPETENCY

I define global competency as the knowledge and skills to help people understand the flat world in which they live, integrate across disciplinary domains to comprehend global affairs and events, and create possibilities to address them. Global competencies are also the attitudinal and ethical dispositions that make it possible to interact peacefully, respectfully and productively with fellow human beings from diverse geographies.

This definition of global competency includes three interdependent dimensions:

1. A positive disposition toward cultural difference and a framework of global values to engage difference. This requires a sense of identity and self-esteem but also empathy toward others with different identities. An interest and understanding of different civilizational streams and the ability to see those differences as opportunities for constructive, respectful and peaceful transactions among people. This ethical dimension of global competency includes also a commitment to basic equality and rights of all persons and a disposition to act to uphold those rights (Gutmann, 1999 and Reimers, 2006).
2. An ability to speak, understand and think in languages in addition to the dominant language in the country in which people are born. As Joel Cohen explains in Chapter 10 in this volume, foreign language skills are analogous to stereoscopic vision to the global mind (the skill dimension).
3. Deep knowledge and understanding of world history, geography, the global dimensions of topics such as health, climate and economics and of the process of globalization itself (the disciplinary and

interdisciplinary dimension) and a capacity to think critically and creatively about the complexity of current global challenges.

We could call these dimensions the three A's of globalization: the affective dimension, the action dimension and the academic dimension. These dimensions for a "teaching space" are defined by three orthogonal vectors: a vector focused on the development of character, affect, and values; a vector focused on skills and the development of the motivation to act and the competency to act; and a vector focused on the development of cognition, academic knowledge, and the ability to draw on distinct knowledge domains to understand global issues. Global education is multidimensional, suggesting that quality global education must attend to each of these dimensions. Some contemporary debates about education quality are limited because they focus on one or the other of these vectors. Excellence in this domain, and perhaps in many others, is about teaching a specialized body of knowledge about global affairs (*academic*) and the ability to use that knowledge to solve practical problems (*action*), but is also about the development of character, of the virtues that would lead people to use their knowledge for ethical global purposes (*affect*).

In the rest of this chapter I explain why this tri-dimensional global competency is a necessity for all people, and I discuss some of the challenges and opportunities for making progress in the near future.

WHY GLOBAL COMPETENCY FOR ALL?

Globalization has led to an increase in the frequency and type of interactions among people of different cultural origins. In some countries this results from immigration. In most, it results also from the increasing use of telecommunication technologies and from the transformed production and trade of goods and services. Immigration, trade and communications present unprecedented opportunities and challenges to most people. These enhanced interactions among people with different worldviews and cultural values affect social expectations and notions of identity. Individuals' or groups' responses to the changes around them depend in part on how they are prepared to understand cultural differences, and to think about globalization and its attendant processes.

Unless schools effectively develop tolerance, cosmopolitanism, deep knowledge of global affairs and a commitment to peace, the likelihood of the civilizational clashes predicted by Samuel Huntington will increase (Huntington, 1993, p. 28).

We live in a rapidly shifting era in which economic opportunities and challenges abound. The increase in the intensity and frequency of interactions among people in different geographies that characterizes globalization impacts job prospects, health, physical security, public policy, communications, investment opportunities, immigration, and community relations. In short, globalization is deeply transforming the context of the lives of many people around the world. Those who are educated to understand those transformations and how to turn them into sources of comparative advantage are likely to benefit from globalization; but those who are not will face real and growing challenges. The preparation to develop these understandings, knowledge and skills must begin early in order to develop high levels of competence as well as help youth recognize the relevance of their education to the world in which they live.

While the economic advantages that accrue to global competency have received more attention than the civic advantages, global competency is helpful not only from an economic standpoint but as a cornerstone of democratic leadership and citizenship.

Because the boundaries between international and domestic problems have become increasingly porous, the demands of government and citizenship now require knowledge of international topics. Elected representatives and voters will be able to make informed decisions about issues such as trade, health epidemics, environmental conservation, energy use, immigration, and especially global stability only if they are educated to understand the global determinants and consequences of those issues and decisions.

Global competencies have been rewarded in years past, and because of this some families, schools and universities have for many years helped a select group of students acquire the ability to speak foreign languages, an interest in global affairs and deep knowledge of global topics. What is changing as a result of globalization is that these skills are necessary for the majority of the world's population, not just for a few. Therefore, global competency should now be a purpose of mass education, not just of elite education.

In the United States, for example, since the end of World War II political elites have agreed on the importance of publicly funding programs in universities to enhance the development of a cadre of experts in foreign languages and foreign area studies that would serve the perceived needs of national security and, more recently, of business competitive advantage. A recent evaluation of those programs, undertaken by the National Academy of Sciences at the request of the U.S. Congress, concludes that they must be redesigned to serve a broader segment of the college population, not just a few specialists (National Research Council, 2007).

Because the demand for international competencies has extended to other occupations beyond the "area studies specialist" and has broadened to become part of the basic competencies necessary for citizenship and work in the twenty-first century, two needs arise: (a) the need to incorporate the opportunities to develop these competencies in the graduate curriculum of other fields of studies beyond area studies, for example in professional studies of education, social work, public health, business or law; and (b) the need to generalize opportunities to develop of the foundations of international competence in the undergraduate curriculum and in K–12 education.

The broad need for global competency is increasingly recognized by students and by parents. A survey of voters by the Partnership for 21st Century Skills, an education advocacy coalition in the United States, found that two in three voters consider global awareness an important skill, while only 13% percent of them thought schools do an adequate job developing them (Partnership for 21st Century Skills, 2007, p. 3).

Support is also growing in the United States for learning a second language. According to a survey conducted by the American Council on Education in 2000, 85 percent of the public thought that knowing a second language was important, compared with 65 percent in 1965, and 77 percent of those surveyed agreed that foreign language instruction should be mandatory in high school (Hayward and Siaya, 2001, p. 22). In 2002, 93 percent of those surveyed said that they believed knowledge about international issues would be important to the careers of their children (American Council on Education, 2002, p. 3). In a youth survey conducted in 2004, 76 percent of students said they would like to know more about the world (Horatio Alger Association of Distinguished Americans, Inc., 2003, pp. 57–58).

In the United Kingdom, a youth survey conducted for the Department for International Development in 2004 showed that 79 percent wanted to know more about what is happening in developing countries, 54 percent thought they should learn about these issues in school and 65 percent were concerned or very concerned about poverty in developing countries (Oxfam, 2006a, p. 4).

HOW CAN GLOBAL COMPETENCY BE DEVELOPED?

The multidimensional nature of global competency means that providing opportunities to develop it must also be a multifaceted process. Some subjects can help to develop that knowledge: world history, geography and foreign languages. But global competency can also be developed in learning to read by reading texts that reflect cultural diversity, and in learning science, by conducting projects that help illuminate the transnational nature of the scientific enterprise. Central to developing global skills is to foster student engagement and interest in world affairs. A good factual foundation and a positive disposition to continue learning throughout life about global affairs can serve students better than many facts taught in boring ways or than a curriculum that caricaturizes world history or social studies.

While the development of each of the three dimensions of global competency may facilitate the development of the others (e.g., learning to read in a foreign language provides access to texts written in that language that can support deep disciplinary knowledge about particular cultures and societies, and this may reinforce a positive disposition toward global affairs), these dimensions represent sufficiently distinct domains that they can be treated, for purposes of policy and programming, as independent.

The *first dimension* includes attitudes, values and skills that reflect an openness, interest and positive disposition to the variation of human cultural expression reflected internationally and a global value framework. In their most basic forms they comprise tolerance toward cultural differences. More advanced are the skills to recognize and negotiate differences in cross-cultural contexts, the cultural flexibility and adaptability necessary to develop empathy and trust and to have effective interpersonal interactions in diverse cultural contexts and a commitment to extending the Golden Rule to the treatment of "others" from different civilizational streams or cultural backgrounds.

These values and attitudes can be developed in a number of ways: reading books that reflect cosmopolitan views and values, interacting with culturally diverse groups of students, engaging in school-to-school international projects, accessing content about comparative topics such as comparative literature or world history or geography, studying artistic creations from different cultures, discussing films focusing on human rights issues, and participating in global groups such as the World Scouts Movement, in Global Youth Movements or in International Sports Competitions.

Cultural awareness can be developed at all levels of the educational ladder and should probably be developed starting at the early ages, when children's basic values are shaped, and should engage multiple performance domains and ways of knowing, including deliberation, formal study, simulations, project-based learning, and experiential education. The opportunities to develop these competencies can effectively be integrated across existing subjects in the curriculum. Providing these opportunities will not necessarily require separate slots in the timetable and as such may be easy to integrate or infuse in the existing curriculum frameworks in many countries.

The resources necessary to support the development of this first set of global competencies include instructional materials in a variety of media, professional development for teachers and administrators and incentives in the accountability systems (standards and tests) to devote some instructional time to these issues. Experiential learning can be very effective to develop these competencies, providing students the opportunity to interact with students from a different cultural background, either in culturally diverse schools, through study abroad or through student collaborations across schools with culturally diverse student populations using technology. For example, iEARN (International Education and Resource Network) is a network of K–12 schools that supports school-to-school collaborative projects (www.iearn.org/projects). Through this network teachers are linked with peers in other parts of the world to collaborate by either joining structured projects or designing their own. Some of the projects include a project on the study of the Holocaust and genocide, a project to exchange folk tales, a project that supports collaboration of urban youth in the publication of a magazine to express differences and similarities of people throughout the world, an environmental project and a project on first nations.

The *second dimension* of global competency is foreign language skills. These allow communication through varied forms of expression of language with individuals and groups who communicate in different languages.

The resources to develop these competencies are skilled teachers of foreign languages, and adequate instructional materials, as well as time in the curriculum to devote to foreign language instruction. Study abroad can help develop foreign language skills. Foreign language instruction can also be supported with programs after school and during the summer, perhaps involving heritage speakers in the communities surrounding each school. Technology is an increasingly important resource to support foreign language instruction.

The *third dimension* covers disciplinary knowledge in comparative fields: comparative history, anthropology, political science, economics and trade, literature, world history and the ability to integrate across disciplines to think about and solve questions about aspects of the process of globalization such as the nature of global trade treaties, how to balance commitment to human rights with commitment to global trade when the latter involves countries where human rights are violated, or how to balance commitment to global institutions with the desire to achieve national foreign policy objectives in a reasonable time frame.

These competencies can also be developed at all levels of the educational ladder, although they should probably be emphasized starting in the middle school curriculum, and deepen in high school and at the college level. Examples of this kind of skill would be knowledge of world history or geography, cultural history, comparative literature, international trade, and development economics. There are also global topics that require drawing on different disciplinary fields. An educated person in the twenty-first century needs to be conversant with such topics and therefore needs the education to comprehend them. For example, the improvement in health conditions worldwide, reduced birth rates in developed nations and higher birth rates in developing nations are changing the demographic world balance. The result is an aging, and declining, population in developed countries and a growing population in developing countries. These demographic trends have implications for global patterns of trade and consumption, energy and resource use, environmental impact and international relations. Understanding the sources of these demographic trends and of the options to deal with them requires some knowledge of cultural norms in different societies, some knowledge of disparities in resource distribution, some knowledge of development economics and some knowledge of comparative politics.

The resources to develop these kinds of competencies are adequate textbooks, supplementary instructional resources—reference books and videotaped materials and current dossiers and reports on current affairs, which can be very fluid and need up-to-date knowledge—supporting materials for teachers, and professional development for teachers as well as places in the curriculum and in the accountability structure that induce attention to these topics. These competencies can be developed by integrating new content and activities both within existing curriculum frameworks as well as in new courses. Negotiating the introduction of new curriculum objectives or the creation of new courses will, in most cases, be significantly more difficult.

These competencies can be developed in the formal curriculum of instruction, but also in after-school projects, in peer-based projects, or in summer programs. For example, Netaid (http://www.netaid.org/) is an organization that provides high school students who want to lead projects to educate their peers about global poverty with professional development and resources to develop such projects. In part, these competencies can also be developed in study abroad and exchange programs and in joint research projects where students collaborate, using technology, across countries. The Global Classroom Project of the U.S. United Nations Association (http://www.unausa.org) helps students in inner city schools learn about the multiple dimensions of different cross-national negotiations and to develop the capacity to take perspective as they work on assignments where they view these negotiations from the point of view of different nations and groups.

Students need authentic experiences that engage them in learning about the world. What is engaging and motivating no doubt differs at various levels of education. The second grader can be engaged by some well-written stories about children growing up in different parts of the world, by good films to support that instruction, and by visits and conversations with college or graduate students from different parts of the world. The middle school child may be more engaged by research projects that allow them to explore questions that involve a comparative dimension that interest them, or by electronic exchanges with classmates in distant parts of the world in a sister school as they work on common projects. The high school student might be more engaged by subject matter in world history and geography that develops expertise to interpret current affairs; by conversations via videoconference with high school peers in distant lands; by study tours, interaction with exchange students, or study abroad opportunities; and by seminars on topical global issues or area studies offered at the college level. Rich library collections of texts and audiovisual material, as well as adequate selections of Internet resources are fundamental to develop students' independence and engagement in taking responsibility for their own learning in this field.

The mix of these three types of competencies and the level at which they should be developed will vary in different professions, and also at the graduate, undergraduate and K–12 levels.

Schools can develop, in partnership with other institutions such as universities, museums, public libraries, publishing companies and the media, knowledge of other countries and cultures and about the processes of interdependency that link countries together at present. Schools can shape engagement throughout life in learning about global affairs, dispositions to value cultural differences, and the ability to draw on understanding of differences as a source to inform a framework of global values. These values include compassion and caring, concern for others, respect and reciprocity; commitment to universal human rights and international covenants (including the expansion of human freedoms and capabilities, and recognition of the basic equality of all people); and commitment to protecting the environment and of addressing global challenges collaboratively. Knowledge, engagement, and values are the cognitive and attitudinal domains that global education should target.

GLOBAL CITIZENSHIP EDUCATION AND HUMAN RIGHTS EDUCATION

The development of global values (the first, ethical, dimension of global competency) can be achieved drawing on the well-established knowledge base in human rights education, teaching students not just knowledge of the rights and their history, but to appreciate and value these rights, to discern how they are upheld in the various communities of which students are a part, and to act toward the work in progress which is the achievement of these rights. Teaching to understand the importance of human rights and to act on this understanding is the cornerstone of global civility and of peace. As the first sentence of the Universal Declaration of Human Rights states, "recognition of the inherent dignity and of the equal and inalienable rights of all members of the human family is the foundation of freedom, justice and peace in the world." Human Rights education provides a framework to examine the multiple ways in which intolerance violates human rights and to recognize and face extreme forms of intolerance and human rights violations such as sexism, racism, ethnocentrism, islamophobia, anti-semitism, aggressive nationalism, fascism, xenophobia, imperialism, exploitation, religious fanaticism and political repression (Reardon, 1997).

To educate for global civility it is imperative to use a common framework that informs the enterprise. This notion has been well developed by philosopher Sissela Bok in her book *Common Values* (1995). Bok explains that common values are essential to the survival of every society and that they are recognizable across societies. She further explains that these values are essential to human coexistence at all levels of interaction, from personal to national and international relations. These common values are necessary to support cross-cultural dialogue and to address military, environmental and other common challenges of humanity (Bok, 1995, p. 13).

The best approximation we have at present to this common framework of values is the Universal Declaration of Human Rights. Those who drafted the declaration struggled mightily with the challenges of drawing from different cultural and philosophical traditions. Though it may be possible to see the Declaration as a work in progress, in the sense that additional rights could be defined or operationalized, the Declaration is a starting point. The work of schools globally could be aligned to teach all children to experience, honor and uphold these rights (not just to know them), and to appreciate that others have the same rights. This would be a sufficient framework for much greater global civility than many schools promote at present.

Beyond direct instruction, the context of education is a fundamental component of global citizenship education. This context includes the opportunities students have to get to know and collaborate with others of diverse cultural, racial, and socioeconomic backgrounds; the climate in the school surrounding relationships among school staff and students as well as among school staff and parents and other members of the community; and the social norms that govern those interactions. These multiple opportunities to develop citizenship competencies are embedded in a community and larger cultural and social context that influences how students interpret what they experience in school and the choices they make about the roles they want to play outside the school. Students have to live their human rights; their schools have to provide authentic experiences in the practice of tolerance. Students need to experience in schools respect for human dignity, equal rights and appreciation of difference and tolerance. In addition to helping develop knowledge about human rights it is necessary that students develop the intrapersonal and interpersonal competences to resolve conflicts peacefully, to confront violence (Reimers and Villegas-Reimers, 2006).

More than direct instruction about human rights and respectful and tolerant education are needed. It is important to gain knowledge and the capacity to act in ways that engage the students' moral reasoning skills and in ways that motivate them to act and to assume personal responsibility for their actions in the global realm. Opportunities to help students to develop and practice skills in real-life settings and to connect abstract knowledge to action are potentially important. Global service learning projects are examples of activities that can bridge the acquisition of knowledge with a disposition to assume personal responsibility for community needs.

THE CHALLENGES AND OPPORTUNITIES FOR GLOBAL EDUCATION

If educating for global competence is desirable, and if we know how to do at least some of it in schools, why then isn't it happening on a massive scale around the world? The problem is a lack of policy priority on this goal, of insufficient development of a knowledge base to support effective global education, and of limited capacities among teachers to engage their students seriously in the development of deep global competency. These are the three critical challenges that must be overcome to effectively repurpose public schools for mass global education. These challenges define then the opportunities: (a) include the development of global competency on the education policy agenda; (b) develop a solid knowledge base about what works well, with what effects, and at what costs; and (c) provide opportunities for teacher preparation and high-quality instructional materials. I devote most of the rest of the chapter to the policy challenge, and make a brief reference to the opportunities to advance a research agenda and the development of instructional materials and opportunities for teacher professional development.

Getting Global Education on the Policy Agenda

In the fierce competition to define the purposes of schools, few of the most active national and local stakeholders have incentives to focus on global education. While the idea that international institutions should be charged with promoting global civility is not new (UNESCO was created after World War II in part so that the seeds of peace could be planted in the minds of people), most advances of UNESCO and other development organizations have not been in this area. The Millennium Development Goals, which are meant to provide guidance and focus to the development community and to nations, are silent about the purposes of education.

Schools have been guided at different times by different purposes, from building nations and national and political identities to helping the poor; from improving national competitiveness to assimilating immigrants; from educating citizens to educating workers. The proposition that schools should aim to educate global citizens competes with alternative purposes. While many nations at the end of World War II could see the necessity of planting the seeds of peace in children's minds, this purpose has been crowded out over the last fifty years. The dominant competing purposes at present are: educating for economic competitiveness, educating for the formation of national identity, and educating to address particular interests of local communities.

The justification of education as an economic investment has become so widespread that few notice that this idea is relatively recent. This idea took particular force with the development of the concept of human capital in the 1950s,[1] and was disseminated by international development institutions. With the increasing globalization of the world economy, many groups, particularly leaders of business firms, have reiterated the rationale that schools should make young people more competitive job-seekers in the world economy. This desire to compete economically was the principal theme of the report *A Nation at Risk* (Gardner et al., 1983) which defined the basic architecture of the reforms of the last two decades in the United States. Little in the argument that schools should make people better workers would lead to the development of skills for global civility. Economic competitiveness is largely about acquiring technical skills to improve one's region or nation's position vis à vis others. Global civility, by contrast, is largely about understanding, solidarity, and empathy with others. Global competitiveness and global civility are not coterminous. Today and in the near future most people around the world will not work in knowledge-intensive industries. While globalization has increased economic exchange and integration, most workers in developing nations remain in agriculture or the more traditional and least knowledge-intensive industries. Plenty of sweatshops or just-in-time factories in free-trade zones use traditional forms of organization with very hierarchical, alienating forms of production. While globalization often means that managers from different cultures now interact with workers from a particular nation, the forms of the interaction—often exploitative and abusive—do not necessarily foster positive cultural exchanges.

The educational goal of forming national identity also competes with the proposed effort of educating for global civility. Perhaps as a result of dislocations caused by globalization, there has been a reemergence of nationalism and populism around the world. Some of these regimes use schools to build legitimacy and to advance political agendas that foster intolerance.

The institutions of education are adept at defining national boundaries in the minds of students and at teaching national symbols and identity. National identity is often constructed by opposition to "others." Public schools in some states advance views that openly challenge global civility, human rights, international covenants, and peace.

In the last twenty years, the trend in educational governance has been toward decentralization to communities and schools, for the purpose of increasing the efficiency and local relevance of what is taught. It is not clear how the localization of education might impact the development of global civility. Some of the most traditional cultural conflicts find expression at the local level, where communities have clear incentives to preserve the values and memories that are at the root of many ethnic, cultural, and religious conflicts. I see no reason to expect cosmopolitanism from local communities.

The Special Role of Policy Entrepreneurs

The consequences of deficient global competency are slow to build up. In the short term, absent a major foreign policy crisis or economic or environmental catastrophe that can be directly attributed to global incompetence, they are invisible to the public and to educators. This is the reason global education is not a more central priority for education around the world.[2]

Where global education gets on the policy agenda of governments or international institutions it will be because policy entrepreneurs make a convincing case that global education relates to problems that are already recognized as important by the public. For instance, insufficient global competitiveness of the workforce, as we have mentioned, may lead to a very narrow approach to developing global competence. Some might argue that to compete in the global economy what schools should do is to teach students to communicate and work productively in teams, solve problems and conflicts, be entrepreneurial and creative, be risk takers and initiators of change, use technology, and be competent in math and science at world standards (Nordgren, 2002). When the capacity of schools to do this well for all students is limited, how can these worthy goals and activities be displaced by adding foreign language study, human rights education, world history or geography or by the study of the process of globalization itself? An answer to that question is that the development of global competency contributes not only to an intrinsically valuable purpose, but also to the development of numerous other twenty-first-century skills.

In the United States, for example, an advocacy coalition including business, education, and policy leaders for the development of twenty-first-century skills has defined the following four topics as the knowledge and expertise students should master to succeed in work and life in the twenty-first century: (a) core subjects and twenty-first century themes, (b) learning and innovation skills, (c) information, media and technology skills, and (d) life and career skills. Knowledge of world languages is one of the nine core subjects they propose (in addition to geography, history, government, science, economics, mathematics, arts, and english). In addition to these subjects the coalition proposes integrating twenty-first-century interdisciplinary themes into core subjects, proposing the following four key literacies: global awareness; financial, economic, business, and entrepreneurial literacy; civic literacy; and health literacy. In addition to contributing to direct knowledge and skills recognized as important in this framework, global education provides a context to develop the four core skills in the framework—for example, to develop learning and innovation skills by providing opportunities for critical thinking and problem solving as well as communication and collaboration; or supporting the development of information, media and technology skills by providing authentic contexts in which to acquire information literacy, media literacy and technical literacy. Global education would also support the development of life and career skills, providing opportunities to develop flexibility and adaptability, initiative and self-direction, social and cross-cultural competency, productivity and accountability, and leadership and responsibility (Partnership for 21st Century Skills, 2008).

It will take social entrepreneurship to articulate the interdependencies between global competency and other twenty-first-century skills, as well as the intrinsic value of global competency as an important twenty-first-century competency in its own right. Coalitions such as the one mentioned can play a critical role making that case. In the United States other organizations are also playing this role, such as the Committee for Economic Development, an influential organization dedicated to making recommendations for private and public policy to advance freedom and economic growth in the United States. The Committee produced a policy document titled *Education for Global Leadership: The Importance of International Studies and Foreign Language Education for U.S. Economic and National Security* (Committee for Economic Development, 2006). The Asia Society has played a similar role of advocating for greater emphasis on global competency in the schools and has supported the creation of a national network of education policy makers and practitioners focused on the identification and exchange of best practices in international education (Asia Society, 2001).

In the United Kingdom, Oxfam has played a similar role, articulating the need for global citizenship education and the potential contributions it can make to the development of more established curricular purposes. Oxfam GB has also developed a rich array of educational materials for teachers at different levels of education (Oxfam Development Education Programme, 2006b and Oxfam GB, 2007).

UNESCO and the United Nations system more generally have for decades advocated for human rights education and peace education in the conferences of member countries and in numerous publications. For instance, in the context of the United Nations Decade for Human Rights Education 1995–2004, there were many conferences, workshops and programs designed to support human rights education. UNESCO formulated also the Integrated Framework of Action on Education for Peace, Human Rights and Democracy, which supported many similar activities.

But social entrepreneurs can contribute to the advancement of global education even in the absence of a supportive policy framework. By making the case for it and by developing specific activities, curriculum, instructional materials or education programs that develop global competency, they can help define the field and accumulate practice-based knowledge that will eventually inform policy in this area. For example, much of the work of the Asia Society mentioned earlier in articulating a vision for global education has been informed by the identification and documentation of specific exemplary cases of good practice developed by teachers, principals and school district leaders.

The work of a single social entrepreneur illustrates the potential of this approach to advancing global education. Peter Copen, a New York businessman who was gravely concerned about the possibility of nuclear confrontation between the United States and the Soviet Union in the 1980s, started a project consisting of providing high school students in a small number of schools in both countries with video speaker-telephones, computers for e-mail, and the funding for student–teacher exchanges. The purpose was to enable the students to engage in collaborative, project-based learning using those three modalities of interpersonal communication. Copen hoped that this would develop a model for replication whereby students would find a way to build enough trust among both societies and that, as this trust scaled up, it would contribute to preventing a nuclear war. Over a twenty-year period, Copen's initiative extended into a nonprofit that sustains a very large network of school-to-school projects, now involving over 20,000 teachers and two million youth in more than 120 countries (http://www.iearn.org/). These efforts of a single individual launched a successful organization that has helped many young people around the world meet and collaborate with students from other countries. When Copen started his work, what he was doing was clearly at odds with education policy—and foreign policy—in the United States and in the Soviet Union. His efforts were met with suspicion and antipathy by many government officials in both countries. Yet, using good marketing and political skills, and hiring the right people, Copen was able to build alliances and find supporters that allowed his counter-cultural intervention to become accepted and to expand.

Notably, iEARN is described as a context to support the development of multiple educational objectives. Its context is best captured in the articulated purpose from the iEARN constitution: "To empower youth and teachers to make a meaningful difference in the health and welfare of people and the planet." iEARN educational objectives are to provide:

A safe and structured environment in which youth can communicate
A community of teachers and learners
A known audience for writing and reading with a purpose
An opportunity to apply knowledge in service-learning projects
An inclusive and culturally diverse community (http://www.iearn.
org/about/index.html, accessed January 14, 2009).

Developing a Knowledge Base to Support Global Education

Because of the relatively more recent attention that global education has received, the knowledge base to inform its development is more limited than the knowledge base to support literacy instruction, math education or science education. There are germane fields where there is a more robust research tradition, such as foreign language instruction, multicultural education, civic education and values education, but in many ways the research on global education is in a pre-scientific stage. This is because there is not, to date, a consensus on what the relevant outcomes are in this field, on how to measure those outcomes, and there is even less consensus on the most accepted methodologies to assess the efficacy of different approaches to develop global education. It took the field of reading instruction, for example, six to eight decades to resolve these issues to a sufficient extent to produce a reliable and accepted knowledge base to inform the practice of literacy instruction (Israel and Monaghan, 2007).

The extant knowledge base is largely descriptive of current initiatives, an important step for sure in drawing lessons from experience. Advancing in the development of this knowledge base is imperative in order to obtain answers to the questions of what educational programs work well, with what effects, for what populations, in what contexts and at what costs. These are essential answers to include this topic on the policy agenda and to make claims on highly competed public resources.

Supporting the Preparation of Teachers and High-Quality Instructional Materials

As mentioned, one of the essential requirements to advance global education is to develop high-quality curricula, instructional materials and opportunities for teacher education. This is where the efforts of most intergovernmental and nongovernmental organizations have focused to date, and their impact has been modest as most schools do not use these materials.

If teachers are to include global education in their schools they need a high-quality curriculum, rich learning environments, access to technology to establish global connections and opportunities to develop their own global understandings and skills. Global education can also be advanced by relying on self-directed efforts of students, supported for example by technology, or on peer education. In some areas it might be possible to tap community resources—for example, incorporating heritage language community members in enrichment foreign language programs or developing partnerships between universities and schools to expand foreign area studies.

UNESCO and the United Nations High Commissioner for Human Rights (http://www.ohchr.org/) through the World Program for Human Rights Education have developed several educational programs and curricula focusing on teaching human rights, on teaching nonviolence, on peace education and on democratic education. Oxfam GB has produced a rich catalogue of books and instructional resources for teachers and students to develop Global Citizenship (UNESCO, 1981 and 2002a).

Some organizations have also developed specific curricula for global education. Oxfam GB has advocated the teaching of controversial contemporary subjects as a way to develop global citizenship, explaining that those are among the most important global challenges students will face and that they therefore need to be prepared to draw their own conclusions, make informed decisions and take considered action on these controversial issues but also because as students engage with those subjects they develop information-processing skills, reasoning skills, enquiry skills, creative thinking, and evaluation (Oxfam, 2006a, p. 5).

This is an approach followed by other programs. For instance, the Choices for the 21st Century Education Program, developed by the Watson Institute for International Studies (http://www.watsoninstitute.org) in Providence, Rhode Island, is a secondary school curriculum that proposes teaching with the news and with online resources foreign affairs topics in ways that present alternative policy options and engage students in an examination and analysis of their tradeoffs while challenging students to consider these issues from multiple perspectives.

The United Nations has developed a program to teach students about the United Nations system and about the global topics which the organization addresses in a series of simulations and competitions that provide students opportunities to reproduce the deliberations and dynamics of the United Nations General Assembly in reaching resolutions.

Teaching economics provides also opportunities to teach about trade and globalization. The International Monetary Fund and the National Council on Economic Education in the United States have developed a curriculum to teach about economic interdependence.

Films and documentaries are also excellent resources to support also instruction and deliberation on global topics. Amnesty International has developed a series of curricula and lesson plans to teach human rights in the context of discussing contemporary films (Amnesty International, 2002).

In addition to films, arts education more generally provides opportunities for students to open their minds to the world, for example with programs such as *dia* in Mexico, which brings art education to public schools (discussed by Claudia Madrazo in Chapter 9 in this book). Arts education is also a very important way to develop creativity and innovation, both essential to help students address global challenges. Arts education, and films, can help evoke empathy for others, help recognize commonality and difference and can help students recognize the common humanity that lies beneath all different forms of cultural expression. For example, in 2002, UNESCO organized a world drawing context to have four- to seven-year-old children represent Peace. The winning entries were published in a book titled *Draw Me Peace*, which is an extraordinary resource not only to facilitate classroom conversations about this abstract concept, through the representations of very young children, but also a valuable tool to help students reflect on the challenges to peace in different parts of the world (UNESCO, 2002b).

Modern information and communication technologies are significant resources to support global education. As mentioned already, iEARN has used technology to facilitate the establishment of school-to-school collaborations across various geographies. Also relying heavily on technology, NetAid, a nonprofit organization, supports the Global Citizen Corps, a youth movement to fight global poverty. Using online professional development, NetAid educates high school students so they can mobilize their peers in efforts to end global poverty.

There is also a growing set of online and computer-assisted tools to support foreign language instruction, including opportunities to practice with native speakers using low-cost telecommunication technologies.

But the development of global competency extends beyond the study of foreign languages and social studies. Technology is providing new opportunities to engage students in the authentic study of science in ways that present well the global and cosmopolitan attributes to the enterprise. For instance, the Globe project managed by the University Corporation for Atmospheric Research in partnership with Colorado State University and supported by the National Aeronautics and Space Administration, The National Science Foundation and the U.S. Department of State is a worldwide hands-on primary and secondary school-based earth science and education program providing students the opportunity to learn by taking scientifically valid environmental measurements, reporting their results, and then using their data, and data from other schools, to collaborate with scientists and students worldwide (http://www.globe.gov/). Along similar lines, the Encyclopedia of Life is a web-based global effort to document and disseminate information on existing species that provides opportunities for students and youth around the

globe to participate in data collection and species classification and interact
with scientists in the project (http://www.eol.org).

CONCLUSIONS

The most important educational questions are, today as in the past, questions
about purpose. Societies and communities need to have clear purposes for the
schools they sustain, just as teachers and principals need purposes to align
their efforts in teaching students, and students need to see that the purpose
of their education is to help them develop and achieve their goals and broader
social goals in life. Paradoxically we don't think sufficiently often about purpose, at any of these levels. As a result, schools, teachers and students spend
great efforts in ways that are dissociated from the purposes they value.

Globalization presents a new and very important context for all of us.
Responding to this context is of course a process, a space of possibility,
rather than a destination. Preparing students with the skills and the ethical dispositions to invent a future that enhances human well-being in this
space of possibility is the most critical challenge for schools in our time.
Global education is the new purpose for these wonderful recent inventions
of humanity we call schools. To do this we need to focus on three objectives
and on three avenues for action. The objectives are to develop global values, foreign language skills, and foreign area and globalization expertise.
The avenues are to develop global competence as a policy priority for mass
education systems; to develop a scientific knowledge base that helps discern
what works well, with what effects and at what costs; and to continue
developing rigorous curricula, instructional materials and opportunities
for teacher education. The path is clear and within reach, and the potential
rewards much greater than some of the costly and complicated approaches
we still use to try to achieve global peace and stability.

NOTES

1. While the roots of the concept of human capital date back to Adam Smith in
   the 1800s, the concept was formalized by Gary Becker only in the twentieth
   century.
2. Of course, even a major global crisis which could be demonstrably linked to
   the lack of global competencies might be insufficient to generate sufficient
   support for major initiatives in global education. As Javier Corrales (2006)
   argues in discussing the politics of education reform, competing priorities,
   institutional weaknesses, and short political time horizons make basic and
   secondary education difficult political projects to enact.

REFERENCES

American Council on Education. 2002. *One Year Later: Attitudes About International Education Since September 11.* Washington, DC: American Council
on Education.

Amnesty International USA. 2002. *The Universal Declaration of Human Rights Poster Series and Teacher's Guide*. New York: Amnesty International USA.

Asia Society. 2001. *Asia in the Schools: Preparing Young Americans for Today's Interconnected World*. A Report of the National Commission on Asia in the Schools. New York: Asia Society, Education Division.

Bok, Sissela. 1995. *Common Values*. Columbia, MO: University of Missouri Press.

Committee for Economic Development. 2006. *Education for Global Leadership. The Importance of International Studies and Foreign Language Education for U.S. Economic and National Security*. Washington, DC: Committee for Economic Development.

Corrales, Javier. 2006. "Political Obstacles to Expanding and Improving Schooling in Developing Countries." In *Educating All Children: A Global Agenda*, ed. Joel E. Cohen, David Bloom, and Martin B. Malin. Cambridge, MA: MIT Press.

Gardner, David P., et al. 1983. *A Nation at Risk: The Imperative for Educational Reform. An Open Letter to the American People. A Report to the Nation and the Secretary of Education*. National Commission on Excellence in Education (ED), Washington, DC: U.S. Department of Education.

Gutmann, Amy. 1999. *Democratic Education*. Princeton, NJ: Princeton University Press.

Hayward, Fred M., and Laura M. Siaya. 2001. *Public Experience, Attitude, and Knowledge: A Report of Two National Surveys About International Education*. Washington, DC: American Council on Education.

Horatio Alger Association of Distinguished Americans, Inc. 2003. *The State of Our Nation's Youth 2003–2004*. Alexandria, VA: Horatio Alger Association of Distinguished Americans, Inc.

Huntington, Samuel. 1993. The Clash of Civilizations. *Foreign Affairs* 72 (3): 22–49.

Israel, Susan, and Jennifer Monaghan, eds. 2007. *Shaping the Reading Field: The Impact of Early Reading Pioneers, Scientific Research, and Progressive Ideas*. Newark, DE: International Reading Association.

National Research Council. 2007. *International Education and Foreign Languages: Keys to Securing America's Future*. Washington, DC: National Academies Press.

Nordgren, Rollin D. 2002. "Globalization and Education: What We Must Know and Be Like for Success in the Global Village." *Phi Delta Kappan* 84 (4): 318–321.

Oxfam Development Education Programme. 2006a. *Teaching Controversial Issues*. Global Citizenship Guides. London: Oxfam GB.

Oxfam Development Education Programme. 2006b. *Education for Global Citizenship: A Guide for Schools*. London: Oxfam GB.

Oxfam GB. 2007. *Oxfam Resources for Schools 2007: Teaching Materials for Global Citizenship across the Curriculum*. London: Oxfam GB.

Partnership for 21st Century Skills. 2007. *Beyond the Three Rs. Voters Attitudes Towards 21st Century Skills*. Tucson, AZ: Partnership for 21st Century Skills.

Partnership for 21st Century Skills. 2008. http://www.21stcenturyskills.org (accessed July 17, 2008).

Reardon, Betty A. 1997. *Tolerance—The Threshold of Peace*. Paris: UNESCO.

Reimers, Fernando. 2006. "Citizenship, Identity and Education: Examining the Public Purposes of Schools in an Age of Globalization." *Prospects* 36 (3): 275–294.

Reimers, Fernando, and Eleonora Villegas-Reimers. 2006. "School Culture and Democratic Citizenship in Latin America." In *Developing Cultures: Essays in Cultural Change*, ed. Jerome Kagan and Lawrence E. Harrison, 95–114. New York: Routledge.

UNESCO. 1981. *Human Rights: Questions and Answers*. Paris: UNESCO.
UNESCO. 2002a. *Best Practices of Non-Violent Conflict Resolution In and Out-of-School: Some Examples*. Paris: UNESCO.
UNESCO. 2002b. *Draw Me Peace*. (World Drawing and Painting Contest for Children Aged 4 to 7 Years). Paris: UNESCO.

15 Education and the Globalization Paradigm

Marcelo M. Suárez-Orozco

How does education respond to change? Over the last two decades economic, cultural, and demographic integration has stimulated debate among scholars in the social sciences and humanities, policy experts, and informed citizens. Globalism and globalization are terms on many people's lips. From the global economic downturn to the rise in inequality, from terrorism to the environment, from free trade to protectionism, from population growth to poverty, from migration to global warming, globalization is increasingly invoked as culprit or as the solution to the big problems of the new millennium. As the recent, immediately contagious economic collapse has made obvious, increasing global interdependence makes the major problems of today and moving forward not easily contained within the boundaries and the paradigm of the nation-state. Nation-states are indeed reacting, sometimes regrouping in fundamental ways around supranational lines, sometimes withdrawing from global engagement, sometimes doing both at the same time. Europe marches toward ever-greater integration—much of it is now *de jure* an internally borderless region sharing growing policy frameworks and currency. The North American region, even with the North American Free Trade Agreement (NAFTA) under siege, continues to integrate economically and culturally—though not in terms of the borders that attempt to police and control human flows. In Asia, the two giants, China and India, seem to be betting that the royal road to development and wealth is now the global highway. The entry of approximately 1.4 billion workers from China, India, and the Russian Federation into the global system of production, distribution, and consumption of goods and services has fundamentally altered the economic playing field and made it increasingly obvious that the fortunes of workers in Ohio are now, more than ever, linked to the fortunes of workers in Fujian province.

Globalization is both a cause and a consequence of these new formations. It is a paradoxical regime. Coastal China's integration in the world economy may turn out to be one of the great experiments in poverty reduction in human history—according to some estimates, China cut the poverty rate in East Asia by half in just a decade. On the other hand, the global economic downturn has unequivocally exposed the limits, some would say "radioactivity," of unregulated free-market capitalism. Latin Americans continue to move against the free trade market regime that came to define the triumphalist "Washington consensus" of the 1990's. Argentina, once the breadbasket of the world and during the 1990s a laboratory for cutting-edge free-market reforms, went from breadbasket to basket case in fast forward. North and South, East and West, globalization for better *and* for worse is touching every corner of the earth.

The forces of globalization are challenging education systems world-wide. The opportunities and constraints, fortunes, and identities of children growing up in Tunis, Texas, or Tel Aviv will be linked to processes in economy, society, and culture that are increasingly global in scope. Yet to date no major research agenda has been developed to examine systematically how globalization might be relevant to K–12 education. While globalization has generated a great deal of debate in economic and policy circles, other implications and applications of the phenomenon remain virtual *terra incognita*. Education is at the heart of the continent of the unknown.

Globalization is first and foremost about movement. Mobile capital, mobile production, mobile distribution, mobile populations, and mobile cultures are transforming nations and regions of the world in ways unimaginable a few decades ago. Globalization is structured by three powerful synergetic vectors of change that have been in the making for several centuries (Coatsworth, 2004): (a) the internationalization of production and distribution of goods and services, fueled by growing international trade, foreign direct investment, and capital market flows (Bloom, 2004); (b) the emergence of borderless information and communication technologies that place a premium on knowledge-intensive work (Turkle, 2004; Battro, 2004; Jenkins, 2004; Maira, 2004); and (c) growing, seemingly uncontainable waves of worldwide migration (Suárez-Orozco, 2004) with attendant cultural and economic changes re-linking global cities to the developing world in new and unprecedented ways.

The globalization of capital and of information is rapidly and irrevocably transforming identity, work, and social relations the world over. But a new, amorphous and eclectic anti-globalization ethos is unmistakable in varied contexts from Seattle to Genoa, from Karachi to Porto Allegre. While disparate ideological frameworks animate globalization's foes, they seem to find global free-market capitalism (embodied by multinational corporations) and global migration (embodied by growing numbers of people from the poor south migrating to the rich north) de-stabilizing, disorienting, and threatening to large numbers of people. In countries "between tradition and modernity," as Charfi and Redissi write (Chapter 12, this volume), globalization raises the unsettling question: how can cultural values, the ethos and eidos of a society, be maintained while everything else is changing with dizzying speed?

For some, globalization raises new and troubling questions about social justice—from child labor in Pakistan to sweatshops in Central America to the role of the third world in managing the toxic high-tech waste problems of the first world. For others, globalization's main threats are to cultural meaning systems, worldviews, the realm of the sacred, and systems of livelihood.

Globalization nevertheless has its own undeniable appeal. Thus we come to globalization's paradox. As it penetrates the local cultural imaginations of low-income countries and destabilizes local economies, livelihoods, and identities, it stimulates desires for consumption that many local economies cannot meet. Globalization's promise, delivered via global media and transnational messages, powerfully affects folk models of status attainment—now more than ever articulated as a project of consumption structured around a homogenized standard of living embodying and promising to satisfy modernity's libidinal logic. Globalization's paradoxical power is that at once it manufactures dystopia and utopia. But for millions of people, now participants in a new global media, globalization's hope is to be realized elsewhere, as migrants. A humorous vignette makes a point opinion polls in the third world have long noted. The new President of Argentina goes to a school and asks children what they want to become when they grow up; an otherwise shy girls raises her hand and replies, "Madame President, when I grow up I want to be a foreigner."

Globalization forms the general backdrop for any understanding of new worldwide cultural and human flows. Immigration is the human face of globalization. By 2009, approximately 200 million immigrants lived in a country other than that of their birth—and more than twice that number are now internal rural to urban migrants—see below. For the first time in human history, all regions of the world are involved in large-scale migration—either as sending, transit, or receiving regions (in some cases all three at once). Some thirty million Africans now live in the Diaspora; in Latin America and the Caribbean there are thirty million emigrants (mostly to the United States); more than fifty million Asians and Oceanians now reside in the Diaspora; in Europe, thirty million migrants now live abroad; in the Near East, twelve million people live as migrants, mostly in France, Germany, and the Russian Federation.

One in twenty Londoners today is an asylum seeker; Leicester in England will soon be the first city in Europe where "whites" will be a minority; Frankfurt is about 30 percent immigrant; Rotterdam is 45 percent immigrant; Amsterdam will be 50 percent immigrant by 2015. Sweden, with a million immigrants, has an immigration rate (12.1 percent of the population) that is almost as high as the U.S. rate (12.3 percent). The United States now has the largest number of immigrants in its history (approximately thirty-eight million, or about the size of the Canadian population). In New York City today, half of all children live in immigrant-headed households. In Los Angeles, over 70 percent of children in schools come from Latino homes, the vast majority of them immigrants or the children of immigrants. The children of immigrant children are the fastest growing sector of both the United States and Canadian, and child populations (C. Suárez-Orozco, M. Suárez-Orozco, and Todorova, 2008).

International migration is only the tip of the global movement of people: A great deal of migration takes place within countries. In China, there are well over 150 million internal migrants—part of the great human flow from the rural hinterlands into the globally linked coastal cities. And in India some thirty rural migrants now arrive every minute at an Indian city—for a total of 700 million migrants by the year 2050. In all, approximately a half-billion human beings are involved in migration, either as migrants (internal or international) or as families left behind. Only China and India have more people than this "Migration Nation" of folk on the move.

Globalization has increased human flows in a variety of ways. First, as the current mass exodus from the Chinese and Indian countryside suggests, where capital flows, immigrants tend to follow to find better work. Second, the new information and communication technologies tend to stimulate flows because they encourage new tastes, new standards of consumption, and new lifestyle choices that cannot be met by local economies and livelihood. Third, the affordability of mass transportation has put migration within the reach of millions who heretofore could not do so. In 2007, there were well over a billion international journeys. Fourth, globalization has stimulated new migration because it has produced uneven results and growing inequality.

Globalization and massive migrations are changing the narratives of national identities and cultural belonging—countries that have not historically had significant migrant populations, such as Spain, are now facing skyrocketing numbers of new arrivals. The economic, social, and cultural consequences are staggering. At the beginning of the twenty-first century the borders between countries and inside them, among peoples and cultures whose differences are obvious, are at once hardened, unstable, and sometimes volatile. These external and internal borders are increasingly noisy and conflict-ridden areas where cultural communication and miscommunication play out in schools, communities, the workplace, and places of worship. Globalization decisively unmakes the once powerful imagined isomorphic fit between culture, language, territory, and the nation (the *Volk* in von Herder's terminology). Today, Dominican culture is thriving in New York City, where roughly one in six Dominicans now lives, just as Kurdish culture—including what are to some troubling kinship and marriage patterns—is found in Sweden where half of all immigrants are Muslims (Wikan, 2007).

The unmaking of the Herderian ideal upsets the symbolic order of the nation, interrupts social practices taken for granted, reshapes political processes, engenders new cultural attitudes, and channels new anxieties of long-term citizens. It has a potential to democratize and yet it also causes conflict and contested identities. Globalization means that foreign languages, allochthonous social practices (sometimes as objectionable to liberal democracies as female genital mutilation), and cultural models (such as arranged marriage) generate anxieties and threaten the cultural imagination of the nation. But (here is another contradiction of globalization), the immigrants are needed to do the unpleasant jobs that over time have become culturally coded as "immigrant jobs" (the Japanese call them the "3 k" jobs for the Japanese words for "dirty, dangerous, and demanding"). In many high-income countries, such as in much of Europe, while anti-immigrant sentiment continues to grow, approximately 100 million new immigrant workers will be needed over the next few decades to deal with labor shortages in countries facing rapidly aging populations and below-replacement fertility rates, and where demands of various national social security systems require higher rates of active workers in the labor market to retirees than current demographic realities can deliver. In Japan, long held as the exception to the North American and Northern European predilection for immigrant labor, regardless of cultural resistance to immigration, immigrants will be needed in large numbers to deal with Japan's aging population.

Globalization generates new dualities, pluralism, and hybrids that nation-states have difficulty managing. We need better conceptual and empirical understanding of these dualities and hybrids. Bi- and multi-lingualism, dual citizenship, and transnational circular movements suggest that immigrant experiences and belongings can no longer most profitably be seen as a linear process of assimilation like that assumed to describe previous generations of immigrants to such countries as the United States. Foreign languages, exotic cultural practices, and new interpersonal sensibilities are normative in today's cities—big global cities, like New York and London, but also increasingly in smaller cities, such as Reggio Emilia. Newcomers learn to live with divided linguistic and cultural identifications, and natives learn to expect them in others. Although multiple cultural or ethnic belongings cause unease to some Americans and increasingly to some Europeans, this multiple mooring is increasingly common for many migrant peoples in the world. Neither the one-to-one practically tribal identity between nation and language that we had imagined to be natural in romantic ideology, nor the Enlightenment fantasy of a single universal logic and language describes most people's experience, either today or during the formative national period.

Globalization necessitates rethinking education broadly conceived because the experiences, identities, opportunities, and outcomes of children growing up today will be increasingly linked to post-national, borderless, global processes in economy, society, and culture. I concur with Professor K. Cheng (Chapter 2, this volume) that education systems tied to the formation of nation-state citizens, workers (and, I would add, consumers) bounded to local economies, local social systems, and local cultural meanings at the expense of neglecting globalization's emerging regime are likely to become redundant. Much of what we call education today is already happening outside formal institutions (Suárez-Orozco and Gardner, 2003).

All social systems nurture certain values, morals, skills, and competencies in the next generation. Globalization complicates matters further by selecting for instrumental and interpersonal competencies, which will be required of children who will thrive in the increasingly borderless societies of the twenty-first century. These competencies include (a) the habits of mind and higher order cognitive skills fostering autonomy and creativity of thought and the capacity to work with others on complex problems that often cut across disciplinary traditions; (b) the ability to communicate and understand others across cultural boundaries; and (c) the development of hybrid identities indexed by the ability to navigate across discontinuous or incommensurable linguistic and epistemic systems. Children growing up today will need to develop the skills to learn, work, love, and live with others, who are increasingly likely to be of very different racial, religious, linguistic, and cultural backgrounds. Globalization will place a great premium on transcultural understandings. New forms of transcultural empathy and perspective-taking will be at a premium for survival and success in the twenty-first century. These competencies and sensibilities will be at the foundation of the leading, most decent and just cultural democracies of the twenty-first century.

While every girl and boy growing up today in Tunis, Texas, or Tel Aviv will need to acquire isomorphic skills, competencies, and sensibilities to engage proactively and successfully globalization's new regime, globalization will be challenged by those who want to preserve the diversity of expressive culture. Everyone recoils at the thought of a homogenous global culture, especially the expressive qualities of culture and the habits of self that constitute the cultural part of every human identity. Globalization's threats to the particular qualities of local cultures, specifically religious identities, values, and worldviews, help explain the recent fury globalization has generated in the streets from Seattle in the North to Buenos Aires in the South.

Globalization is dystopic when it threatens and undermines values, worldviews, ethos or interpersonal relations, and especially the sacred. Because globalization is predicated on homogenization of labor markets, of consumer tastes, of ideas about the good life as a material project, it becomes more important than ever to understand defenses of difference. A UNESCO study claims that about half of the world's 6,000 languages are "dying" and are likely to disappear. Societies that nurture in today's boys and girls the emergence of the instrumental skills, competencies, and interpersonal sensitivities needed to engage and thrive globally while not subverting or undermining and indeed strengthening the expressive domains of local cultures—languages, values, worldviews, and the realm of the sacred—will have the edge in globalization's new regime.

Globalization, then, can be broadly defined as processes of change that tend to de-territorialize important economic, social, and cultural dynamics from their traditional moorings in nation-states. Four powerful vectors of change have direct repercussions for K–12 education:

1. We need to examine more systematically the skills and sensibilities that are required and conditioned by new computer-based information technologies. Antonio Battro (2004) has claimed that a human "digital intelligence" proceeds from a universal binary logic but requires the capacity to manipulate symbol systems and places a premium on knowledge-intensive work; Sherry Turkle (2004) has alerted us to the limitations, missed opportunities, unanticipated paradoxes, and areas of concerns of the "new fellowship of the microchip."

2. We need better conceptual and empirical work on how new media, information, and communication technologies spread cultural models (often generated from and based on the United States) that both attract and repel those from other cultural and religious traditions. We must examine more closely the implications of new research which rejects the claim that globalization is a mimetic process of repetition that generates cultural homogeneity and endless uniformity. On the contrary, allochthonous cultural practices, facts, and artifacts are constitutive of the cosmopolitan logic and ethos that make difference normative in global cities. Global formations are given local meanings, saturated with local knowledge and local epistemologies. Eating a Big Mac in China is a very different cultural experience than eating a burger in Boston—food for thought (Watson, 2004, *inter alia*). Carl von Sydow's idea of the oicotype might be highly relevant here, too: cultural borrowing often takes place when cultural facts or artifacts are "changed to fit culturally the preferred pattern in quite different cultural settings" (Dundes, 1965, p. 220).

3. We need better conceptual and empirical work on the post-nationalization of production and distribution of goods and services, predicated on direct foreign investment, transnational capital flows, and diminishing costs of transportation and communication. These changes undermine the classical nation-state model and reward those who can work comfortably and rapidly with people and products from around the world. Professor K. Cheng's work (Chapter 2, this volume) makes important headway into this problem.

4. We need better conceptual and empirical work on the new global migratory flows. These engender, *inter alia,* transitory populations in schools and throw together individuals speaking numerous languages and reflecting diverse cultural traditions. These flows generate new identities and ways of belonging. How would reforming education in Arab countries be relevant to the seven million Muslims being educated in Europe today? At a time when Tunisian, Algerian, and Moroccan economies and societies are deeply dependent on the

diasporic citizens pursuing their fortunes as immigrants and refugees in Europe, how do we rethink education in the sending countries?

These four currents constitute the central tendencies of globalization today, though the process has been centuries in the making. Scholars of education concerned with how globalization is transforming education and what education must do to remain relevant must attend to the following claims:

1. *Globalization rewards the emergence of certain cognitive and inter-personal skills.* The skills required for problem finding, problem solving, articulating an argument and deploying verifiable facts or artifacts to substantiate it, learning to learn, and working and net-working with others who are increasingly likely to be from different national, linguistic, religious, and racial backgrounds should be of particular interest to anyone interested in education for globalization. Globalization may privilege individuals who are cognitively flexible and are capable of establishing many weak ties, rather than or in addition to the strong deep ties that were honored in the past. In the words of Levy and Murnane (2007), the ability to perform "expert thinking" and the ability to deploy sophisticated communication skills will have a significant premium in the twenty-first century.

   While disciplinary grounding remains important, the big chal-lenges of the global era—global warming, deep poverty, terrorism, infectious diseases, the degradation of the environment, unprecedented refugee and illegal migration flows—are no longer best understood within single disciplines. Their solutions call for interdisciplinary col-laborations and synthetic thinking. Howard Gardner argues that the "synthetic mind" may indeed turn out to be one of the key Five Minds for the Future (Gardner, 2007). These skills, competencies, habits of mind, and sensibilities will be required of young persons regardless of national origin or cultural upbringing. The convergence hypothesis is that globalization is deterritorializing the skills and competencies it will reward, thereby generating a powerful convergence on what students the world over will need to know.

2. *Local understandings, definitions, and attitudes toward globaliza-tion matter more today than ever.* In many countries, especially those "between tradition and modernity" (Charfi and Redissi, Chapter 12, this volume), anti-globalization remains strong. There is little empiri-cal understanding or theoretical framing of the conditions that gen-erate and perpetuate anti-globalization attitudes and practices. We need better understanding of when globalization emerges in local contexts as an opportunity versus as a threat. We need basic research to examine under what conditions the skills, habits of mind, and interpersonal sensibilities called forth to thrive under globalization are compatible and easily integrated into local cultural structures,

narratives, and rituals, and when they are readily rejected. We need to better understand how media and popular culture affect attitudes toward globalization. How are global formations given local meanings—positive, neutral, negative, or mixed? More research is needed on the role of "glocalization"—the emergence of local isomorphs of global forms—and how these mechanisms might facilitate or impede global understandings. While the focus of this line of work will fall on individuals who are directly involved with education, I think it is important to construe education quite broadly to include a range of stakeholders.

Globalization will continue to be a powerful vector of worldwide change. We need better understanding of how education will be transformed by globalization and how it, in turn, can shape and manage the course or courses of globalization. We need a major research effort to examine how education most broadly defined can best prepare children with the relevant twenty-first-century skills to engage globalization. We need better theoretical understandings of globalization's multiple faces—economic, social, and cultural. We need more dialogue between scholars, practitioners, and policy makers.

REFERENCES

Battro, Antonio M. 2004. "Digital Skills, Globalization, and Education." In Suárez-Orozco and Qin-Hilliard, 2004, 78–96.

Bloom, David E. 2004. "Globalization and Education: An Economic Perspective." In Suárez-Orozco and Qin-Hilliard, 2004, 56–77.

Coatsworth, John H. 2004. "Globalization, Growth, and Welfare in History." In Suárez-Orozco and Qin-Hilliard, 2004, 38–55.

Dundes, Alan, ed. 1965. *The Study of Folklore*. New York: Prentice Hall.

Gardner, Howard. 2007. *Five Minds for the Future*. Cambridge, MA: Harvard Business School.

Jenkins, Henry. 2004. "Pop Cosmopolitanism: Mapping Cultural Flows in an Age of Media Convergence." In Suárez-Orozco and Qin-Hilliard, 2004, 114–140.

Levy, Frank, and Richard Murnane. 2007. "How Computerized Work and Globalization Shape Human Skill Demand." In *Learning in the Global Era: International Perspectives on Globalization and Education*, ed. Marcelo M. Suárez-Orozco, 158–174. Berkeley, CA: University of California Press.

Maira, Sunaina. 2004. "Imperial Feelings: Youth Culture, Citizenship, and Globalization." In Suárez-Orozco and Qin-Hilliard, 2004, 203–234.

Suárez-Orozco, Carola. 2004. "Formulating Identity in a Globalized World." In Suárez-Orozco and Qin-Hilliard, 2004, 173–202.

Suárez-Orozco, Carola, Marcelo M. Suárez-Orozco, and Irina Todorova. 2008. *Learning a New Land: Immigrant Students in American Society*. Cambridge, MA: Harvard University Press.

Suárez-Orozco, Marcelo M., and Howard Gardner. 2003. "Educating Billy Wang for the World of Tomorrow." *Education Week*, Oct. 23: 34–44.

Suárez-Orozco, Marcelo M., and Desirée B. Qin-Hilliard, eds. 2004. *Globalization: Culture and Education in the New Millennium*. Berkeley, CA: University of California Press.

Turkle, Sherry. 2004. "The Fellowship of the Microchip: Global Technologies as Evocative Objects." In Suárez-Orozco and Qin-Hilliard, 2004, 97–113.

Watson, James L. 2004. "Globalization in Asia: Anthropological Perspectives." In Suárez-Orozco and Qin-Hilliard, 2004, 141–172.

Wikan, Unni. 2007. "Rethinking Honor in Regard to Human Rights: An Educational Imperative in Troubled Times." In *Learning in the Global Era: International Perspectives on Globalization and Education*, ed. Marcelo M. Suárez-Orozco, 272–290. Berkeley, CA: University of California Press.

Part VII

Perspectives on Assessment and Educational Goals

16 Evaluating Basic and Secondary Education

Ana Carolina Letichevsky

The challenge of an educational evaluation lies in the complexity of educational processes, which start at birth, develop through social interactions with people, objects, and facts, and involve multiple agents and institutions. Agents of basic and secondary education include parents, teachers, technical-pedagogical teams, classmates, and friends. Participating institutions include the community, the school, and the family. The educational process combines reason and emotion in a relationship encompassing contents, attitudes, language, and people. Education plays a decisive role in building citizenship. Through education, a society seeks to assure that its citizens receive public goods, services, and knowledge; the capacity to live with other cultures at home and abroad with tolerance and solidarity; and the possibility of character development. Much of this complexity has been beyond the scope of educational evaluation.

Professionals in education have traditionally been concerned with evaluation of school performance. For centuries, schools have been using tests to verify if students have acquired the expected knowledge about contents and subjects to which they have been exposed. Originally, only students were evaluated, and evaluation aimed to estimate students' proficiency in the contents taught.[1] The instruments used for data collection were tests involving contents; only the individual results of each student were analyzed; and there was no interest in formulating a value judgment about the efficacy of the school or educational system. The use of results was generally very restricted and negative: students classification and punishments were frequent. In this role, evaluation produced fear.

More recently, evaluation has gone beyond the classroom walls. The need to plan and implement evaluative processes has become increasingly evident to administrators, researchers, scholars of education, teachers, users of educational systems, and the community at large, be it to create and implement new policies, to estimate the proficiency of students, to try to understand and improve the educational process, to know the characteristics, advantages, and limitations of schools, or to account for education to society.

Nowadays, evaluation is understood as a documented process of systematic data collection and precise information, aiming at, through a value judgment, answering questions raised *a priori*. This process must explain the criteria of excellence that permits the production of the value judgment mentioned previously with regard to the following: (a) merit of the focus of attention, which may be a student, school, or system (in terms of the internal quality of its components and operation) and (b) relevance to goals of education (which refers to its effects and result, that is, its impact), with the purpose of providing information to improve the evaluative focus and to make pertinent decisions (Penna Firme, Blackburn, and Putten, 1998).

It is difficult to determine the exact origin of evaluation as judgment. There have been records of the practice of evaluation since 2000 BCE (Dubois and Mayo, 1970). However, the concept of evaluation as understood today is the result of a trajectory, a construction, and a reconstruction, which involve a broad range of factors. Only in the nineteenth century, knowledge of evaluation started to be systematized and documented from practical political and social order needs. Madaus and Stufflebeam (2000) presented a historical perspective on the growth of evaluation theory and practice in seven periods: Age of Reform; Age of Efficiency and Testing; Tylerian Age; Age of Innocence; Age of Development; Age of Professionalization; Age of Expansion and Integration. Guba and Lincoln (1989) presented the concept of evaluation in four generations: measurement, description, judgment, and negotiation. During certain periods, the history of evaluation mingles with that of education.

With the formalization of evaluation as an area of study and practice, theoretical-methodological advancements started to suggest that evaluation should go beyond measurement by describing performance in the light of the objectives of learning. The next step was adding value judgment so that the results of evaluation began to depend on criteria of excellence in judgment. Then, a new restlessness appeared with regard to a failure in managing to accommodate the pluralism of values held by different stakeholders (Guba and Lincoln, 1990). Thus values must be negotiated with the one who orders the evaluation, the one who carries out the evaluation, and the one who is affected (positively or negatively) by its results. Unfortunately, in some cases, evaluation results of basic and secondary education are still used to punish students, teachers, and schools, and are underused to improve education. A new evaluation of learning cannot limit itself to the application of a test, no matter how well prepared it is. A test is one of the evaluative instruments of an evaluation, and the use of these instruments is only a moment in the process. There is a need for continuity, not only in the judgment of values, but also in using the results to improve the learning process.

Discussions of educational evaluation require consideration of how the results will be used to improve education and of what standards are to be adopted. If the people involved in the practice of evaluation reach a consensus and fulfill the requirements of the consensus, the quality of the evaluation is assured. A joint effort of professional organizations and practicing evaluation professionals made it possible for the Joint Committee on Standards for Educational Evaluation to publish, in the 1990s, thirty individual standards organized around four criteria: utility, feasibility, propriety, and accuracy.[2] The order of these criteria is not accidental. The Joint Committee recommends that an evaluation should not be performed if it is not useful to some audience, feasible in political or practical terms, and proper in terms of fairness. If these three criteria are met, then it is necessary to look for accuracy, which is the technical adequacy of the evaluation. Michael Scriven (2004, p. 183) wrote: "In my view, one of the most important questions professional evaluators should regularly consider is the extent to which evaluation has made a contribution to the welfare of humankind and, more generally, to the welfare of the planet we inhabit."

Therefore, whenever an educational evaluation is planned, before it is implemented, it is important to ask: How will this evaluation contribute to improving education? The answer to this question is directly related to the quality and the utility of the results. It is possible that, throughout the evaluation or even after it ends, other uses, not originally foreseen, may appear. Nevertheless, if it is not possible to answer this question of use in a clear and convincing manner, it is necessary to review the planning, or even question the carrying out, of the evaluation.

The evaluation of the teaching system of basic and secondary education is a challenge, not only because it is difficult to define in a clear and universal way the objectives of these teaching levels, but also because a significant number of educators resist being evaluated. Furthermore, a complete evaluation of the system and its agents may become impossible in time and costs. Even so, facing the challenge of democratically constructing and implementing an evaluation is worthwhile, as its impact is so meaningful to education and society broadly.

METHODOLOGICAL CONSIDERATIONS

Despite the great diversity of evaluative approaches and methodologies used worldwide, a series of stages appears, or at least should appear, in most evaluative processes.

One of the first stages in an evaluation is the creation of those evaluative questions one intends to answer (Worthen, Sanders, and Fitzpatrick, 1997). Such questions consider merit and relevance related to the focal object of the evaluation. This is a crucial moment in the design of the evaluation, as those questions will be present in all the other stages of the evaluation. For this reason, current approaches to evaluation insist that different stakeholders must participate in this phase. When organizing the questions, it is important to keep in mind that they should allow for concrete answers even if the answers will be obtained at different times.[3] Usually, questions concerning merit may be answered more immediately than those referring to educational impact.

Therefore, when one decides to conduct an evaluation of basic and secondary education, it is necessary, in view of one's goals, to construct evaluative questions and to establish criteria of excellence based on a broad negotiation among those involved. The negotiation among the stakeholders must start as soon as possible and continue until the conclusion of the evaluation. The negotiation, the clarity of the evaluation objectives, and the explicit expression of intentions on the use of results will generate a commitment to evaluation on the part of the stakeholders, which is fundamental to the evaluation's success. It is crucial to involve, in the best possible way, students, teachers, administrators, technical-pedagogical teams, parents, and other representatives of organizations and institutions associated with the purposes of education.

To quantify evaluative questions, indicators are usually constructed or adapted. These indicators build the bridge between the observed data and the evaluative questions (Penna Firme, Tijiboy, and Stone, 2006). The definition of criteria of excellence for the indicators and explicit, clear presentation of the definition are fundamental to ensure the transparency of the process. The criteria of excellence express the expected results for behaviors, with regard to each indicator. Based on those decisions, it is possible to select sources of information and techniques of data collection. Several techniques of data collection and diverse sources of data are combined to obtain information about different interest groups and different audiences involved. Ideally, the respondents in an educational evaluation should be at least students, teachers, administrators, and parents. The selection and documentation of the techniques and methods of analysis are fundamental.

In choosing the most appropriate technique of data analysis, it is important to be clear about the evaluative question(s) one is trying to answer, since a technique that is appropriate to seek the answer to one question may not be appropriate for answering another.

Also, the instruments of data collection must be sufficiently sensitive and precise to enable the formulation of judgments. In this sense, when verifying academic proficiency, it is important to contemplate not only those aspects related to contents, but also those related to competencies and abilities. To the extent possible, it is important to include social and moral competencies that are indispensable to the development of citizenship. At the same time, information related to the socioeconomic profile, the aspirations, the trajectory of life, and the family situation of the students, among others, must be collected.

With regard to teachers, administrators, and parents, it is essential to inquire into the conditions and procedures that constitute the educational environment of the students, which may favor or hinder thorough development. The use of appropriate procedures in data collection is fundamental to ensure the quality of the data. It is through appropriate data processing that useful information for decision making will be generated. Only those answers that really provide information about what is being measured should be considered. Blank test forms, or a single answer pattern, or any other evidence that the filling out of the instrument was not honest, should be left out.

Information on the results of the evaluation should be provided to different stakeholders, from the students to those responsible for the administration and for educational policy making.

It is important to distinguish between the evaluation of each student, carried out by the teacher in the classroom, and that of the teaching system. Both are essential, but their objectives differ and, consequently, they are guided by different evaluative questions. The teacher who evaluates the student in the classroom has several opportunities to collect information by a variety of techniques (tests, written assignments, oral presentations, non-obtrusive methods, portfolio, and observing the student among other students). This evaluation is formative, going on through the whole academic year, and at the end of the year, it provides a summative perspective.[4] Systems (and, in some cases, schools) are the main focus of the evaluation of teaching systems. Evaluations of systems are fundamental to provide information for the formulation of public policies and macro actions for the improvement of the system or of the school. Those evaluations are formative for the systems, teachers, and schools, and are summative for the students.

All teachers of basic and secondary education need better training in evaluation. The precarious theoretical, methodological, and practical training in evaluation generally provided in teacher training courses has generated countless problems, from distortions in the concept of evaluation to an inappropriate use of its results. The deficient training of teachers in evaluation prevents them from receiving, discussing, questioning, and using any form of system evaluation. It is highly probable that an improvement in the evaluation of the educational systems will occur only to the extent that teachers are qualified to become critical users of evaluation systems.

Other parts of society also lack proper training in evaluation. This deficiency is expected considering that, as mentioned before, evaluation is a relatively new area. In this sense it is recommended to sensitize those involved before an evaluative process is initiated. Furthermore, evaluations developed by laws or issued by decrees, without previous negotiation with those evaluated or affected by their results, find great difficulty in being implanted and often fail to generate information of high quality. People who respond to evaluative instruments need to understand the importance of evaluation and know its objectives in order to provide reliable information. In educational evaluation, it is important to make it clear that the results will serve to improve education to the extent that they detect: (a) areas in which teachers need to be better trained; (b) contents, competencies, and abilities in which students need to be better trained; (c) school factors that maximize school efficiency and which, therefore, must be reinforced; and (d) school factors that reduce the efficiency of the schools and which, therefore, must be treated.

It is amazing that, despite all the development in the theory of evaluation, elementary mistakes are made in many countries, such as using the results of evaluations of systems and/or schools for punishment or reward. However, in some cases, substantive efforts are being made to fill out those gaps in the evaluations of schools or systems. What is sought is the full development of an evaluation that, beyond purely academic areas, can incorporate technical pedagogical competencies, arts, sports, leadership, emotional development, social responsibility, and ethical development, among other areas.

LESSONS FROM THE BRAZILIAN EXPERIENCE IN BASIC AND SECONDARY EDUCATION

Brazilian education is going through a transition in which the development of evaluative processes occupies an outstanding position. From the Brazilian experience in the evaluation of basic and secondary education, two especially important experiences are highlighted here: the Evaluation System for Basic Education (SAEB) and the National Examination of Secondary Education (ENEM).

In the 1990s, Brazil, like some other countries, taking a global perspective and responding to international demand, restructured its teaching system, especially in basic education. A new law, called Law of Directives and Bases of Education, adopted National Curricular Parameters by levels of teaching, as well as systems of external evaluation. Brazil's educational policy has tried to reform the educational system to accompany changes in the world of work and in social conditions.

SAEB

In 1995, the federal government implemented the Evaluation System for Basic Education (SAEB). SAEB was the first initiative of the federal government to implement large-scale evaluations in the country. SAEB is a biannual evaluation, carried out through representative samples of all twenty-six states in Brazil and the Federal District. The exam consists of a test given to the student, a socioeconomic questionnaire for the student, a questionnaire for the teacher, a questionnaire for the school, and a questionnaire for the principal. In 2003, 218,521 students were evaluated in 6,179 schools in grades four and eight of basic education, and in the third year of secondary education only in the disciplines of Portuguese and mathematics. Through SAEB, a scale of proficiency was used in Brazil at the national level for the first time. To construct and maintain the exam, the Item Response Theory[5]

(IRT) was adopted, which made continued monitoring of results possible. The scale of proficiency is interpreted,[6] facilitating the development of specific programs in each state for the improvement of education.

To have the results of this evaluation used, in fact, in each state of the country has been a constant challenge to evaluators, educators, and politicians committed to the cause. One positive result right at the beginning of the implementation was that SAEB triggered a discussion about evaluation in the schools, involving at first teachers and administrators and, afterwards, parents and students. Also, the need to use the results created a greater interaction between the school system and the university system.

ENEM

In Brazil, the objectives of the Ensino Médio (Secondary Education) are to consolidate and deepen the knowledge acquired by the student in Ensino Fundamental (Elementary Education), making it possible for this student to continue his studies, to have access to productive activities, and to exercise citizenship. The interaction between formal education and the life as a citizen promotes the development of individuals who are capable of performing autonomous actions.

ENEM is an annual examination given to students who have finished Ensino Médio. It consists of objective questions and a composition. ENEM differs greatly in methodology and use from the other large-scale exams held in Brazil. Methodologically, it differs in its organization and correction as well as its inclusion of a composition. It differs dramatically in use because it offers those who take it an instrument for self-evaluation. The result of the exam, which is voluntary, is given only to the student. The student decides the best way to use it.

By its ninth year in 2006, ENEM had improved as an instrument for evaluating the young Brazilian's basic competencies to enter the world of work and the practice of citizenship. The exam "considers the young citizens playing distinct but complementary roles as readers and writers of the world." The objective part of the test has as its main purpose the evaluation of the participant as a "reader of the world." This part is elaborated as an instrument that seeks to measure five competencies and twenty-one abilities, forming wholes associated to the competencies.[7]

In all the previous exams the objective part was always composed of sixty-three questions. Three questions were prepared for each of the twenty-one abilities. All the questions are of the multiple-choice type, with five choices, of which only one is correct. The intention is to provide easy questions, difficult questions, and questions of medium difficulty. All questions have the same value, and the total points obtained are placed on a scale from zero to one hundred. Besides the students' general score on the objective part of the tests, their performance is also graded on each of the five competencies. All questions in the objective section are original, transdisciplinary, and intended to present an entirely original problem-situation, leading the respondent to adopt solutions involving contents from more than one discipline.

The essay aims to evaluate the participant as a "writer of the world." The student must produce a text based on a proposal presented to him or her. As in the objective part, the proposal or theme of the essay also involves a problem-situation. The student is expected to solve it by using the knowledge acquired through formal education and during day-to-day life. The essay is evaluated with respect to the same five competencies used in the objective part, adapted for the production of text. Each of the five competencies is evaluated at four levels. The student's grade for the essay is obtained by calculating the arithmetical mean of his or her specific grades in each of the five competencies. The aggregate of the examination results (without identification of the respondents) is presented in a "pedagogical report" sent to the schools and governmental Secretariats of Education.

As mentioned before, besides taking the test, the examinees must complete a socio-economic questionnaire provided with the student's Manual (which contains information about the test). This report makes it possible to learn about different aspects of the examinees, such as personal identification, family status, school background, and professional life (if applicable). The information collected through the socioeconomic questionnaire is used not only to obtain a profile of those who took the examination in the country and in each state but also to allow diverse studies of the student's development and the characteristics related (positively or negatively) to their performance on the test.

In 2005, 3,004,491 students registered for the examination. Students, schools, and communities in general started to mobilize and strive for democratization of the examination.

This type of examination was initially resisted in Brazil because teachers, students, and university professors were more used to traditional examinations where each question referred to certain content of a specific discipline. In the initial years when ENEM was given, students were afraid they would not be able to solve questions with formats, structure, and formulation different from those they were used to. Teachers feared how their students would perform and realized they would have to exchange their conventional teaching methods, based on the acquisition of contents, for a new form, organized according to the development of competencies and abilities. University professors, especially those responsible for the formulation of entrance examinations, also resisted initially (some still do). They found it difficult to change their expectation that a student who wishes to attend a university must have attained proficiency on a whole lot of specific contents. In many cases, the student was required only to take an objective test, not to answer questions involving reasoning or to write a paper.

Therefore, it was necessary to intensify the "sensitivity training" of teacher and students in the first and second years of ENEM. However, the points that may have been decisive in making the examination acceptable to the students was that taking it is voluntary; the anonymity of the students is preserved; and identification of the examinee is made only with his/her consent, when he/she wishes and the way he/she desires.

FINAL REMARKS

The climax of an educational evaluation may be the full use of both its process and its results (Patton, 2005) in the consolidation, reformulation, and construction of educational goals. This climax is reached through dialogue and negotiation among the authors of and actors in the educational process, in the continuous search for consensus, always with due respect for differences. The great challenge is to go on evaluating and building educational goals in a world in constant transformation.

NOTES

1. Currently evaluation is understood as a much broader concept that also includes assessment.
2. The utility standards are intended to ensure that an evaluation will serve the practical information needs of intended uses. The feasibility standards are intended to ensure that an evaluation will be realistic, prudent, diplomatic, and frugal. The propriety standards are intended to ensure that an evaluation will be conducted legally, ethically, and with due regard for the welfare of those involved in the evaluation, as well as those affected by its results (Joint Committee on Standards for Educational Evaluation, 1994).
3. The logical model is a tool that has been used by evaluators to describe the connections between the material and human resources available, the activities carried out in the different stages of the program implementation, and the expected results in short, medium, and long terms.
4. The difference between summative and formative evaluation was proposed by Michael Scriven in 1967.
5. In this theory, models are constructed that permit the creation of a relationship between the probability of a certain response given to an item by an individual and his or her having acquired a component of the area evaluated.
6. For some levels of the scale, the knowledge and abilities shown by the students are described.
7. The competencies are the following: 1. Command of the cultural norm of the Portuguese language and use of the mathematical, artistic, and scientific languages; 2. Construction and application of the concepts of different areas of knowledge to understand natural phenomena, historical and geographical processes, technological production and artistic manifestations; 3. Selection, organization, and relation, represented in different ways, in order to make decisions and confront problem-situations; 4. Relating of information represented in different formats to available knowledge in concrete situations in order to build consistent argumentation; 5. Use of knowledge acquired

in school to develop proposals of intervention to enhance the common good in reality, respecting human values and considering socio-cultural diversity (Ministry of Education of Brazil, 2008).

REFERENCES

Ministry of Education of Brazil. 2008. INEP/ENEM: Relatório Pedagógico 2007. Brazil, DF: INEP. http://www.inep.gov.br/download/enem/Relatorio/ENEM_2007.pdf.

Dubois, Philip H., and D. Douglas Mayo, eds. 1970. *Research Strategies for Evaluating Training.* AERA Monograph Series on Curriculum Evaluation. Chicago: Rand McNally.

Guba, Egon G., and Yvonna S. Lincoln. 1989. *Fourth Generation Evaluation.* Newbury Park, CA: Sage.

Guba, Egon G., and Yvonna S. Lincoln. 1990. "Can There Be a Human Science? Construtivism as an Alternative." *Person-Centered Review* 5 (92): 130–154.

Joint Committee on Standards for Educational Evaluation. 1994. *The Program Evaluation Standards*, 2nd ed. Thousand Oaks, CA: Sage Publications.

Mandaus, G. F, and Daniel L. Stufflebeam. 2000. "Historical Perspectives on Evaluation." In *Evaluation Models*, ed. T. Kellaghan, Daniel L. Stufflebeam, and G. F. Mandaus, 3–22. Boston: Kluwer.

Patton, Michael Quinn. 2005. "The Challenges of Making Evaluation Useful." *Ensaio: avaliação e políticas públicas em educação: revista da Fundação Cesgranrio* 13 (46): 67–78.

Penna Firme, Thereza, R. Blackburn, and J. V. Putten. 1998. "Avaliação de docentes e do ensino." In SOUZA, E. C. B. M. (Org.), *Curso de especialização em avaliação à distância.* Brazil, DF: Universidade de Brasília, UNESCO.

Penna Firme, Thereza, J. A. Tijiboy, and V. I. Stone. 2006. *Avaliação de programas sociais: como enfocar e como pôr em prática.* Belo Horizonte, Brazil: Modus Faciendi.

Scriven, Michael S. 1967. "The Methodology of Evaluation." In *Perspectives of Curriculum Evaluation*, ed. Ralph Tyler, Robert Gagner, and Michael S. Scriven, 39–83. AERA Monograph Series on Curriculum Evaluation. Chicago: Rand McNally.

———. 2004. Reflections. In *Evaluation Roots: Tracing Theorists' Views and Influences*, ed. Marvin C. Alkin, 183–195. Thousand Oaks, CA: Sage Publications.

Worthen, Blaine R., James R. Sanders, and Jody L. Fitzpatrick. 1997. *Program Evaluation: Alternative Approaches and Practical Guidelines.* New York: Longman Publishers.

17 For What Should Schools Be Held Accountable?

Richard Rothstein and Rebecca Jacobsen

Contemporary demands that public schools be held accountable for their performance invite a reconsideration of educational goals, because the first question any accountability system must ask is, "accountable for what?"

School accountability systems should avoid three complementary failures: first, a tendency to hold schools accountable only for the most easily measured outcomes, ignoring others that may be as or more important; second, the likelihood that schools will shift resources and attention from important outcomes to only those for which schools are held to account; and third, a disproportionate effect of this goal displacement on economically and socially disadvantaged students, leading to a widening of outcome gaps in goal areas less easily standardized for testing purposes.

In the United States, each of these failures is increasingly present. Government surveys of elementary school teachers' time allocation find an instructional shift from science and social studies to math and reading during the last fifteen years, as federal and most state accountability systems have imposed sanctions on schools for low scores on math and reading tests alone (Morton and Dalton, 2007).

Private surveys confirm these trends, suggesting even greater shifts for disadvantaged students, subsequent to adoption of the federal No Child Left Behind Act (NCLB), which requires annual testing in math and reading.

The Council for Basic Education (CBE) surveyed school principals in several states in fall 2003. It found that principals in schools with a high proportion of minorities were more likely to have reduced time for history, civics, geography, the arts, and foreign languages, to devote more time to math and reading. In New York, for example, twice as many principals in high-minority schools (where half or more of students are minority) reported such curricular shifts as did principals in mostly white schools. In high-minority elementary schools, 38 percent of principals reported decreasing the time devoted to social studies (usually meaning history), but in low-minority schools, only 17 percent reported decreasing such time (von Zastrow and Janc, 2004; von Zastrow, pers. comm., Dec. 6, 2005).

A 2005 survey by the Center on Education Policy (CEP) found that 97 percent of high-poverty districts had new minimum time requirements for reading, while only 55 percent of low-poverty districts had them (Center on Education Policy, 2006, p. 97). CEP had previously found that where districts had adopted such minimum time policies, about half had reduced social studies, 43 percent had reduced art and music, and 27 percent reduced physical education. Some districts reduced more than one of these areas (Center on Education Policy, 2005, p. 22).

This is how one former teacher described her recent experiences:

> From my experience of being an elementary school teacher at a low-performing urban school in Los Angeles, I can say that the pressure became so intense that we had to show how every single lesson we taught connected to a standard that was going to be tested. This meant that art, music and even science and social studies were not a priority and were hardly ever taught. We were forced to spend ninety percent of the instructional time on reading and math. This made teaching boring for me and was a huge part of why I decided to leave the profession (Duran, 2005, p. 23).

Some have expressed concern about these developments. The historian David McCullough concluded, in testimony before a U.S. Senate committee: "Because of No Child Left Behind, sadly, history is being put on the back burner or taken off the stove altogether in many or most schools, in favor of math or reading" (Dillon, 2005). Retired Supreme Court Justice Sandra Day O'Connor now co-chairs a "Campaign for the Civic Mission of Schools" which laments that, under NCLB, "as civic learning has been pushed aside, society has neglected a fundamental purpose of American education, putting the health of our democracy at risk" (Campaign for the Civic Mission of Schools, 2006). And U.S. Senator Robert Byrd has reacted to civics receiving insufficient attention in public schools by successfully sponsoring a bill requiring that every educational institution in the country teach about the federal Constitution each September 17. It can hardly be considered a reasonable solution to have Congress mandate specific days for instruction for each of the many education goals now being diminished under the testing pressure of NCLB.

Supporters of restricting accountability to math and reading often assert that teaching basic skills has been the traditional role of schools, and other goals have recently been added, to the detriment of math and reading. This view is not supported by history. As Joel E. Cohen notes in his introduction to this volume (p. 14), when Thomas Jefferson provided the first coherent American description of a public education system, enabling a student "to calculate for himself, and to express and preserve his ideas, his contracts and accounts, in writing" was but one goal in a series whose emphasis was on moral and political development. For the Founding Fathers generally, political goals were paramount. Some, like Jefferson, emphasized the preparation of potential voters to make wise decisions in the selection of their representatives. Others like George Washington feared, more than did Jefferson, that a non-monarchical political system would find it difficult to maintain order unless schools disciplined young people to respect authority. In his first state of the union message, in 1790, Washington urged Congress to consider how to promote educational institutions to teach Americans not only "to value their own rights" but "to distinguish between oppression and the necessary exercise of lawful authority," and "to discriminate the spirit of liberty from that of licentiousness, . . . with an inviolable respect to the laws" (Washington, 1790, p. 3). In his farewell address, Washington worried about voters who might be tempted to elect demagogues, warning that "it is essential that public opinion should be enlightened" by schools (Washington, 1796, p. 25). To Washington, it was important that a public university could bring together youths of different backgrounds where they can develop a common national identity (Ellis, 2001, p. 154). Wanting students to experience and accept diversity as a goal of education did not originate with contemporary affirmative action proponents.

As Cohen also observes, political goals had continued prominence in early public school systems, as expressed, for example, in the annual reports of Horace Mann, Massachusetts' first state schools superintendent. Following a tour of Europe, Mann praised Prussian schools for students' discipline and order. But he noted that universal public education did not itself ensure democratic values. Prussian students, after all, became literate, but this literacy was used to support autocracy. So Mann suggested that public schools in a democracy could not be held accountable for academic proficiency alone; they must inculcate democratic moral and political values, so that literacy will not be misused: "[I]f Prussia can pervert the benign influences of education to the support of arbitrary power, we surely can employ them for the support and perpetuation of republican institutions. . ., and if it may be made one of the great prerogatives of education to perform the unnatural and unholy work of making slaves, then surely it must be one of the noblest instrumentalities for rearing a nation of freemen" (Mann, 1844, p. 23).

In another report, Mann stressed health and physical fitness as important school goals. If schools fail to attend to these, Mann noted, the costs are borne by the entire community, in lost worker productivity and in the burdens of caring for the infirm, so it is in the community's interest to ensure that all children receive instruction in health habits. These included physical fitness as well as sophistication about issues of public sanitation and hygiene, such as provision of pure drinking water and sewage systems in the growing cities of an industrializing nation. "For this thorough diffusion of sanitary intelligence, the Common School is the only agency," Mann concluded (1848, p. 52).

Throughout the twentieth century as well, leading educators and policy makers have often proclaimed a broad set of school goals and bemoaned the threat to these goals posed by standardized testing. In 1938, for example, the National Education Association (at the time, not a teachers' union but a quasi-governmental organization representing teachers, administrators, university faculty and policy makers in education), echoing Horace Mann's reflections following his visit to Prussia, proclaimed: "[T]he safety of democracy will not be assured merely by making education universal"; in other words, simply by making all Americans literate. "The task is not so easy as that. The dictatorships [Germany, Italy, Japan and the Soviet Union] have universal schooling and use this very means to prevent the spread of democratic doctrines and institutions" (Educational Policies Commission, 1938, p. 16). Teaching of democratic values and habits must be an explicit focus of schools, and could not be assumed. The commission, prefiguring our contemporary dilemmas, went on to warn:

> Most of the standardized testing instruments [and written examinations] used in schools today deal largely with information. . . . There should be a much greater concern with the development of attitudes, interests, ideals, and habits. To focus tests exclusively on the acquisition and retention of information may recognize objectives of education which are relatively unimportant. Measuring the results of education must be increasingly concerned with such questions as these: Are the children growing in their ability to work together for a common end? Do they show greater skill in collecting and weighing evidence? Are they learning to be fair and tolerant in situations where conflicts arise? Are they sympathetic in the presence of suffering and indignant in the presence of injustice? Do they show greater concern about questions of civic, social, and economic importance? Are they using their spending money wisely? Are they becoming more skillful in doing some useful type of work? Are they more honest, more reliable, more temperate, more humane? Are they finding happiness in their present family life? Are they living in accordance with the rules of health? Are they acquiring skills in using all of the fundamental tools of learning? Are they curious about the natural world around them? Do they appreciate, each to the fullest degree possible, their rich inheritance in art, literature, and music? Do they balk at being led around by their prejudices? (Educational Policies Commission, 1938, pp. 153–154)

Twenty years later, a report by the Rockefeller Brothers Fund, responding to the concern in the late 1950s with training a scientific elite that could

compete with the Soviet Union, qualified its proposals for scientific education by asking how "may we best prepare our young people to keep their
individuality, initiative, creativity in a highly organized, intricately meshed
society? ... Our conception of excellence must embrace many kinds of
achievement at many levels.... There is excellence in abstract intellectual activity, in art, in music, in managerial activities, in craftsmanship, in
human relations, in technical work" (Rockefeller Brothers Fund, 1958, pp.
14, 16). The Report's emphasis was on excellence, no longer on preparation
for democracy or social justice, but its authors (chaired by future Governor
and Vice President Nelson Rockefeller, with future Secretary of State Henry
Kissinger as staff director) were in accord with previous generations' insis-
tence that school goals could not encompass academic achievement alone.

The Report warned that testing would become increasingly important,
as a way of sorting future scientists and leaders for advanced training. But
"[d]ecisions based on test scores must be made with the awareness of the
imponderables in human behavior. We cannot measure the rare qualities of
character that are a necessary ingredient of great performance. We cannot
measure aspiration or purpose. We cannot measure courage, vitality or
determination" (Rockefeller Brothers Fund, 1958, p. 29).

Nearly thirty years later, a committee of the National Academy of Education issued this warning:

> At root here is a fundamental dilemma. Those personal qualities
> that we hold dear—resilience and courage in the face of stress, a
> sense of craft in our work, a commitment to justice and caring in our
> social relationships, a dedication to advancing the public good in our
> communal life—are exceedingly difficult to assess. And so, unfor-
> tunately, we are apt to measure what we can, and eventually come
> to value what is measured over what is left unmeasured. The shift is
> subtle, and occurs gradually. It first invades our language and then
> slowly begins to dominate our thinking. It is all around us, and we
> too are a part of it. In neither academic nor popular discourse about
> schools does one find nowadays much reference to the important hu-
> man qualities noted above. The language of academic achievement
> tests has become the primary rhetoric of schooling (Review Com-
> mittee of the National Academy of Education, 1987, p. 51).

Citing this warning, the Department of Education's National Center for
Education Statistics (NCES) established a "Special Study Panel on Education Indicators" that published a 1991 report urging a national indicator
system that reflected this balance of educational goals. The report urged
that, in addition to academic competence in the core subjects, measured
"learner outcomes" should include tolerance, comprehending pluralism,
self-direction, responsibility, commitment to craft, and other measures
(Special Study Panel on Education Indicators for the National Center for

Educational Statistics, 1991, p. 64). But NCES never proceeded to develop such a system and, as the testing frenzy grew, the warning of the National Academy was forgotten.

In 2005, we attempted to synthesize the descriptions of goals for public education established through 250 years of American history. We defined eight broad goal areas that seemed to be prominent in each era, although certainly emphases changed from generation to generation. We then presented these eight goal areas to representative samples of American adults, of school board members, of state legislators, and of school superintendents, asking respondents to assign a relative importance to each of the goal areas. Rothstein et al. (2008) described the survey methodology and detailed results. Average responses of all adults, board members, legislators, and superintendents were very similar. If an accountability system were to hold schools responsible for achievement of a balanced set of outcomes, the system would have to be structured as shown in Table 17.1, at least according to these surveyed groups.

Table 17.1   Views on Relative Importance of Public Education Goals

Goal Area	Relative Importance of Goal Area (Weights, in %)[1]
Basic Academic Skills in Core Subjects Reading, writing, math, knowledge of science and history.	22
Critical Thinking and Problem Solving Able to analyze and interpret information, use computers to develop knowledge, apply ideas to new situations.	18
Social Skills and Work Ethic Good communication skills, personal responsibility, the ability to get along well with others, and work with others from different backgrounds.	12
Citizenship and Community Responsibility Know how government works, how to participate in civic activities like voting, volunteering, and becoming active in communities.	11
Physical Health A foundation for lifelong physical health, including good habits of exercise and nutrition.	9
Emotional Health Tools to develop self-confidence, respect for others, and the ability to resist peer pressure to engage in irresponsible personal behavior.	9
The Arts and Literature Participate in and appreciate the musical, visual, and performing arts and developing a love of literature.	9
Preparation for Skilled Work Vocational, career, and technical education that will qualify youth for skilled employment that does not require a college degree.	10

[1] The weights shown are a simple average of the average responses for each of the four surveyed groups.

What is most curious about these survey findings is that they articulate the goals even of state representatives and school board members, two groups of public officials who have been aggressive in the last two decades about establishing school accountability systems that expect performance only in basic skills. This gap between the preferences for educational goals expressed in our survey and the educational standards established through political processes reflects a widespread policy incoherence. Before legislators rush to implement poorly designed accountability systems, the full range of school goals should be more carefully considered.

REFERENCES

Campaign for the Civic Mission of Schools. 2006. *Call to Action.* April 17. http://www.civicmissionofschools.org/ (accessed July 19, 2006).

Center on Education Policy. 2005. *From the Capital to the Classroom. Year 3 of the No Child Left Behind Act*, 22, Table 1–1. Washington, DC: Center on Education Policy. http://www.cep-dc.org/pubs/nclby3/press/cep-nclby3_21Mar2005.pdf (accessed July 19, 2006).

Center on Education Policy. 2006. *From the Capital to the Classroom. Year 4 of the No Child Left Behind Act.* Washington, DC: Center on Education Policy. http://www.cep-dc.org/nclb/Year4/CEP-NCLB-Report-4.pdf, Figure 4-A, p. 97 (accessed July 19, 2006).

Dillon, Sam. 2005. "From Yale to Cosmetology School, Americans Brush Up on History and Government." *The New York Times*, September 16.

Duran, Jacquelyn. 2005. *An Adequate Teacher: What Would the System Look Like?* Unpublished paper, Teachers College, Columbia University, Course ITSF 4151. December 23.

Educational Policies Commission. 1938. *The Purposes of Education in American Democracy.* Washington, DC: National Education Association of the United States and the American Association of School Administrators.

Ellis, Joseph J. 2001. *Founding Brothers: The Revolutionary Generation.* New York: Alfred A. Knopf.

Mann, Horace. 1844. *Seventh Annual Report of the Board of Education Together with the Seventh Annual Report of the Secretary of the Board.* Boston: Dutton and Wentworth, State Printers.

Mann, Horace. 1848. *Twelfth Annual Report of the Board of Education Together with the Seventh Annual Report of the Secretary of the Board.* Boston: Dutton and Wentworth, State Printers.

Morton, Beth A., and Ben Dalton. 2007. *Stats in Brief: Changes in Instructional Hours in Four Subjects by Public School Teachers of Grades 1 through 4* (Report No. NCES 2001–305). Washington, DC: U.S. Department of Education, National Center for Education Statistics.

Review Committee of the National Academy of Education. 1987. "Commentary by the National Academy of Education." In Lamar Alexander, chair, *The Nation's Report Card: Improving the Assessment of Student Achievement. Report of the Study Group. With a Review of the Report by a Committee of the National Academy of Education. Robert Glaser, Chairman.* Washington, DC: Office of Educational Research and Improvement, U.S. Department of Education, and the National Academy of Education.

Rockefeller Brothers Fund. 1958. *The Pursuit of Excellence: Education and the Future of America—The "Rockefeller Report" on Education.* Special Studies Project Report V. New York: Rockefeller Brothers Fund.

Rothstein, Richard, Rebecca Jacobsen, and Tamara Wilder. 2008. *Grading Education: Getting Accountability Right.* Washington, DC: Economic Policy Institute; New York: Teachers College Press.

Special Study Panel on Education Indicators for the National Center for Educational Statistics. 1991. *Education Counts: An Indicator System to Monitor the Nation's Educational Health* (Report No. NCES 91–634). Washington, DC: U.S. Department of Education, National Center for Education Statistics.

von Zastrow, Claus, with Helen Janc. 2004. *Academic Atrophy: The Condition of the Liberal Arts in America's Public Schools.* Washington, DC: Council for Basic Education.

Washington, George. 1790. "First Annual Message," January 8. In *The State of the Union Messages of the Presidents, Volume I, 1790–1860,* ed. Fred L. Israel, 1966. New York: Chelsea House-Robert Hector Publishers.

Washington, George. 1796. "The Farewell Address." In *Washington's Farewell Address: The View from the 20ᵗʰ Century,* ed. Burton Ira Kaufman, 1969. Chicago: Quadrangle Books.

Part VIII

Defining Educational Quality as a Basis for Educational Policy

18 Quality Education
A UNESCO Perspective[1]

Mary Joy Pigozzi

INTRODUCTION

A new approach to understanding the quality of education is needed
because the current understanding is no longer functional. In addition, in
many instances the education that is offered is no longer pertinent to the
societies in which it is offered. Underpinning this wish to reconsider "what
is quality" is a desire to focus on learning.

WHAT DRIVES THE GOALS OF EDUCATION TODAY?[2]

Traditionally, the quality of education has been an internal affair, the
responsibility of the educational authorities at governmental and institutional levels. Today, however, the quality of education is no longer the
exclusive preserve of educational authorities and professionals. Ministries
other than the Ministry of Education are taking an interest. The same is
true for NGOs, businesses, and the general public—all putting different
pressures on education. The ramifications of this extend far beyond the
walls of individual ministries or educational institutions. To explain why
this is occurring and why the quality of education has become a higher
profile issue, it is necessary to take several key factors into account.

First, the growing importance of the quality of education cannot be
divorced from the heightened salience of education policy and education
reform within public policy, mainly because of the acknowledged linkages
between education and economic performance, participation in the global
economy, and the building of knowledge societies. Much concern about the
quality of education derives from the belief that poor quality will frustrate
efforts to use education as an effective lever of economic growth and development in this age of accelerating globalization.

Second, the nature of the problem has been redefined. Traditional
approaches to the quality of education often relied upon proxy measures
such as increases in financing and other inputs to educational provision.
While clearly not irrelevant or unhelpful, such outlays may not prove decisive

when another criterion for defining and measuring the quality of education is used, namely, measurable educational outcomes (knowledge, competencies, skills, and behaviors). Governments and citizens are increasingly concerned about the discrepancy between outlays and outcomes. People want to know what is learned and what works in teaching and learning.

Third, such questions are fueling a growing trend toward greater government interest in and use of evidence through which student learning attainment may be monitored both nationally and cross-nationally. This interest has two important dimensions. The first is whether students are learning the right things to lead a decent life in a fast-changing world. The second is closely related. Monitoring of student performance over time and in comparative perspective, including across national boundaries, can provide information vital for assessing how well or how badly education systems are preparing young people for future adult roles as creative, thinking citizens who can sustain themselves and contribute to the well-being of their families, communities, and societies.

Fourth, such information is becoming more politically sensitive as it points to the unevenness of quality both within and between education systems. Quality levels vary widely from one education system to another and, within a single education system, there may be sharp variations in quality, for example between public and private schools, or between urban and rural schools, or between education for the majority and education for minorities, immigrants, the marginalized, and so on. Even in the same classrooms, boys and girls can have significantly different learning experiences. The unevenness of quality is a critical issue facing education systems and is particularly important in regard to the widening education gap between countries, the tasks of development, and the effects of internal disparities on social cohesion.

Fifth, the growing diversification of societies, largely as a result of migration, urbanization, and cultural change, joined with increased sensitivity to the national, regional, gender, cultural, ethnic, and religious bases of individual and group identity, is placing fresh demands upon education systems and is challenging assumptions about the purpose and functions of education. Problems of discrimination, racism, and violence within schools affect learning opportunities and learning achievement.

Sixth, and directly related to the preceding point, are questions about the fundamental purposes of education. Disparity in educational quality often mirrors other disparities, which many view as directly tied to the fulfillment of human and other rights. Thus education is being asked to become one tool, of many, that can build societies based on peace, equality, and democratic practice.

"QUALITY EDUCATION" AS A DYNAMIC CONCEPT

These different pressures have resulted in the concept of quality education coming to the fore as learners, parents and communities, educators, leaders, and nations acknowledge that what is learned and how learning occurs is as important as access to education. The old problems that have plagued educational quality remain, and they are further complicated by new challenges such as the role of education in relation to peace and security and the HIV and AIDS pandemic, for example.

While most people understand intuitively what they mean by "quality of education," there may not be a common understanding of the term at the beginning of the twenty-first century. Now education is increasingly understood to be more than reading, writing, and arithmetic and extends to the expanded vision of education articulated at the Jomtien Conference on Education for All in 1990 and re-affirmed at the Dakar World Education Forum (UNESCO, 2000).

The understanding of what constitutes a quality education is evolving. The conventional definition remains important. It includes literacy, numeracy, and life skills, and is linked directly to such critical components as teachers, content, methodologies, curriculum, examination systems, policy, planning, and management and administration. Basic academics remain essential.

There is a demand, however, for education to reflect upon its relevance to the modern world. While in the past much of the emphasis on education related to cognitive understanding and development, now there is a need to also address the social and other dimensions of learning. Education is expected to make a contribution to addressing sustainable human development, peace and security, universal values, informed decision-making, and the quality of life at individual, family, societal, and global levels.

THE RELATIONSHIPS BETWEEN ACCESS AND QUALITY

There is a common misunderstanding that access to education must always precede attention to quality. This is not the case. In some cases, learners are not taking advantage of available school places, and in other cases, learners drop out of schools when what schools offer is not seen as relevant to their current or future needs. In both cases, students vote with their feet. Contrary to the common misunderstanding, educational access and quality are distinct concepts but are intricately linked, especially when supply and demand are considered. While quality is impossible without access, access without quality is often meaningless to those for whom access is made possible.

RIGHTS-BASED EDUCATION AS THE CONCEPTUAL UNDERPINNING OF QUALITY EDUCATION

UNESCO promotes quality education as a human right and supports a rights-based approach to the implementation of all educational activities. There are three important aspects of education as a human right:

- Participation in quality education in itself;
- The practice of human rights in education; and
- Education as a right that facilitates the fulfillment of other rights.

Our work is based on a number of international instruments[3] that identify education as a human right. Several of these international instruments indicate the desired nature or quality of this education. Together, these instruments go far beyond single articles to a web of commitments to a deep and broad understanding of educational quality.

Education must be placed and understood in terms of the larger context. A quality education must reflect learning in relation to the learner as individual, family and community member, and part of a world society.

A quality education understands the past, is relevant to the present, and has a view to the future. Quality education relates to knowledge building and the skillful application of all forms of knowledge by unique individuals who function both independently and in relation to others. A quality education reflects the dynamic nature of culture and languages, the value of the individual in relation to the larger context, and the importance of living in a way that promotes equality in the present and fosters a sustainable future.

FRAMING QUALITY EDUCATION IN RELATION TO THE MODERN WORLD

For learning, the relationship between the learner and the teacher is critical. The inputs, processes, and environments that foster or hamper learning are key as well. They affect learning at the *level of the learner* in her or his learning environment and at the *level of the system* that creates and supports the learning experience. Each of these two levels can be divided into five dimensions. These ten dimensions of a quality education are summarized next and are illustrated in the Figure 18.1. The act of learning is at the center, and it is surrounded by two levels. The inner one is that of the learner, and the outer one is of the learning system. Both of these levels operate within a specific context, which can vary considerably from location to location.

THE LEARNER LEVEL

UNESCO is concerned about five key dimensions of quality education at the level of the learner from a rights perspective.

Seeking Out Learners

Education must be available without discrimination. This underscores the UNESCO commitment to reach out to those who have not been reached traditionally, including the poor, girls, working children, children affected by emergencies, children with disabilities, and those with nomadic lifestyles. All learners have a right to a quality education as the basis for lifelong learning.[4]

Quality education actively seeks out learners and assists them to learn using a wide range of modalities, recognizing that learning is linked to experience, language and cultural practices, gifts, traits, the external environment, and interests.

We learn in different ways, each emphasizing different senses and abilities. A quality education is one that welcomes the learner and adapts to learning needs. It is inclusive. A quality education strives to ensure that all learners, regardless of sex, age, language, religion, and ethnicity, for example, are reached—that they have the possibility of participating in and learning from organized learning activities.

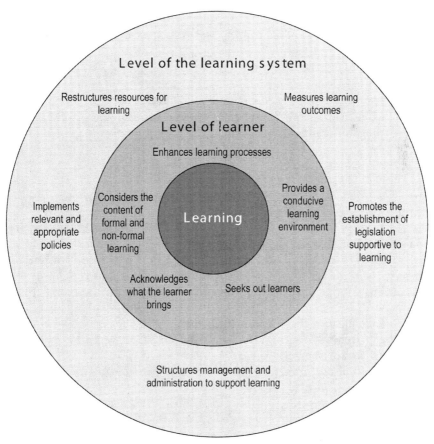

Figure 18.1 A quality education—a framework.

What the Learner Brings

What the learner brings to her or his learning and to that of a group is extremely important. It can vary from work skills to traumatic experiences, to excellent early childhood development opportunities, to illness or hunger, for example. A quality education has to consider the learner as an active participant and a central part of educational efforts. All of a learner's characteristics determine how the learner learns, behaves in class, interacts with the group and teacher, and how s/he interprets the knowledge presented. A quality education therefore has to recognize, and actively respond to, and take advantage of the diversity of learners.

Content

Content is well understood as a component of quality, but needs to be re-examined to be relevant to the changes that have occurred in the world. Materials relevant to learners are needed for curricula in literacy, numeracy, and facts and skills for life, including education on rights, gender equality, respect for the earth and other life forms, health, nutrition, HIV and AIDS, peace, and respect for and appreciation of diversity.

Equitable access to sufficient educational materials has long been recognized as essential for learning. Low-cost materials can facilitate learning as well as expensive ones. But the materials themselves need to be reviewed in light of what they convey about rights, obligations, responsibilities, gender, stereotyping, and religion, for example.

Processes

Processes of education are a frequently overlooked aspect of quality. How learners are enabled to frame and solve problems, how different learners in the same group are treated, how teachers and administrators are treated and behave, and how families and communities are engaged in education all affect the quality of education. Differential treatment of children demonstrates by example at an early age that some people do not have the same rights as others, and this kind of action must not be tolerated, however commonly it may be practiced.

Quality educational processes require well-trained teachers able to use learner-centered teaching and learning methods, and life-skills approaches. The term "learner-centered" must be reconstructed to address issues of disparity and discrimination with regard to culture, language, and gender, for example.

How knowledge, skills, and values are transmitted is as important a part of curriculum as *what* knowledge, skills, and values are learned, because the process is part of what is learned. Within the learning environment learners must be able to express their views, thoughts, and ideas—to participate fully, associate freely, and feel comfortable about who they are, where they come from, their sex, and what they believe in. They need to be treated with the dignity that is inherent in them. Without these facilitating processes, learners will not develop or cement the self-esteem that is essential for decision making throughout life. Educational processes can also help learners develop a sense of self-discipline that will help them pursue their goals throughout their lives.[5]

The Learning Environment

The learning environment must also be considered part of educational quality. There must be adequate hygiene and sanitation facilities accessible to all and, if possible, health and nutrition services in the vicinity. School policies and their implementation must promote physical and mental health, safety, and security. While the physical environment is better understood, the psycho-social one is at least as important and deserves serious attention. Practices such as gender discrimination, bullying, corporal punishment, and forced work must be eliminated.

Lack of safety and security may be very obvious from the prevalence of physical dangers such as beatings or rape. More insidious are invisible forms of harassment and violence in education, particularly gender-based violence. Violence in all forms, any action intended to cause emotional or physical harm to a person, will affect learning. The perpetrators may be other students, teachers, or school administrators. The vulnerability of girls to violence must continue to be highlighted.

THE SYSTEM LEVEL

UNESCO is concerned about five important dimensions of quality education at the system level from a rights perspective.

Managerial and Administrative Structure and Processes

The structure and organization of education usually are the philosophical underpinning for what occurs throughout the system, whether in the university, the school, or the curriculum development unit of a ministry of education, for example. A quality education requires a system that supports effective learning.

Education systems exhibit a culture of their own, often a culture that reflects (perhaps necessarily) the dominant culture of the nation or of a region in the nation. In some cases, it still reflects an imposed culture. Knowledge of the cultural norms and practices in operation in a particular educational context or situation facilitate the "negotiation" of that situation in both obvious and subtle ways.

Education must be structured and organized to be learner-centered. Learner-centered education concerns not only the learners but also the systems, environments, and materials around learners. Currently very few educational institutions and/or bureaucracies are learner-centered. Where learners are working in nonhazardous labor, the structure and organization of education must take this into account. Timetables must also be flexible enough to be able to keep children at risk from dropping out or otherwise losing their right to education.

The education system must be fair and transparent to all. Rules and regulations need to be clear, with responsibilities and related procedures well articulated and implemented. Teachers need to be facilitated in their work by a managerial and administrative system designed to improve learning outcomes.

Well-run schools include opportunities for bringing difficult issues into the open, a key first step to addressing them. Education must be approachable by parents and members of the surrounding communities. They must feel positive and comfortable about their appropriate roles in the educational process. This approachability requires an enabling structure and organization of the education system at all levels.

The structure, organization, and management of education play an important role in providing the checks and balances that are necessary in any system. Involved institutions, such as teacher training colleges and research institutes, are also key in promoting a quality education. Yet the system cannot be separated from the people who operate it and interpret its rules on a daily basis.

Implementation of Good Policies

Typically, ministries of education set policies. However, the policies may not be widely known and understood by all, particularly in the classroom. It is helpful to raise awareness among administrators, teachers, and students about these policies and to ensure that mechanisms implement and enforce the policies. It is pointless to have rules and procedures if they are not observed.

Successful efforts to promote, implement, and enforce good policies have involved teachers and students broadly in setting and respecting them. All school policies need to be consistent with national legislation, which should also be regularly reviewed and updated to ensure relevancy.

Education is not independent of the rest of society, nor of policies developed and implemented in other sectors of the country. For example, a quality education requires coherent and supportive policies in areas such as responsible media, health education, youth, early childhood development, and lifelong learning opportunities.

Appropriate Legislative Framework

Legislation is essential for ensuring that the principles inherent in the right to education are put into action daily in a sustained way. As with policies, both education legislation and other related legislation must be in place, understood by the general public as well as experts, and implemented.

An enabling legislative framework must do more than pay lip service to the right to education, defined broadly. It must facilitate the necessary changes in the education system at the macro and micro levels. A quality education must ensure that there are sufficient places for all children. Legislation needs to address the obligations to provide education (defined broadly to include both access and quality), to allocate resources (human, time, and financial), and to set the overall expectations of the system.

It is important to obligate the *state*, the trustee of the nation, to provide education for all. Too often, compulsory education is seen as a legal framework that places parents and children, especially females, in the negative role of criminal or victim.

Other legislation is critical as well, however. For example, the Convention on the Rights of the Child indicates that children under fifteen years of age must not have their learning diverted due to involvement in hostilities. International law also states the minimum age for full-time work. National labor and education laws must be consistent with these agreements.

In many instances, compensatory action is needed to ensure equality of opportunity. Current data and practice in an increasing number of countries suggest a very strong case for affirmative action, initiated legally, to ensure educational opportunities for those negatively affected by discrimination.

Resources

A quality education requires resources of money, human capability, and time. While some countries have budgeted to emphasize education as a key engine for national development and a means to build democratic societies, others cannot. Allocating resources to support quality education requires a long-term view. For example, international law calls for free compulsory education. While universality is not yet a reality in many countries, plans must be put in place and immediate action initiated toward this end. In the short run, costs of education must be distributed equitably.

Measurement of Learning Outcomes

This chapter began by stressing the importance of learning. The last of the ten dimensions of quality addresses learning outcomes. A better understanding of what is wanted from a quality education has expanded significantly the desired learning outcomes. The main types of learning outcomes to be pursued are:

- Knowledge: the essential cognitive achievements that all learners should reach (including literacy, numeracy, core subject knowledge);
- Values: solidarity, gender equality, tolerance, mutual understanding, respect for human rights, non-violence, respect for human life and dignity;
- Skills or competencies: a secure command of how to solve problems, to experiment, to work in teams, to live together and interact with those who are different and to learn how to learn; and
- Behaviors: the willingness to put into practice what has been learned.

Our ability to measure learning achievement varies considerably for different kinds of outcomes. Many indicators of learning achievement (or their proxies) are already in use, and some systems measure learning achievement and use the results to implement and assess educational policies, programs, and practices. More effort has gone into addressing knowledge and competencies and less into values and behaviors.[5] Additional work is needed. As understanding of the various dimensions of quality evolves, some of the commonly used indicators might need to be reconsidered as well.

It is possible, and crucial for improvement, to monitor the quality of education. To do so will take, in some instances, a rethinking of what to measure, how to balance qualitative and quantitative measures, and how to translate some qualitative measures into quantitative ones that can be meaningfully compared. While cross-national comparisons are important, they might not be the most immediate need.

CONCLUSION

Does this conception of a quality education set the bar high? Emphatically yes! But this approach allows education systems the flexibility to determine the ways and means they will use to approach the bar. Education systems and their processes cannot realistically be expected to change overnight. A vision of quality that takes into account its various dimensions sets the standard. Teachers, schools, communities, systems, and nations are responsible for determining how this vision should be interpreted and, incrementally, put in place.

NOTES

1. An earlier version of this chapter has been published as: Pigozzi, Mary Joy. 2006. "What is the 'Quality of Education?' (A UNESCO Perspective)" in *Cross-National Studies in the Quality of Education: Planning their Design and Managing their Impact*, ed. Kenneth N. Ross and Ilona Jürgens Genevois, 39–50. http://unesdoc.unesco.org/images/0014/001470/147093e.pdf.

2. This portion of the chapter is taken, with minor amendments, from the annotated agenda of the Ministerial Round Table of Ministers of Education, UNESCO, Paris, 4–5 October 2003, which was prepared by the author and Mark Richmond. http://unesdoc.unesco.org/images/0015/001533/153324E.pdf.
3. Including the December 10, 1948 UN General Assembly resolution 217 A (III) on the Universal Declaration of Human Rights and the Convention on the Rights of the Child.
4. In relation to the processes and content of education as they relate to Education for All (EFA), UNESCO is also engaged in an activity to assist countries to monitor progress in achievement of life skills. It has developed a position paper which uses the four pillars of education from the Delors Commission to frame life skills (UNESCO, 2005).
5. A number of mechanisms exist, or existed, to measure learning outcomes. Some of the better known are: Trends in International Mathematics and Science Study (TIMSS), Programme for International Student Assessment (PISA), Southern and Eastern Africa Consortium for Monitoring Educational Quality (SACMEQ), and the International Association for the Evaluation of Educational Achievement (IEA) cross-national studies. Most of these focus on cognitive achievement, although a variety of efforts are underway to measure values, skills, and behaviours. National level studies such as the UNESCO Monitoring Learning Achievement (MLA) project, which attempted to measure life skills as well as numeracy and literacy, and Minimum Levels of Literacy (MLL) in India and Assessing Basic Competencies (ABCs) in Bangladesh were attempts to develop locally appropriate and manageable assessment systems.

REFERENCES

UNESCO. 2000. *The Dakar Framework for Action, Education for All: Meeting our Collective Commitments.* Paris: UNESCO.
UNESCO. 2005. *Draft: Life Skills: The Bridge to Human Capabilities.* Paris: UNESCO.

19 Quality Education
What Is It, and Who Decides?
Briefing Paper for a Policy Maker

George M. Ingram

SUMMARY

Mr. Secretary/Senator: You asked a simple, straightforward question as to what is meant by quality in the sixth Education for All goal: *Improving all aspects of the quality of education.*

Unfortunately, there is no consensus or single answer. Quality is a relative term. The goal of quality education involves a relentless pursuit of ever-improving learning. It is evolutionary and cannot be short-circuited. It can be hastened or retarded, but not leapfrogged. Quality of education is a dynamic concept that varies depending on who asks the question, the nature of the circumstances and context, and what one views as the purpose of education, and it can change over time. Any answer starts with, "It depends. . . ." The literature is rich with concepts of quality education and the components required for creating a quality education. A principal conundrum is how to define and deliver quality education in difficult situations.

PURPOSE

The definition of quality depends on who is asked and the person's view of the purpose of education. The various purposes of education include: nation building based on certain values, ideology, or theology; preserving or changing traditional values and myths; achieving national economic competitiveness; gaining individual employment or economic security; maintaining family or community values; promoting world peace and human rights.

The definition of quality also depends on the audience: student, parent, school, community, nation, or world. For the student, quality may be defined in terms of grades, how engaging are the subject matter and instruction, or the usefulness of the schooling in finding a job. For the parent, quality may be defined in terms of maintaining certain values, contributing to family goals, or securing employment for the child. For the school, quality may be defined in terms of success in graduating students, students moving to the next stage of schooling, or student scores on national achievement assessments. For the community, quality may be defined in terms of community values, ranking of a school according to national tests, or a sufficient number of graduates adequately educated and trained so as to attract investment. For the nation, quality may be defined in terms of building a national consensus around a political philosophy or religion, maintaining or overcoming a perception of the nation's history, or making the country competitive in the global economy. At the international level, the purpose may be promoting world peace and order and a sense of world community.

Kai-ming Cheng (Chapter 2, this volume) makes a case, convincing to educated people concerned with modernizing their nation's economy and making it competitive at the global level, that today's education systems are outmoded because they were designed to fit an industrial model rather than today's knowledge-based society. In this new society, work has shifted from routinization to constant evolution in order to respond to customer needs. In the job market, creativity, design, innovation, teamwork, and continuous learning are valued, whereas most education systems produce compliance and are based on uniform standards. The argument is persuasive for an Organisation for Economic Co-operation and Development (OECD) nation or an Asian Tiger, but maybe not for a country that needs first to produce enough food—to make its farmers more efficient—to feed its citizens.

Similarly, Mohamed Charfi and Hamadi Redissi (Chapter 12, this volume) make a persuasive case that education in Arab nations is outmoded. They suggest a prescription for joining the needs and teachings of liberalism and religion in a way that both inculcates religious values and beliefs but also reveals knowledge and truth. The result would appear to be improved, high-quality learning, but not to someone who believes in a theocracy or a purely secular state.

NATIONAL AND GROUP DIFFERENCES

The purposes and expectations of education vary among different governments, institutions, and income and social groups. The government of a democratic nation will seek a vastly different national consensus and values through the education system than will the government of an autocratic or theocratic nation, and those differences can affect what is taught, how it is taught, and even who is taught. Many parents and students in a poor developing country are likely to have a different view of what they want from education than those in a rich nation, although the wealthy in both countries may have comparable views. The poor farmer in Bangladesh, the middle-class family in Paris, and the wealthy family in California will have vastly different needs and expectations for the education of their children.

Even within a nation and community, the expectations of the rich and poor, the urban and rural, and the religious and secular, will differ.

CORE COMPETENCE

If there is a commonality that cuts across these differences, it is the concept that education should prepare a student to be a constructive, contributing member of society by delivering a minimum quality of competence in literacy, numeracy, life skills, and problem solving. Some educational systems focus more heavily or solely on delivering religious content, but they are the exception. Many educational systems are expected to deliver values, but there is a wide range of differences in what those values should be.

ELEMENTS

There are various approaches to the issue of what is required to produce an education of quality. UNICEF (2000) and UNESCO (2004) identify five critical components:

- *learners*—healthy, well-nourished, ready to participate and learn
- *environments*—healthy, safe, protective, gender-sensitive, adequately resourced
- *content*—relevant for acquisition of life skills and knowledge
- *processes*—trained teachers using child-centered pedagogy
- *outcomes*—knowledge, skills, and attitudes linked to national goals

To these five components, the Global Campaign for Education (2002) adds a sixth:

- *responsiveness*—responsive to the diverse needs of children and accountable to parents

David Stephens (2003) offers a different approach to quality:

- *relevance*—to context, needs, and humanity
- *efficiency*—in setting and meeting standards
- *something special*—going beyond normal expectations
- *inclusion*—of all children, irrespective of gender, ability, or wealth

And a third approach is to use a context-input-process-outcome framework (UNESCO, 2004).

Among specific elements that various analysts identify as important to quality education are: support and involvement of parents and community;

language of instruction (mother tongue in early years); relevant curriculum content and learning materials; family environment, and preparation and health of students; process of teaching (child-centered teaching, active participation of students); safe, healthy, and gender-sensitive environment (e.g., for girls, latrines and women teachers); a system to assess learning outcomes; effective management and governance (decentralization, local engagement, and accountability); school heads as instructional and school leaders; adequate resources; and access to opportunities that require basic education (secondary school, employment). Above all, teachers—their preparation, support, training (pre- and in-service), compensation, morale, and commitment—are at the center of the learning process.

QUALITY IN RESOURCE-POOR ENVIRONMENTS

Definitions, analyses, and presentations on quality education most often describe what is required to produce quality education in ideal circumstances—strong political commitment, adequate resources, supportive and involved parents and community, trained teachers and systems to support them, healthy students, and so on. In a seminal report in 2002, the World Bank identified key benchmarks based on an assessment of characteristics of developing countries with well-performing education systems:

- average teachers salary: 3.5 times per capita GNP
- pupil/teacher ratio: 40:1
- non-teacher salary proportion of recurrent spending: 33 percent
- average repetition rate: 10 percent
- education spending as a proportion of government budget: 14 to 18 percent
- primary education proportion of education spending: 50 percent

While these common characteristics are the hallmarks of education systems that are succeeding, they should be seen as benchmark guides, not as essential requirements, as the characteristics of some successful education systems do not match all of these criteria.

Since you asked how the United States stacks up against these benchmarks, Mr. Secretary/Senator, I can report that U.S. education spending as a proportion of the government budget is 17 percent, within the range of 14 to 18 percent for developing countries. The reported U.S. pupil/teacher ratio of 16:1 is far lower than the benchmark of 40:1, while the U.S. pays teachers on average 1.5 times the per capita GNP, compared to the benchmark multiple of 3.5. In short, the U.S. has more teachers per pupil and lower salaries relative to the benchmarks. The proportion of recurrent education spending that is not for teachers' salaries is 19 percent compared to the benchmark of 33 percent.

The unaddressed issue is how to maximize quality in less-than-ideal circumstances. Experience has taught us how to deal with less-than-ideal circumstances. Teachers and students can produce learning tools from locally available materials, and radio is a valuable mechanism for delivering training to remote areas. The lack of adequately trained teachers in rural areas may be mitigated by recruiting locally and lowering qualification standards, then providing ongoing support and training.

Missing is a systemic analysis of what would define quality education and how it would be maximized in a resource-poor environment—crowded classes, poorly trained and compensated teachers, inadequate materials, and unengaged parents. For example, most discussions of quality education emphasize child-centered instruction and active student participation. But how realistic is that approach in a classroom of eighty or one hundred students, poorly nourished, crowded on narrow benches, without an aisle so the teacher cannot engage students in the middle of the classroom, much less those at the back, and where she likely does not know their names and may not speak their mother tongue? In such a situation, teachers have little opportunity to effectively engage students in active learning. So what methodologies would maximize the learning experience, particularly for a poorly trained teacher with minimal education?

Nor does the education literature discuss what quality education should mean for students who are outside the reach of a classroom. Hard-to-reach and vulnerable populations include street children, rural dwellers, disabled children, HIV/AIDS orphans, dropouts, child laborers, night travelers in Uganda, and children with mental, physical, and emotional disabilities. Interventions are being attempted to reach these groups. But what are realistic, relevant goals? What type of learning is relevant for such groups? What is the educational quality that should be sought?

A NOTE OF REALITY FROM THE CLASSROOM

When I asked my niece, Cassia Douglass, a teacher of young students in the Dominican Republic, what quality education is, she responded with a comprehensive picture of what a teacher contends with to create a quality learning environment:

> Teaching, learning, assessing, planning, motivation, social and emotional, hands-on, working together, managing and administering, seeing the big picture but also being able to see each person as an individual, and always being able to recognize what is valuable about what you already know but also learn new things every day.

And, when she asked her customers—her fifth grade class—to define quality education, they said:

- To be a good person with people and not hurt others. Mutual respect.
- To be kind with kids and explain everything.
- Teachers show me, tell me how I should do things like talk, and always say please. Having a good education is what gives you your reputation.
- Teachers need to make students like the work they do by doing it in a fun way, then students want to work.
- To show kids to be responsible and good people.
- A way of being and acting. You can have it if your parents or teachers correct you in anything you are doing wrong or not properly.
- Teachers teaching well.
- To show kids to be responsible.
- Something to use when we are grown.
- Listening and learning.
- Being respectful with people.
- Having good manners and showing respect to others and adults. It is doing what your parents tell you to do, not whatever you want.
- When you learn all you need to learn.
- To teach all kids good manners and make them know why education is important.
- Getting taught in a way that everyone can understand the material.
- When teachers teach and respect students; when there is a role made for smaller kids.
- To be perfect boy or girl.

REFERENCES

Global Campaign for Education. 2002. *A Quality Education for All: Priority Actions for Governments, Donors and Civil Society.* Johannesburg: Global Campaign for Education.

Stephens, David. 2003. *Quality of Basic Education.* Paper commissioned for the *EFA Global Monitoring Report 2003/4, The Leap to Equality.* Paris: UNESCO.

UNESCO. 2004. *The Quality Imperative: 2005 EFA Global Monitoring Report.* Paris: UNESCO.

UNICEF. 2000. *Defining Quality in Education.* Paper presented at the meeting of The International Working Group on Education Florence, Italy. New York: United Nations Children's Fund.

World Bank. 2002. *Education for Dynamic Economies: Action Plan to Accelerate Progress Towards Education for All (EFA).* Washington, DC: World Bank.

20 The Challenge of Defining a Quality Universal Education
Mapping a Common Core

Laura Hersh Salganik and
Stephen J. Provasnik

The Universal Basic and Secondary Education (UBASE) project has posed the question: What would constitute a quality education? To answer this question, we describe our understanding of the purpose of universal education and then propose a specific approach to defining a quality education applicable for all. At the heart of the approach is a framework, developed through a broad consensus-building process, to help guide the selection of key competencies which can describe the contents of an education that is applicable and high-quality for countries with different institutions and curricula. Based on this framework, we put forth three specific areas of key competencies as a common basis for developing quality universal basic and secondary education: acting autonomously, using tools interactively, and interacting in socially heterogeneous groups. Last, we review the contributions of other UBASE scholars to demonstrate how these three areas of key competencies not only accord with their viewpoints but help unify seemingly different ways of defining a quality education.

WHAT IS UNIVERSAL EDUCATION?

If everyone in a country were to undertake some sort of education, one could say that education was universal in the country, but this would not be a *universal education*. As we understand it, to have a universal education means to have a singular, common educational experience with the same broad purpose for all. This definition is perhaps easiest to understand by taking a moment to review the origins of universal education.

The practice of universal education developed in Europe in the sixteenth century in the wake of the emergence of the concept of the individual.[1] Although we now take it for granted, the idea of the individual created great social and cultural waves when it first emerged and began to undermine the corporate character of medieval society.[2] Prominent among these waves were the Protestant Reformation and the Catholic Counter-Reformation, which sought to create the means for individuals to secure their own salvation (a change from the earlier notion of corporate salvation[3]). To that end, the states and principalities in Protestant Prussia and Catholic Austria hit upon the idea of using schools to foster a particular sense of individual conscience and agency among all their subjects—one that would enable their subjects to preserve their own souls and be loyal subjects through their own volition. The required education for all was defined by an outcome: indoctrination or knowledge of the faith's doctrine, which was believed to engender religious piety and loyalty to the sovereign.[4]

As the states' religious purposes for instituting universal education became less pressing over the next centuries (with the end of Europe's religious wars), states found universal education to be a practical way to form subjects as autonomous individuals who would obey laws and support the public good because of reason, rather than because of fear of punishment or violence. Thus, schools to provide a universal education evolved into an integral part of the modern European nation-state (Meyer, Ramirez, and Soysal, 1992).

Over the twentieth century, the ends of a universal education continued to evolve in Western nation-states such that state-school systems instituting universal education are now understood to form responsible citizens, independent thinkers, competent (competitive) workers, or some combination of all three. Although ostensibly different from the earlier purposes of universal education, there is an underlying commonality with the past: universal education remains (a) an institution with a common aim for all to become individuals who take on particular responsibilities or can act in particular ways, depending on the social and economic conditions of the times; (b) an institution serving the interests of states, the collective decision maker of the curriculum (both explicit and hidden) that is made common to all; and (c) an institution implemented through formal schooling.[5]

These characteristics pose various challenges for any attempt to make a high quality education both universal and worldwide, primary among which is how to define it—or, more precisely, a common core—that can be applicable for all and be of high quality for all. Key competencies we believe can effectively address this challenge.

KEY COMPETENCIES

Before we explain how key competencies provide a way to define a quality education suited to universal education and a practical approach for pragmatically anchoring education policy-making to what people need to be able to do, it is helpful to understand the origins of the idea of key competencies.

For much of the twentieth century, a quality education was defined by characteristics of inputs such as qualified teachers, adequate school resources, and/or a sound curriculum. These are, after all, widely believed to be primary factors in the quality of an education in any school. In the past few decades, however, many countries and most international organizations dedicated to improving education in developed and developing countries have begun to view such inputs as important but not sufficient to achieve a quality education. Instead they increasingly focus on outcomes, such as graduation rates, level of educational attainment, and student achievement, to drive educational improvements. As a result, outcomes such as academic achievement and rates of secondary school completion have gained a prominent place in educational policy discussions.

In addition, especially since the late 1980s, when social and economic changes associated with new technologies (e.g., the silicon chip that made possible the micro-computer, cell phones, computerized appliances, etc.) and globalization (of world markets and the rise of free trade after World War II) have prompted discussions in Western nations about whether existing structures of schooling designed for an earlier time were relevant for preparing young people for the demands of life today.[6] In Europe and the United States, these discussions originated, by and large, in the economic and labor sectors and eventually led to a range of proposals for curricular reform (to promote desired academic and social outcomes) and for measured outcomes (to ensure accountability). The range of proposals within individual countries was broad; but across Western nations, the proposals had common themes. Proposals called for school systems to "revise the content of schooling," "to build bridges across disciplines," to rethink the existing notions of separate vocational and pre-university academic education, to prepare students for a "new workplace," and "to hold schools and school systems accountable" for results. In addition, these proposals typically drew upon a common vocabulary, using adjectives such as "life," "key" or "core" to describe "skills" or "competencies" (Salganik and Stephens, 2003; Weinert, 2001).

The way in which outcomes were to be operationalized to effect these proposals, however, was hazy. By the mid-1990s, it was evident in a number of Western countries that, while policy-makers were increasingly focusing on measures of outcomes, the extant measures were limited in their policy uses and did not reflect new ideas about what students needed to learn. Measures of educational performance were disconnected from other outcomes and unrelated to broader discussions about curriculum, standards, what young people need for a successful life, and the purpose of schooling generally. What policy-makers and educational reformers needed were broader measures of educational outcomes and a conceptual framework for relating different outcomes to each other (Salganik, 2001).

International efforts to make outcome measures more useful for policy led to an international project, under the auspices of the Organisation for Economic Co-operation and Development (OECD),[7] to develop a broader vision of the endpoint of education that could guide the development of indicators of educational outcomes: individuals with the competencies they need to lead successful lives and contribute to successful societies. This project—Definition and Selection of Competencies: Theoretical and Conceptual Foundations, or DeSeCo, for short—explored whether a limited set of *key competencies* could be identified that could serve as a guide for the development of broader measures of teaching and learning outcomes and, more generally, for the formulation of educational policy and practice.[8]

DeSeCo initiated an international interchange among scholars from different disciplines as well as policy-makers and policy researchers. The goal of this interchange was to develop a conceptual and theoretical foundation for identifying and understanding key competencies for OECD countries, though participants recognized that it would be potentially relevant beyond the OECD as well.[9] The central guiding question of the project was: Beyond reading, writing, and computing, what competencies are needed by individuals to live a successful life and for society to face the challenges of the present and the future in modern, democratic societies?

Given the wide array of terms and lists related to this topic already existing (Salganik and Stephens, 2003; Weinert, 2001), the goal of the project was not to produce yet another list of desired attributes for individuals. Rather, the idea was to create a broad overview of the topic—a frame of reference[10]—that in addition to responding to the question could guide discussion about education; ground debate about the goals of education pragmatically (i.e., in what people need to be able to do as individuals in a modern society); facilitate a common understanding; and support the development of indicators, policy, and practice.

In the next section, we describe the building blocks of this frame of reference: the concept of competence, the concept of key competence, an explicit view of highly valued outcomes (what constitutes success for individuals and for society) and common demands of life in today's world, and a three-fold categorization of key competencies.[11] We believe this frame of reference is relevant internationally and can guide the process of reaching consensus on key competencies that are applicable worldwide and constitute a common core for a quality *universal* education for all, while leaving to the discretion of each country the choice of educational content and teaching method. In addition, this frame of reference grounds educational reform and policy-making on a conceptually logical and resolutely pragmatic foundation. In the last section of this chapter, we discuss the relevance of this approach for non-OECD countries.

DESECO'S FRAME OF REFERENCE

The purpose of DeSeCo's frame of reference is to provide a means of distinguishing between key competencies and other competencies and, ultimately, selecting key competencies. In addition, once key competencies are selected, an explicit frame of reference anchors their meaning so that they are not merely textual descriptions open to any interpretation. Thus we start this explanation with DeSeCo's concept of competence.

Concept of Competence

DeSeCo's definition of competence focuses on the demands facing individuals and the actions, choices, or behaviors needed to meet these demands. A competence is defined as "the ability to successfully meet complex demands in a particular context through the mobilization of psychosocial prerequisites (including both cognitive and noncognitive aspects)" (Rychen and Salganik, 2003b, p. 43).

This definition incorporates three critical elements. First, it includes demands placed on individuals in different areas of life, including in the family, the workplace, civic life, and social or personal life. It also allows demands to be expressed at different levels of abstraction—sometimes broadly, such as the need to cooperate with others, and sometimes specifically, as for an occupation, situation, or particular area of life. What is critical in this conceptualization of competence is that a competence entails being able to meet a demand facing an individual (e.g., the need to be able to use a map to get to a destination in an unfamiliar place) and not just an academically desirable ability (e.g., naming all the cities on the map).

Second, this definition of competence recognizes that a range of internal prerequisites combine to allow individuals to meet demands. These prerequisites may include knowledge, cognitive skills, practical skills, attitudes, emotions, values and ethics, and motivation—multiple factors that interact among themselves in a complex manner that eventually results in an action (see Figure 20.1).

Many of these internal attributes—including both cognitive and noncognitive ones—have been thought of as competencies (e.g., knowledge), but, according to this definition of competencies, they are not. Indeed, in this formulation, knowledge may be important even to meet demands that are typically not characterized as cognitive. Similarly, to meet demands often characterized as "cognitive," attitudes, emotions, values and ethics may play an important role. Thus, it may do little good to possess particular internal attributes (e.g., knowledge, values, etc.) unless one has the entire constellation of attributes that contributes to behavior, choices, or action that meet the particular demand. This is evident, for example, in how motivation, knowledge, and skills[12] are all called into play and interact dynamically to allow individuals to meet the demands of everyday life. Each element is critically important; no one element works without the others.

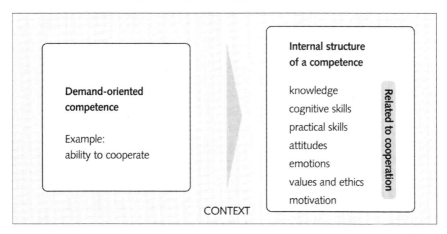

Figure 20.1. The demand defines the internal structure of a competence. Reprinted with permission from *Key Competencies for a Successful Life and a Well-Functioning Society* by D. S. Rychen and L. H. Salganik, ISBN 0–88937–272–1, p. 44, © 2003 by Hogrefe & Huber Publishers.

The third critical element of the definition is the role of context. Competencies are played out in the social and physical environment—and thus their specifics, as well as the specifics of their internal components, are profoundly influenced by the individual's particular situation. For this element, DeSeCo drew from Pierre Bourdieu's notion of social fields (Bourdieu, 1980, 1982; Swartz, 1997). According to this theory, individual action takes place within dynamic systems or sets of social interests and challenges, which are referred to as social fields. Meeting demands in a social field involves understanding and being able to operate within the system of capital of the field. As competencies vary on the scale of abstraction, social fields vary according to specificity. They can be broad, such as spheres of life, or they can be quite specific, such as a particular context (e.g., a work situation or family situation). With the inclusion of context in its definition, the concept of competence recognizes that there is variation in how competencies are manifested over time and place, even within developed countries.

Concept of Key Competence

DeSeCo defined competencies as "key competencies" if they:

> [1] contribute to highly valued outcomes . . . in terms of an overall successful life and a well-functioning society . . . [2] are instrumental for meeting important, complex demands and challenges in a wide

spectrum of contexts . . . and [3] are important for all individuals (Rychen, 2003, pp. 66–67).

Several ideas in this definition are worth further explanation.

First, individual behavior is recognized as affecting not only the individual but also the larger society. Thus, while a key competence contributes to an individual's successful life, at the same time, it also contributes to a well-functioning society. An example of such a "win–win" result that could be the outcome of a key competence is social capital, in the sense of social networks grounded in trust, which benefits the individual and his or her larger community.

Second, key competencies are important for different areas of life, such as the economic sector, civic life, the family, interpersonal relations, individual and public health, and are not directed solely toward individuals' basic survival or society's basic functioning. Thus, key competencies may contribute at the individual level to successful participation in the labor market, civic and political life, and interpersonal relations, as well as health and general satisfaction with one's life. Key competencies may contribute at the social level to a productive economy and democratic processes as well as social cohesion and peace.

Last, key competencies are neither reserved for the elite—they are for everyone—nor are they a second-rate substitute for academic knowledge and skills—they challenge everyone. Competencies that are needed only by some or are relevant for a narrow area of life may be important for those individuals or in those contexts, but they are not key competencies. This understanding of key competencies accords with the conceptual analysis of universal education presented earlier, whereby a universal education means a singular, common educational experience with the same purpose for all. It also demonstrates the logic of applying key competencies to the task of defining universal education goals: Identifying key competencies is functionally the same as outlining the common core for universal education.

Highly Valued Outcomes

Given this definition of key competencies, the selection of key competencies depends crucially on how one defines "highly valued outcomes in terms of an overall successful life and a well-functioning society." How one defines such outcomes, of course, depends on a value judgment about what is a successful life and a well-functioning society. Moreover, this value judgment needs to be one that can be universally shared—that is, one based on a common set of values or a common vision of a desired world. Thus, before attempting to articulate what is a successful life and a well-functioning society, DeSeCo addressed the question of whether there is or can be a universal normative set of values and/or a vision of a desired world across OECD countries and potentially in transitional and developing countries.

DeSeCo determined that it is reasonable to assume that a normative set of values and a normative vision of a desired world are possible given that international agreements and conventions—for example, the Universal Declaration of Human Rights, the World Declaration on Education for All, the Rio Declaration on the Environment and Development—are based on normative grounds "which specify basic human rights, democratic values, and sustainable and integrated environmental, economic, and social development as desirable goals for all societies" (Rychen, 2003, p. 69). These agreements are based on the notion that there are sufficient common ideas and values to support collective world enterprises (Delors and Draxler, 2001).

This conclusion was reinforced by the philosophers' contribution to DeSeCo on the topic of the "good life." Canto-Sperber and Dupuy (2001) argue that all humans share certain psychological needs and capacities (e.g., the aspiration to go beyond necessity, to learn from the past and plan for the future, to think, remember, imagine, have feelings and emotions). These common aspects, along with major moral theories, justify their conceptual criteria for a good life: accomplishment, the elements of human existence ("choosing one's own course through life and having a life which is properly human"), understanding of oneself and one's world, enjoyment, and deep personal relations (Canto-Sperber and Dupuy, 2001, p. 74).

Based on these very basic and fundamental common aspects as a normative starting point, DeSeCo next tried to articulate what is a successful life and a well-functioning society (Gilomen, 2003b). It was beyond the project's scope to conduct a rigorous in-depth analysis of this topic, but the project set forth initial thoughts based on a review of the literature. In sum, DeSeCo proposed eight principal dimensions for a successful life and six for a well-functioning society.

A Successful Life

Any consideration of "what is a successful life?" must recognize that that question involves both subjective and objective elements; success can be assessed from either an objective perspective, using external criteria, or from a subjective one, using the criteria and perceptions of the individual whose life it is. In addition, individual accomplishments are always to some extent contingent on resources available to the individual. In the context of these caveats, DeSeCo proposed eight principal dimensions of a successful life (Gilomen, 2003b):

1. Economic positions and resources (gainful employment, income, and wealth).
2. Political rights and power (participation in political decisions and in interest groups).

3. Intellectual resources (participation in formal education, availability of learning foundations).
4. Housing and infrastructure (quality of housing, infrastructure of surrounding environment).
5. Personal health and security (subjective and objective health, personal security).
6. Social networks/social capital (family and friends, relatives and acquaintances).
7. Leisure and cultural activities (participation in leisure and cultural activities).
8. Personal satisfaction and value orientation (personal satisfaction, autonomy in value orientation).

These dimensions incorporate elements that are outcomes strictly speaking but also others that fall more easily in the domain of resources and access to resources. Further, they are not presented as of equal importance. Although the underlying assumption is that an overall successful life will take account of all these dimensions, their relative importance will vary across individuals and across contexts (Gilomen, 2003b).

A Well-functioning Society

Although similar to desired individual outcomes, DeSeCo's definition of a well-functioning society focused on institutions, social structures, and desired societal-level characteristics—such as equity and how resources are distributed. DeSeCo identified a general consensus around several critical features of quality societies to suggest a set of dimensions of a well-functioning society that are in line with the basic normative stance described previously (Gilomen, 2003b). These dimensions are:

1. Economic productivity.
2. Democratic processes.
3. Solidarity and social cohesion.
4. Human rights and peace.
5. Equity, equality, and absence of discrimination.
6. Ecological sustainability.

These social characteristics, along with the dimensions of an individual's successful life, cover a broad array of aspects of life. Inevitably, there will be conflict between individual and social outcomes and also across different areas that make up success for society or individuals. As will be seen in the following text, understanding and dealing with these conflicting demands constitutes an aspect of key competencies needed by individuals.

Common Demands of Life in Today's World

The final component for identifying key competencies within DeSeCo's frame of reference is a definition of the common demands of today's world. Without demands in common, key competencies cannot be universal. It is clear that even within the OECD, different countries and different groups within and across countries have different concrete circumstances and have different cultural traditions and social institutions. These all contribute to variation in specific demands facing individuals. Yet, as with the normative starting point, there are characteristics that these societies share and demands that individuals living in them face in common. Without conducting an in-depth analysis of modern, democratic societies, we can state briefly that common challenges arise from increasing interdependency throughout the world, new forms of transportation and communication, and the movement of populations.[13] Furthermore, old and new problems such as poverty, inequality of opportunity, preserving the environment, increased competition, and alienation and violence are certainly not the exclusive province of one country or another (Rychen, 2003). Facing uncertainty and complexity is the rule rather than the exception in today's world, wherever one lives.

Beyond these social, physical, and psychological demands, there is also a specific common mental challenge that emerges from the nature of modern life: the demand for reflectivity and reflective practice. This is the demand for a level of mental development that allows individuals to take a critical stance toward their own lives, to see themselves as products of their own making and not merely products of socializing processes, to create a value system that allows them to prioritize among conflicting demands, and to take responsibility for what happens to themselves. In short, it is a demand for individuals to achieve what Kegan (2001) terms the "self-authoring order of mental complexity" (p. 197) or to become the playwrights of their own lives.[14]

DeSeCo found broad agreement across OECD countries that this sort of reflectivity was needed by individuals today to address complex and potentially conflicting demands as well as to take an active role in grounding their actions in their own value systems. DeSeCo contributors agreed that merely recalling knowledge, thinking abstractly, and being well socialized are no longer sufficient (if they ever were) for individuals to meet the demands facing them today.

One reason this capability is so important is that issues often cannot be resolved through an either–or solution. Individuals need to recognize and deal with tensions, "for instance between equality and freedom, autonomy and solidarity, efficiency and democratic processes, ecology and economic logic, diversity and universality, and innovation and continuity—by integrating seemingly contradictory or incompatible goals as aspects of the same reality" (Rychen, 2003, p. 78). Beyond recognizing these tensions,

262 Laura Hersh Salganik and Stephen J. Provasnik

individuals need to make decisions and take responsibility that their decisions and actions are consistent with their goals and values. This is such a basic requirement for compctence in any area that DeSeCo recognized reflectivity as a basic element in its frame of reference.

The elements just described provide a theoretical and conceptual foundation for defining key competencies. They do not, however, provide guidance for actually selecting the key competencies that are needed for individuals to live a successful life and for society to be well-functioning. For this, DeSeCo's frame of reference includes a three-fold categorization from which key competencies can be selected.

Three-fold Categorization of Key Competencies

DeSeCo developed its three-fold categorization of key competencies based on (a) the understanding that key competencies are competencies needed by all individuals to lead a successful life and contribute to the success of society (DeSeCo's common normative framework), (b) the common demands of life, and (c) scholarly contributions. This conceptualization of the three categories, together with the information about the use of key competencies in OECD countries, formed the basis for identifying the exemplar key competencies in each category. The categories (and exemplar key competencies in each category) are as follows.[15]

1. Interacting in Socially Heterogeneous Groups

Human beings are dependent throughout their lives on ties with others, not only for physical survival but also for their sense of self and social meaning. This category addresses interaction with others, and given the pluralistic character of modern democratic societies, the focus is on socially heterogeneous groups—"different others." Because "[w]e live in a network of close relationships," this category of interacting in socially heterogeneous groups "concerns the development of social bonds and coexistence with people whose backgrounds may be different from one's own, who do not necessarily speak the same language (literally or metaphorically) or share the same memories, history, culture, or socioeconomic background" (Rychen, 2003, p. 87). Key competencies under this category benefit individuals both in instrumental ways and by enriching their understanding of themselves and society. These competencies work to strengthen social cohesion and alleviate fragmentation and social strains associated with increasing individual diversity. (This group of key competencies addresses the general concerns associated with such terms as "social skills," "social competencies," and "intercultural competencies" found in lists of key competencies submitted to DeSeCo.) DeSeCo identified three exemplar key competencies in the category of interacting in socially heterogeneous groups.

The ability to relate well to others. This key competence focuses on initiating, maintaining, and managing personal relationships, for instance with family members, friends, neighbors and co-workers. Empathy—taking the role of the other person and seeing things from his or her perspective—is an important prerequisite to relating well to others. It leads to reflection about options for actions, with the realization that one's own view is not necessarily shared by the other person. Awareness and management of one's emotions are also important for relating well to others.

The ability to cooperate. Many demands of modern life cannot be met by one individual alone. Cooperation—working together with others toward a common goal—is a key competence mentioned repeatedly in the DeSeCo material. Joining forces with others is necessary in work teams, families, civic organizations, unions, management groups, indeed in just about every social environment. Cooperating involves balancing one's own desires with commitment to the group and its goals and norms, balancing responsibility for active participation with the need to share leadership and support others, understanding one's roles and responsibilities in relation to the group and its goals, constructing alliances with others, allowing for different shades of opinion, and making compromises (Rychen, 2003).

The ability to manage and resolve conflicts. Conflict occurs in all aspects of life, and the ability to manage and resolve conflict is the third key competence identified by DeSeCo in this category. It is an unavoidable by-product of individual freedom, and rather than seeking to avoid and eliminate it, conflict should be approached in a constructive manner. This means considering the desires and needs of others, looking for win–win solutions rather than exclusively achieving one's own goals, and recognizing when others' needs take precedence over one's own. "For individuals to take an active part in conflict management and resolution, they need to analyze the issues and interests at stake (e.g., power, recognition of merit, division of work, equity), the origins of the conflict, and the reasoning of all sides, and recognize that there are different possible positions" (Rychen, 2003, p. 90).

2. Acting Autonomously

Acting autonomously is the category of key competencies that focuses on an individual's sense of identity and empowerment to exercise control over his or her own life. It should not be interpreted as meaning that individuals can do whatever they want or can freely act in isolation from others. Rather, acting autonomously is complementary to acting in socially heterogeneous groups; all our actions take place in the context of other people and of social norms and institutions. Key competencies in this area enable individuals to develop a value system, "to act rather than to be acted upon, to shape rather than to be shaped, and to choose rather than to accept choices decided by others. Acting autonomously refers to participating effectively in the development of society, in its social, political, and economic institutions (e.g., to take part in decision processes), and functioning well in different spheres of life—in the workplace, in one's personal and family life, and in civil and political life" (Rychen, 2003, p. 91). The image of individuals determining life outcomes is most commonly associated with those who have power in society, but key competencies related to acting autonomously are just as important for those at the margins of power if they are to conceive of potential for change and take action to improve their lives. It is recognized that autonomy has to be considered relative to the rules of the social field in which an individual operates—for example, the rules of autonomy are influenced by institutional norms (e.g., military, bureaucratic, religious, schools). However, even in these spheres, there are situations in which stepping outside of institutional norms and exercising individual autonomy is recognized as consistent with a wider value system. Three exemplar key competencies were identified in this category.

The ability to act within the "big picture." This key competence involves not only understanding that individual actions take place within a larger normative and socioeconomic context, but also acting in accordance with the wider implications of one's actions. The "big picture" is frequently multi-faceted, including not only the local situation but also a wider view of the community and ultimately a global perspective. This competence allows individuals to understand the larger issues at stake and the consequences of their actions in a larger context, so that individuals' actions are just and responsible, even when not easy or convenient (Rychen, 2003). It requires individuals to have an understanding of the larger physical and social world, envision the impact of different courses of action, and choose actions that are consistent with one's values at different levels of the system.

The ability to form and conduct life plans and personal projects. This key competence enables individuals to see the development of their lives as an object of their actions. Initially, this entails being aware of one's own obligations, goals, and dreams. Then, it requires an orientation toward the future and the ability to prioritize among different possible ends, understand one's own strengths and weaknesses, balance resources, learn from the past, monitor progress, and make adjustments (Rychen, 2003). It is also associated with terms used in policy discussions such as "self-directed learning," "strategic competencies," and "self management."

The ability to defend and assert one's rights, interests, limits, and needs. This key competence recognizes that in modern Western societies, individuals are responsible for making myriad decisions, and both the norms and formal rules related to them are increasingly complex. It is often the case that an individual's rights, interests, and needs are in conflict with those of others. As a result, autonomous action is needed both to assure rights related to the self (such as fair opportunities in society) and in the interest of collective life (such as adequate health care or education for all, effective democratic institutions). Many rights are established in formal laws, but these rights should be seen by individuals as a resource, not a guarantee. "The development of this competence empowers individuals to assert both personal and collective rights, ensure a dignified existence, and gain more control over their own lives" (Rychen, 2003, p. 97).

3. Using Tools Interactively

Like interacting in groups, using tools is a universal activity for human beings. Here, the term "tool" is used in the broadest sense of the term, to include not only physical tools but also socio-cultural ones such as language, information, and knowledge. The adverb "interactively" signifies that what is needed is not just the technical skills to operate a tool (e.g., reading or making a phone call with a cell phone); to use a tool interactively is to understand the potential of the tool for allowing us to do new things, to interact with the world in a different way, to endeavor to accomplish new goals. Our experiences using various tools should "shape how we make sense of and become competent in the world, how we deal with transformation and change, and how we respond to long-term challenges" (Rychen, 2003, p. 98). When we encounter a new tool, we recognize its potential to allow us to do new things—live in different places, communicate with others differently, express new ideas, solve new problems, or undertake new activities that we could not do before—and take action accordingly. Three exemplar key competencies were identified in this category.

The ability to use language, symbols, and text interactively. Here the focus is on using language, symbols, and text to participate in society and accomplish personal goals. Thus, it requires, for example, the ability not only to read or manipulate numbers correctly, but also to reflect on the content's relevance in one's life and draw on attitudes and values to use the language, symbols, or text as a tool to relate to the world. This key competence is related to "communication competence" and also to some uses of the "literacy," although the meanings of these terms vary widely.

The ability to use knowledge and information interactively. This key competence draws attention to the importance of knowledge and information for individuals and society. But again, what is important is not just to have knowledge or information; what is important is to use it to make decisions or take actions. "It assumes critical reflection on the nature of information itself, its technical infrastructure, and its social, cultural, and even ideological context and impact. Information competence is necessary as a basis for understanding options, forming opinions, making decisions, and taking informed and responsible actions" (Rychen, 2003, p. 101). Using knowledge and information interactively is needed not only for activities generally thought of as cognitive but also for those considered as predominantly social. Knowledge and information are important for understanding others and interacting with others in a manner that is consistent with one's values.

The ability to use technology interactively. Human beings are confronted with advances in technology when new technologies are developed or when they are introduced where they were not available before. In today's world, information and communication technologies in particular have placed new demands on individuals. Using new technology interactively entails not only learning how to operate it and agreeing to adopt it, but also adapting to what it makes possible. Examples from the developed world are the use of the cell phone and e-mail. They are not simply a different medium for making a telephone call or sending mail—they have changed the way people communicate with others. There are many other technologies that have changed the way we live (e.g., cars, televisions, DVDs, microwave ovens, and the Internet, to name a few that have affected the West in living memory). Recognizing the potential to do new things with such technologies and acting in a manner that is consistent with what one values in making use of that potential is at the heart of using tools interactively.

Key Competencies in Action

We have described these exemplar key competencies individually, which is important to do for reaching consensus on them and for designing curricula and assessments. However, in real life none of these key competencies would be used in isolation from the others because of the multifaceted nature of demands on individuals and the interrelated nature of the competencies. In real-life situations, individuals need to draw on multiple key competencies, coming from different categories, especially when meeting practical demands described at a broad, abstract level—e.g., participating in a club or political interest group, deciding how to vote, contributing to sustainable development. In such cases, the particulars of the social field, including those related to normative aspects of different cultures within and across countries as well as of the particular situation, are an important factor in structuring the constellation of competencies needed by the individual.

For this reason, DeSeCo proposed that the idea of a *constellation* is a useful way to think about groups of key competencies: "A constellation of key competencies, therefore, is a culturally and contextually specific instantiation of key competencies in response to the specific nature of the demands of the local situation" (Rychen, 2003, p. 105). Examples of factors affecting the structure of the constellation are the level of urbanization, cultural norms, property rights, technology, civic organization, and social and power relations. Figure 20.2 graphically illustrates this point—that the importance of a key competence to achieving a desired outcome can vary in different contexts.

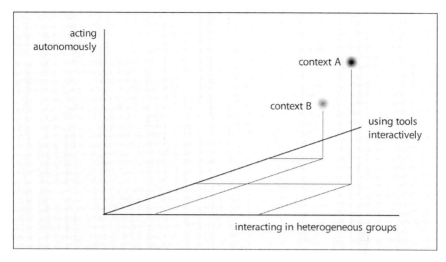

Figure 20.2 The relative importance of the three categories of key competencies in different contexts. Reprinted with permission from *Key Competencies for a Successful Life and a Well-Functioning Society* by D. S. Rychen and L. H. Salganik, ISBN 0–88937–272–1, p. 105, © 2003 by Hogrefe & Huber Publishers.

In Figure 20.2, competencies related to acting autonomously and interacting in heterogeneous groups are more important in Context A than in Context B, whereas competencies related to using tools interactively are more important in Context B than in Context A. Although oversimplified, the point is that using key competencies to define a common core for an education is neither a "one-size-fits-all" approach nor a strait-jacket approach. The relative importance of the key competencies can vary given the needs of different countries, social fields, or other particulars of the social and economic environment.

Given such flexibility, we believe the approach we have outlined here can provide a better guide for policy and programmatic decisions related to the goals of education than the more commonly found lists of attributes and outcomes whose interconnections are not made explicit. Moreover, because this approach is explicit about its normative orientation, we believe it can ground policy debate about the goals of education in what people should and need to be able to do as individuals in modern society and, thereby, check the tendency of educational policy debate about *what is a quality education* to drift into discussions of ideological goals devoid of practical considerations.

APPLICATION TO NON-OECD COUNTRIES

As noted previously, participants in the DeSeCo project developed the frame of reference to identify key competencies that would be relevant in

OECD countries. However, they also recognized that their work could have broader applications beyond the OECD[16] given that improving education and lifelong learning strategies are on the political agenda worldwide—as evidenced by contributions to DeSeCo (Ouane, 2003; Riordan and Rosas, 2003), efforts of the World Bank (2002), and the UBASE project itself. Moreover, the global trend toward standardization of institutions; the influence of international organizations, such as the World Bank, the OECD, the United Nations Educational, Scientific and Cultural Organization (UNESCO), and the United Nation's International Labour Organization (ILO); and the adoption of universal objectives expressed by the international conventions that form the normative basis of DeSeCo all support the hypothesis that DeSeCo's three-fold categorization would be relevant and useful for developing and transitional countries. To know whether they truly are relevant and useful, however, will require further consideration and research. Toward that end, the next section of the chapter draws on the work of other contributors to this volume to consider this approach's worldwide applicability, ultimately arguing that DeSeCo's frame of reference is applicable and can contribute to policy dialogues beyond the OECD.

Considering DeSeCo's Approach beyond the OECD

First, the approach taken by DeSeCo comprehends education in the same way that the UBASE project and its contributors have: as a means to many positive, non-economic social outcomes at the individual and societal level, as well as economic ones. This broad purpose for education is explicitly at the heart of the UBASE project, which at its inception identified the needs for UBASE as humanitarian, sociological, political, and economic (Bloom and Cohen, 2002). This conception is also echoed in the goals of education proposed by other UBASE contributors to this volume: for example, building global understanding (Mahbubani, Chapter 3); linking education to life, livelihood, peace, and social justice (Ramachandran, Chapter 8); fostering global civility (Reimers, Chapter 14); and ensuring a balanced education that includes teaching citizenship and community responsibility, and social skills and work ethic (Rothstein and Jacobsen, Chapter 17).

Further, DeSeCo's concept of competence—premised on the idea that multiple attributes (knowledge, values, motivation, cognitive and practical skills, attitudes, and aspects of context) must be brought together for competencies to take root—matches the broader, multi-dimensional understanding of learning called for by several UBASE contributors in their chapters on what constitutes a quality education. For example, Mary Joy Pigozzi (Chapter 18, p. 237), in her contribution on UNESCO's perspective on a quality education, noted that "[w]hile in the past much of the emphasis on education related to cognitive understanding and development, now there is a need to also address the social and other dimensions of learning." Camer Vellani (Chapter 7, p. 98), drawing on his experience in Pakistan, wrote that a quality education recognizes that "[m]ultiple factors modulate an individual's knowledge, which in turn influences behavior; prominent among them are moral reasoning, social and economic status in society, and beliefs derived from religious teaching, tradition and culture."

Building on the concept of competence, the concept of key competence—with its emphasis on being applicable to everyone; being grounded by the important, complex demands of modern life; and leading to a successful life and a well-functioning society—aligns remarkably well with the policy dialogue about education in developing countries. Making education relevant to the demands of modern life was identified as one of the world's principal educational needs by UNESCO and representatives of nations from around the world at the Jomtien Conference on Education for All in 1990 and the Dakar World Education Forum in 2000. At both conferences, participants reaffirmed the need for "[b]asic academics" but at the same time recognized the need for "education to reflect upon its relevance to the modern world" (Pigozzi, Chapter 18, p. 237). This is the same need that initially led the OECD to examine the value of key competencies, and it is the reason the concept of key competence makes sense for universal education—it offers a way to make education relevant to the world by linking educational policy, curricular development, and educational accountability to the demands of real life faced by all.

Thus nothing about DeSeCo's approach limits it to OECD nations. However, this does not mean that DeSeCo's particular three-fold categorization of key competencies is the most relevant for non-OECD nations, especially developing nations. Indeed, one can easily imagine the case being made that this frame of reference is too Western-centric or that for some developing nations more narrowly targeted competencies, say in individual hygiene or training for industrial or agricultural work, are more important.

Relevance of the Areas of Key Competencies

Reviewing the essays and commentaries submitted for the UBASE project, we found that none of them identified narrowly targeted competencies as key to a quality education for developing nations. On the contrary, all called for broad definitions of a quality education, and each identified educational needs or approaches that fit within DeSeCo's frame of reference and/or within one or more of DeSeCo's three categories of key competencies. The majority of the scholars identified self-reflectiveness or critical thought or "reflectivity"—at the heart of DeSeCo's frame of reference for identifying key competencies—as a major part of any quality education (Charfi and Redissi; Levinger; Meier; Mahbubani; Pigozzi; Rothstein and Jacobsen; Suárez-Orozco; Vellani, this volume). Several noted the need for a respect for democratic processes and/or for human rights to inform and guide a quality education, which accords with DeSeCo's common normative starting point for its frame of reference.[17] Moreover, the three categories of educational needs identified by two of the scholars—Beryl Levinger and Marcelo M. Suárez-Orozco—corresponded astonishingly well with DeSeCo's three categories of key competencies. The educational needs and approaches these scholars identified support the relevance for non-OECD nations of DeSeCo's frame of reference and its three specific categories as a starting point for identifying key competencies.[18]

The most common educational needs cited by these scholars correspond to the key competencies grouped under the rubric of interacting with socially heterogeneous groups—that is, the ability to relate well to others, the ability to cooperate with others, and the ability to manage and resolve conflicts. This category of key competencies encompasses what Deborah Meier (Chapter 13, p. 178) refers to as "informed empathy for others unlike ourselves" and what Kishore Mahbubani's (Chapter 3, p. 71) labels the global need "to promote more cross-cultural understanding." It also covers some of the skills that Mary Joy Pigozzi (Chapter 18, p. 244) identifies as important "learning outcomes" within the UNESCO perspective of a quality education—"to work in teams, to live together and interact with those who are different. . . ." This category addresses the need identified by Fernando Reimers (Chapter 14) for education to reduce socially transmitted hate and intolerance, which has been at the root of worldwide occurrences in the twentieth century of discrimination, racial/ethnic oppression, and genocide. It also seems consistent with Levinger's (Chapter 5, p. 86) analysis that the sort of education that can responsibly equip a girl in a West African village for the future she will face must include "processes that add to the store of social capital in the community"—that is, processes by which "the relations—formal and informal—that bring people together to take action" develop "the glue that holds a society's institution's and citizens together." Moreover, it touches on all three of the qualities that Suárez-Orozco (Chapter 15, p. 208) suggests globalization selects for in all countries: (a) "habits of mind and higher order cognitive skills fostering . . . the capacity to work with others on complex problems . . . ," (b) "the ability to communicate and understand others across cultural boundaries," and (c) "the ability to navigate across discontinuous or incommensurable linguistic and epistemic systems." Given the great degree of immigration (both intra- and internationally), exacerbated ethnic tensions in regions of economic transition, and the shrinking "global village" that are among the common characteristics of globalization's effect on all nations, it is not hard to see why key competencies under this category are relevant to all nations.

The key competencies grouped under the rubric of using tools interactively—that is, the ability to use language, symbols, and text interactively; the ability to use knowledge and information interactively; and the ability to use technology interactively—are perhaps most consistent with the commonly held expectations for education, for example teaching literacy and numeracy. These competencies also address the needs for constructive or contributing members of society (cited by Ingram, Chapter 19) and for what Levinger (Chapter 5, p. 84) calls "metacognitive skills that contribute to the transfer of knowledge and to the solution of novel problems." This category also can address the need for what Suárez-Orozco (Chapter 15, p. 208) identified as "the ability to navigate across discontinuous or incommensurable linguistic and epistemic systems." Given that the thrust of these competencies is so fundamental, it is hard to imagine any type of education that does not develop some facet of these competencies.[19]

The key competencies grouped under the rubric of acting autonomously— that is, the ability to act within the "big picture"; the ability to form and conduct life plans and personal projects; and the ability to defend and assert one's rights, interests, limits, and needs—are the most debatable competencies for nations with strong traditional, especially tribal, cultures because autonomy is at the heart of modernity. And for many, to foster autonomy within a traditional culture is to sow the seeds of social conflict. Yet, this category resonates with the educational needs identified by Levinger's analysis (of the sort of education needed by a West African girl to escape poverty) and Vellani's assessment (based his experiences in Pakistan). For Levinger (Chapter 5, p. 85), it is essential to develop "skills that prepare learners to avail themselves of development opportunities"—for themselves, their families, their communities, and their nations. According to Vellani (Chapter 7, p. 99), all students need to learn "to apply moral reasoning; to acquire a broad range of knowledge about the physical world as a part of the universe; to appreciate life as an unusual phenomenon and understand its history and precarious sustenance in an ecosystem; to appreciate the constancy of human biology and the diversity of civilization and cultures; to understand the existence of the spiritual constituent of human thought and the diversity of its expression; to express creativity." This category, likewise, addresses the need for what Suárez-Orozco (Chapter 15, p. 208) identified as "the habits of mind and higher order cognitive skills fostering autonomy and creativity of thought." Such professional opinion about educational needs, however, does not mean competencies related to autonomy will be valued in traditional cultures.

Broader Demand for Autonomy

We believe there is good reason to believe that a demand for fostering autonomy exists broadly worldwide because there are clear signs that autonomy is sought in parts of the world that in the past were considered resistant or opposed to the modern, individual self implicit in promoting autonomy. For example, in Russia, a country long focused on collectivist and socialist values, the need "to help each young person to develop a reflective and autonomous personality" was ranked among the highest educational needs in 1998 by educational policy-makers and officials in Moscow as well as local elites in Kemerovo and Vladivostok (Bain, 2001). The same premium on autonomy was reported by elites in China, Hong Kong, Japan, Korea, Malaysia, and Taiwan (nations that have been regarded as paragons of collectivism) in the Sigma Survey conducted between 1996 and 1998. This surprising result was highlighted by William Cummings (2001), in his discussion of the survey's finding:

> Whereas past accounts of the [education values stressed by countries around the] Pacific Basin stressed the penchant for orderliness and control including the tendency to use values education to shape habits of national loyalty and obedience, the elite respondents of the twenty settings participating in the Sigma Survey suggest a new era may be emerging with an increased emphasis on personal autonomy and responsibility (p. 296).

Indications that autonomy is more broadly sought than in the past are not confined to elites or to nations experiencing rapid economic growth. In Guatemala, the Mayan community, which fought a decades-long civil war as part of their effort to preserve their traditional culture and heritage, established the Instituto de Cultura Maya in 1984 to "regain control of their cultural inheritance."[20] The Institute has sought to do this by standardizing a written Mayan alphabet, creating curricular materials for primary schools in the various Mayan languages, and promoting the teaching of Mayan culture in primary school to Mayan children in their mother tongue—all of which is designed to foster self-respect and individual autonomy among Mayan children so that Mayans as a collective can preserve their traditional culture in the face of hegemonic Hispanic culture and modernity. This is a strategy, however, that upends the conventional notion that traditional culture and modern autonomy are incompatible.[21] Further, in rural African communities, traditionally accepted practices (e.g., rape to secure a young girl's hand in marriage, female genital mutilation as a rite of womanhood, etc.) have been challenged within the communities by younger generations that have learned of human rights but do not seek to abandon their traditional cultures or communities.[22] These challenges suggest that autonomy may not necessarily be contrary to the traditional cultures as much as disturbing to existing power relations. Such examples are largely anecdotal and are merely suggestive. Yet they support the idea that key competencies related to "acting autonomously" are meaningful and relevant beyond OECD countries. This is not to say that they will necessarily be desired universally, as they are part and parcel of modernity. And, as the first section of this chapter made clear, to institute universal education is to tacitly impose a modern social order with a state-directed education system and a norm of autonomous individuals, all of which will not be welcome in some places.

Caveats

Our argument thus far has focused on the value of key competencies and DeSeCo's frame of reference for all nations seeking to provide quality universal education. We are not claiming, however, that this approach offers any simple way to institute quality universal education in every area of the world. We see DeSeCo's frame of reference with its three categories of key competencies as a fruitful starting point for any serious effort to formulate a broad standard for quality UBASE. However, adopting this approach will require vetting the frame of reference in a wider international community, exploring its implications for teaching and learning, and interpreting the categories of key competencies for different national contexts. Beyond that, states need to plan and implement suitable policies and practices for schooling that foster individual students' development of key competencies.

Furthermore, we are not claiming that this approach is a panacea to solve the perennial problems of implementing a quality education in every area of the world, regardless of the social and economic context. For example, in areas of subsistence farming one can institute all of the outward activities of schooling and compel attendance with some degree of success, but children whose parents had no formal schooling and who see that educated individuals of similar birth enjoy no better standard of living than their own parents may see no value in formal education and have no motivation to learn in school. As a result, such children may end up completing no more than two or three grades of a primary education. For those who do complete a basic education, there is the problem that Vellani (Chapter 7, this volume) illustrates, that disillusionment sets in when the proportion of the educated unemployed grows as a result of the growth in the population and low investment in development. Such institutional problems cannot be forgotten if one wants to improve education quality.

Lastly, while we believe this approach offers a new direction, it is hardly radical: it does not require completely remaking schooling, and it builds resolutely on the work of many, many individuals and organizations, most notably, UNESCO. UNESCO created an International Commission on Education for the Twenty-first Century in 1993 to look at "What kind of education is needed for what kind of society tomorrow?" The commission's final report, *Learning: The Treasure Within*, identified four "pillars of education" or "four types of learning": "learning to know, that is acquiring the instruments of understanding; learning to do, so as to be able to act creatively on one's environment; learning to live together, so as to participate and co-operate with other people in all human activities; and learning to be, an essential progression which proceeds from the previous three . . . [and] that emphasizes the development of the complete person" (Delors, et al., 1998, p. 86). DeSeCo's work remaps these four types of learning within its broader frame of reference, which also calls upon policy-makers to be explicit about, for example, what "learning to live together" means in terms of behavior of individuals, and educators to specify and instill the prerequisites individuals need in order to act in ways that fulfill this goal.

A COHERENT MAP FOR DEFINING QUALITY
UNIVERSAL BASIC AND SECONDARY EDUCATION

The task of defining a quality universal education is not a simple one, but it is also not completely impossible. As this chapter has explained, there are various institutional elements of universal education that shape how a *quality* universal education can be defined, and there are myriad possible approaches to answer the question of what is a quality education. We have reviewed the DeSeCo Project's effort both because its frame of reference works within these institutional constraints and because we believe it offers a promising approach to the task.

As described, DeSeCo's approach is promising for several reasons. It employs the concept of key competence, which fits the basic requirement of universal education: that it would impart—at a general level—the same "something" to everyone—a common core. In addition, it meets the practical need to be relevant to the demands of the modern world for both developed and developing nations, allowing the specifics of countries' key competencies to vary according to each country's social and cultural context. It can fit within the existing institution of schools and schooling both because it serves as a *guide* to orient educational change, rather than a *blueprint* to prescribe educational reform, and because it echoes many themes that are already in public discourse about education.

Moreover, DeSeCo's approach has a theoretical and conceptual foundation that has been already vetted through an international and interdisciplinary process. Although its framework, including its three-fold categorization of key competencies—acting autonomously, using tools interactively, and interacting in socially heterogeneous groups—needs to be vetted further and refined in a wider arena, it represents a sizeable intellectual and international endeavor to address questions that are fundamental for defining quality UBASE. Among these, in particular, DeSeCo's approach keeps at the top of the agenda the question that is at the heart of the educational enterprise of shaping society by shaping individuals: what do individuals need to be able to do?

APPENDIX A: SCHOLARS' CONTRIBUTIONS
ON KEY COMPETENCIES

To assemble material on key competencies, DeSeCo, at the start of the project, asked scholars from different academic disciplines (anthropology, economics, philosophy, psychology, and sociology) and different countries (France, Switzerland, the United Kingdom, and the United States) "which competencies are key?" Their ideas represented a range of viewpoints about what is important for individuals to learn. The following is a brief synopsis of each of their contributions.

Philosophers Monique Canto-Sperber (Centre National de Recherche Scientifique, Paris) and Jean-Pierre Dupuy (Ecole Polytechnique, Paris) established a set of values that are useful for defining a good life and are consistent with major moral theories: accomplishment, choosing one's own course through life, understanding oneself and one's world, enjoyment, and deep personal relationships (Canto-Sperber and Dupuy, 2001). In addition, they established the premise that the human mind cannot be reduced to a set of abstract rules or algorithms that describe the workings of a machine. Based on these values and this premise, the authors identified five broad dimensions of competence: (a) coping with complexity (recognizing patterns); (b) perceptive competencies (discriminating between relevant and irrelevant features); (c) normative competencies (choosing the appropriate means to reach a given end, appreciating various possibilities, making and applying moral judgments); (d) cooperative competencies (cooperating with others, trusting others, taking the role of the other); and (e) narrative competencies (making sense of what happens in life to oneself and others, describing the world and one's own real and desirable place in it). These competencies they believe can be construed as dimensions of a five-dimensional space, with subcompetencies and skills pertaining to several, if not all, of the five areas of key competencies.

Psychologist Helen Haste (University of Bath, England) began from the premise that humans are adaptive, social beings whose competencies both derive from these attributes and allow them to meet the demands of particular historical periods and social contexts (Haste, 2001). She proposed management of the tension between innovation and continuity as an overarching meta-competence, and she identified five broad areas of key competence: adaptively assimilating changing technologies; dealing with ambiguity and diversity; finding and sustaining community links; managing motivation and emotion; and the competence to focus on morality, responsibility, and citizenship. She described the competent individual as one who "is self-sufficient, able to focus attention and plan, with a future orientation, is adaptable to change, has a sense of responsibility, has a belief that one can have an effect, and is capable of commitment." Haste suggested that it is useful to think of competencies through thinking of individuals as "Tool Users" in the sense that tools (including language) are "part of an active dialogue between the individual and the environment" (Haste, 2001, p. 96). Competencies, then, are more than skilled use of the tool; they involve recognizing what the tool makes possible, integrating new ways of understanding or making sense of the world, and introducing new activities into our lives.

Sociologist Philippe Perrenoud (University of Geneva) focused his analysis on "ordinary actors, the woman or man in the street, doing their best to survive and live as well as possible" (Perrenoud, 2001, p. 126). What competencies do they need to preserve their autonomy, without infringing on that of others, and to avoid being abused, alienated, dominated, or exploited? Drawing on Bourdieu's concept of social fields, Perrenoud proposed a set of transversal key competencies: being able to identify, evaluate, and defend one's resources, rights, and limits; to form and conduct projects and develop strategies, individually and collectively; to analyze situations and relationships; to co-operate, act in synergy, and share leadership; to build and operate democratic organizations and systems of collective action; to manage and resolve conflicts; to understand, apply, and elaborate rules; and to construct negotiated orders beyond cultural differences.

Economists Frank Levy (Massachusetts Institute of Technology) and Richard Murnane (Harvard University) argued that recent social changes related to technology and globalization have transformed the competencies needed in the workplace (Levy and Murnane, 2001). They used relevant economic theory and available empirical results, as well as their own research with hiring practices of high-performance firms, to identify those competencies that predict economic success and individual income. These competencies include reading and mathematical skills (not only for their instrumental use but as the basis for lifelong learning); oral and written communication abilities; skills to work productively in different social groups; emotional intelligence and related abilities to co-operate well with other people; and familiarity with information technology. As a result of their grounding in economic theory and research, these competencies are identified in a particular field and for a specific group (e.g., employees in the labor market), but are seen as relevant across social fields and groups.

Anthropologist Jack Goody (University of Cambridge) rejected the idea of identifying common key competencies per se on grounds that theory must always be considered in the context of practice (Goody, 2001). Recognizing that there may be some very general qualities required by modern life, Goody focused on the intractability of specifying key competencies that can span cultures, social contexts, and individuals *within* any one country, let alone *between* countries at a sufficient level of specificity to guide practice. Relevant for UBASE, he also cautioned against limiting the work to developed countries because it is bound to be used in a larger context and have a homogenizing effect, which he views as negative.

These scholars' ideas are very heterogeneous, but this is hardly surprising considering that the scholars structured their approaches to identifying key competencies around different organizing ideas, central questions, and conceptual frameworks. With the exception of Goody, however, they each proposed a set of key competencies needed by the individual for what the authors define as success, reflecting their overall approaches. While seemingly disparate on the surface, these sets of key competencies have many underlying common themes. To work toward developing a synthesis, DeSeCo asked two scholars to review these five papers and identify commonalities among them.

One commonality that *developmental psychologist Robert Kegan (Harvard University)* saw across these sets of key competencies was the need for individuals to reach a particular level of mental complexity (Kegan, 2001). Kegan drew from his evolutionary theory of mental development in which individuals' "ways of knowing" change from childhood through adulthood.

Young children, for instance, are very literal and mimetic in their thinking about the world, while adolescents can think abstractly, construct values and ideas through self-reflection, and subordinate their interests to those of a group. These mental capacities indicate maturation, but they are not sufficient for adults to meet the often conflicting demands of the modern world. To do that, it is necessary to go one step further, to step back from one's own socialization and create one's own system for prioritizing and resolving conflicting demands, and then to act—to be the author of one's own script, or "self-authoring." In his review, Kegan observed that each of the papers described competencies in a way that expects individuals to have sufficient mental development beyond the socializing process to a point at which they are mindful of their socialization but, in the face of challenges and conflicting demands, they do not view their lives as bound by an "unquestioned set of arrangements" (Kegan 2001, p. 199).

Sociologist Cecilia Ridgeway (Stanford University) identified two broad areas of common ground among the essays: (a) the ability to join and function effectively in social groups and (b) the importance of personality attributes (Ridgeway, 2001). She considered the first to be a truly universal key competence, necessary for material and psychological survival of human beings. The reason for this, she argued, is that in modern democratic societies, it is necessary for people to join and operate democratically in multiple, complex, and socially heterogeneous groups. The components that she found to contribute to this competence included taking the role of the other, finding mutually agreeable solutions in the face of conflicting interests, motivation to act democratically, and cognitive complexity and ideational flexibility. Ridgeway thought that the second area of common ground—personality attributes—includes self-concept (which supports individuals' ability to act with confidence) and emotion management (which allows individuals to deal with frustration, disappointment, and failure).

APPENDIX B: VIEWS FROM POLICY AND PRACTICE ON KEY COMPETENCIES

Given that its work was ultimately directed at the policy arena, DeSeCo asked individuals from relevant organizations to comment on the scholars' contributions and invited OECD countries to contribute reports about how key competencies were used at the national level and which key competencies were identified.[23] DeSeCo learned that identifying common key competencies across countries and social contexts is not without challenges and complexities, but that at the same time the concept of competencies is already in wide use, and there are many similarities in how it is used and in what competencies are considered important.

The question of whether it is appropriate to think that there may be common key competencies, even within countries, was raised by several respondents. The New Zealand report commented that the value placed on autonomous individual behavior reflects a Western paradigm, which is not consistent with the values of the Mäori and Pacific peoples' cultures (Kelley, 2001). Some respondents noted that differences between Western capitalist ideas about property and the values of middle-Asian communal economies may mean that one needs different key competencies for different groups (Oates, 2003). Respondents also identified citizenship as an area where common key competencies may not be possible, for while meeting demands related to being a citizen may be a common key competence, the particularities of doing so differ in different political and cultural contexts (Fratczak-Rudnicka and Torney-Purta, 2003).

The majority of respondents, however, concurred that, in spite of contextual differences, which everyone recognized, it is possible and worthwhile to identify key competencies and use them to guide policy and practice. Delors and Draxler noted that all collective human endeavor is based on the assumption that there are some things that unite individuals, and they cited the United Nations and democratic governments as examples of institutions that assume certain common ideals and values (Delors and Draxler, 2001). They rejected the argument that the fact that these commonalties are sometimes situational or seen as idealistic and ideological makes them irrelevant. Consistent with the idea mentioned previously that key competencies should be anchored in a normative starting point, they pointed to their experience with UNESCO's International Commission on Education for the Twenty-first Century. Despite the different perspectives related to cultural viewpoints, pragmatic versus ideal starting points, and differential application of these values, the commission

> discovered a much greater agreement about the nature of competencies than one would assume. The ability to make moral judgments and apply them, to describe the world and our own real and desirable place in it, the ability to marshal our own skills to constructing a future that involves living in society (with its freedoms and constraints), and so on, are universally recognized as competencies for a "successful life" (Delors and Draxler, 2001, p. 215).

DeSeCo also found that the idea of key competence has been a useful conceptual tool in different social fields in many OECD countries for formulating and discussing policies that respond to broad demands seen as associated with rapid technological changes, globalization, and movement toward a "knowledge economy." Although the emphases have been different, the idea of key competence as a means for expressing a broad view of capabilities needed by individuals has resonated in education and in the economic sector, and also in other fields such as youth development and citizenship:

- In education, key competencies are often associated with broadening of both general and vocational education and also with reforming education for social renewal. In some countries (generally Austria, Germany, and Switzerland), they have been a policy vehicle for promoting curriculum changes that integrate across schools subjects, either directly through curriculum reform or indirectly through school-leaving requirements. In others (generally the Nordic countries), key competencies have been used in national expressions of the goals of education (Salganik and Stephens, 2003).

- In the economic sector, the use and value of the concept of worker competencies and skills has become quite standard. "Workers in all types of industry are involved in a growing number of activities which are related to the new technologies, but above all, to new tasks, new responsibilities and new resources" (Callieri, 2001, p. 228). As a result, worker competencies and skills are frequently seen as "the first strategic factor that can be used to boost productivity and market competitiveness" (Callieri, 2001, p. 228). Competence development and management as a legitimate guiding framework for organizational decision-making is seen as an addition (or alternate) to the traditional focus on formal qualifications and a means for integrating the notion of lifelong learning into the business management process (Farrugia, 2001). From the labor perspective, there is the concern that these strategies are used by business to promote their own interests,[24] although in some countries (Sweden and Denmark), unions have also used the idea of key competence as a means to promote increasing the opportunities for workers (Callieri, 2001; Farrugia, 2001; Oliva, 2003; Ritchie, 2001).

- Outside of the formal education system, discussions about key competencies have arisen in initiatives meant to contribute to the social, emotional, physical and/or intellectual development of youth. For example, in the United States, the 4-H program conducted a research study to conceptualize life skills in each of the four "H"s: Hands, Health, Head, and Heart. A similar effort has also taken place in the Netherlands. Concern in the civic sector has focused on behaviors associated with participation in democratic society.

- A number of national-level projects have conducted research and developed statistics and indicators related to key competencies. Responding to the National Educational Goal for "every adult American to be literate and possess the knowledge and skills necessary to compete in the global economy and exercise the rights and responsibilities of citizenship" (National Education Goals Panel, 1999), the United States initiated Equipped for the Future: What Adults Need to Know and Be Able to Do in the 21st Century (EFF), which conducted an extensive consensus process to ask adults what skills they thought they needed in their roles as citizens, family members, and workers, and to identify the skills that underlay these activities. Switzerland, Canada, and Denmark have conducted research and developed indicators structured around key competencies. Related research in France has focused on the importance of context for developing indicators of skills and competencies.

At the international level, a number of large-scale survey efforts have measured characteristics related to key competencies across countries. The Adult Literacy and Lifeskills Survey (ALL) assessed literacy, numeracy, and problem-solving in 2003 and builds on the International Study of Adult Literacy (IALS), conducted during the 1990s. Most international studies of school-age youth have focused on school subjects. For example, in 2001 and 2006 the IEA's Progress in International Reading Literacy Study (PIRLS) assessed fourth graders' early reading skills. However, recent efforts to measure competencies more broadly include the Programme for International Student Assessment (PISA) conducted by the OECD and the IEA Civic Education Study. PISA measures reading, mathematical, and scientific literacy, and in 2000, 2003, and 2006 measured cross-curricular competencies such as self-regulated learning and problem solving. The IEA Civic Education Study measured civic knowledge, skills, and attitudes of fourteen- and eighteen-year olds. In addition, the OECD is currently developing the Programme for the International Assessment of Adult Competencies (PIAAC), for administration in 2011. PIAAC is intended both to "identify and measure differences between individuals and countries in competencies believed to underlie both personal and societal success" and to "gauge the performance of education and training systems in generating required competencies."[25]

After the OECD countries submitted these reports to DeSeCo, psychologist Uri Peter Trier (University of Neuchâtel, Switzerland) conducted an analysis of them (Trier, 2003). His conclusions about which competencies are identified as key in the different OECD countries are shown in Table 20.1.

Table 20.1   The Most Common Demands for Individual Competencies in Twelve OECD Countries, by the Frequency with Which They Were Mentioned in Country Reports for DeSeCo

High	Medium	Low
Social competencies/ Cooperation	Value orientation	Cultural competencies (aesthetic, creative, intercultural, media)
Literacies/Intelligent and applicable knowledge	Self-competence/ Self-management	Health/Sports/Physical competence
Learning competencies/ Lifelong learning	Political competence/ Democracy	
Communication competencies	Ecological competence	
	Relation to nature	

Source: (Trier, 2003, p. 45).

ACKNOWLEDGMENTS

The authors would like to thank Joel Cohen for his helpful comments on earlier drafts of this chapter. We would also like to thank Heinz Gilomen, Eugene Owen, Valena White Plisko, and Scott Murray for their support of the project Definition and Selection of Competencies: Theoretical and Conceptual Foundations (DeSeCo) at the Swiss Federal Statistical Office (SFSO), the U.S. Department of Education's National Center for Educational Statistics, and Statistics Canada, and acknowledge the leadership of Dominique Simone Rychen, Program Manager at SFSO, throughout the duration of the work.

NOTES

1. The idea of a universal education makes little sense without the abstract idea of some underlying commonality and an understanding of all persons as agents capable of making decisions and acting to affect themselves and others. Indeed, without these notions, the practical reality of everyday life experience is more likely to lead one to conclude that not all people can or should learn the same things. For a sociological account of the social construction of the concept of the individual as having the "capacity for responsible agency," see Meyer and Jepperson (2000). On the relationship between "the rise of individualism" and mass education (and how "[m]ass education is meaningless and in fact practically inconceivable where the primary social unit is the family, clan, village, or other group collectivity"), see Boli and Ramirez (1986). Historians differ as to exactly when and why Europeans developed the concept of the individual, but clearly a sense of individualized relationships (and the tensions between individual and collective responsibilities) captivated public interest by the sixteenth century, when Shakespeare's plays on this theme were popularly received. For differing historical accounts, see Ullman (1966) and Morris (1972).

2. Medieval society (or, more precisely, society under the ancien régime) owed its corporate character to a feudal governing system, introduced in the eighth and ninth centuries during the Norman and Saracen invasions, that some historians refer to as "corporativism." Under this system, "the ruler decentralized responsibilities and rights, in the hope that barons and townships would perform functions for him that he, the king, could not afford, or did not have the strength, to perform himself." As long as the social order was organized by corporativism, the fundamental units of society were not individuals but rather "corporate groups of individuals" (e.g., manors, parishes, towns, guilds, universities and academies, commercial and financial companies, etc.). Each of these corporate groups had "its own carefully delimited rights and responsibilities," creating "a vast agglomeration of chartered freedoms, ranging from the aristocrat's right to receive tolls at a bridge to a peasant's right to pasture a cow in a common field" (Sachar, 1990, pp. 4–5).

3. The medieval notion of corporate salvation held that the actions of the clergy could save the entire church of the faithful from eternal damnation but that individuals could do nothing to effect their individual salvation.

4. For an historical account of these developments, see Van Horn Melton (1988).
5. The term *institution* can refer either to an established practice or form of organization, or to an established society or corporation. The latter is the more common usage; however, in this chapter, we use the word *institution* in the former sense—to indicate a human practice or form of organization that has become conventional and, as a result, may be regarded as natural, inevitable, or necessary.
6. See, for example, Cheng (Chapter 2, this volume).
7. Established in 1961, the OECD is an international institution, sponsored now by thirty member nations committed to democracy and the market economy, to help governments compare policy experiences, seek answers to common problems, identify good practice, and coordinate domestic and international policies. For more information, see http://www.oecd.org.
8. DeSeCo was led by the Swiss Federal Statistical Office, with additional support from the U.S. Department of Education, National Center for Education Statistics (NCES), and Statistics Canada.
9. After conducting an analysis of projects related to indicators of competencies conducted during the 1990s in OECD countries, the project commissioned a series of papers beginning with the concept of competence. Scholars from a number of disciplinary perspectives (anthropology, economics, philosophy, psychology, and sociology) were then asked to identify theory-grounded sets of key competencies, and policy-makers and representatives of leading social and economic institutions, including unions and business organizations, commented on the scholars' work. In addition, a country consultation was organized within the OECD to review national experiences in the definition and selection of key competencies and issues related to the development and assessment of competencies. Appendix A and Appendix B summarize this material. Two international symposia were held to provide an opportunity for reflection and dialogue among the research community, policy analysts and policy-makers at the national level, leaders in social arenas, and representatives of international organizations. The various contributions and the elaborated findings can be found in Rychen and Salganik (2001, 2003a) and Rychen, Salganik, and McLaughlin (2003). They are also summarized in OECD (n.d.). For more information, see www.deseco.admin.ch.
10. One helpful way to understand what is meant by a frame of reference is the following: "Every organization in carrying out its mission and role operates within a set of guidelines, a frame of reference against which it measures and weighs what it should be doing, what it is doing, and, finally, how well its accomplished tasks meet its criteria. In many cases, the framework is fully articulated and spelled out in directives or other pronouncements of the organization; in other instances, the history of performance stands as the object illustration, and little if anything is found in written, explicit form" (National Research Council, 1986, pp. 26–27).
11. For further details on DeSeCo's frame of reference, see Rychen and Salganik (2003a), primarily Rychen and Salganik (2003b), Rychen (2003), and Gilomen (2003a, 2003b), Rychen (2004), OECD (n.d.).
12. The term *skills* is often used in a manner similar to competencies; however, *skills* also carries meanings and connotations that are associated with reducing an activity into pre-defined steps or a low level of difficulty, which distinguish it from the notion of competence as a complex action system (Rychen and Salganik, 2003b; Weinert, 2001).
13. For a more detailed discussion, see Suárez-Orozco (Chapter 15, this volume).
14. For a fuller discussion, see Kegan (1994).

15. These are described in greater detail in Rychen (2003).
16. Such recognition was evidenced by concerns about identifying key competencies that would be relevant worldwide (Carson, 2001; Goody, 2001; Perrenoud, 2001).
17. DeSeCo's frame of reference's common normative starting point includes democracy, human rights, and sustainable development. The scholars who noted a need for these values included Carroll, Charfi and Redissi, Pigozzi, Reimers, and Rothstein and Jacobsen.
18. The only educational needs and approaches that these scholars mentioned that are not explicitly named as part of DeSeCo's frame of reference and its three categories of key competencies were (a) creativity and (b) seeking to optimize the components of the educational system such as management and administration, teacher quality, and teaching materials. These differences, however, do not compromise the applicability of DeSeCo's approach. Depending on how one defines creativity, it can be understood to be a product of acting autonomously and self-reflectiveness, or it can be easily accommodated within the prerequisites for each key competence. Optimizing the components of the educational system, on the other hand, is a strategy posited on the assumption that what is needed for quality education is to make the system work better. In an oversimplified fashion, this is to say, if teachers, principals, curricula, and school environments were of high quality, then student learning would be of high quality and the goals of education would be met. The DeSeCo Project, however, consistent with a recognition of the institutionalized nature of schooling and the recent discourse about outcomes, is based on the assumption that the strategy of optimizing the system is incomplete in what it can achieve and that if we are to achieve competencies for all, it is important to be guided by a comprehensive vision of these competencies.
19. The use of tools is so fundamental that since at least the eighteenth century (when Benjamin Franklin is supposed to have first suggested it) human beings have been defined by some thinkers as tool-using animals. This definition rests both on the mistaken belief that no other animal employs tools and on the fact that it is difficult to imagine any life that is human without the employment of physical, social, or mental tools (Sagan and Druyan, 1992, p. 390).
20. From one author's interview with the head of the Instituto de Cultura Maya in 2000 as part of an evaluation of USAID Girls' and Women's Education Activity Projects in Guatemala (Brush et al., 2002).
21. For a fuller explanation of this conventional notion, see Kitayama and Duffy (2004).
22. On challenges to the traditionally accepted practice of rape to secure a young girl's hand in marriage, see Wax (2004).
23. This section draws heavily on Salganik and Stephens (2003) and Trier (2003).
24. Ritchie (2001) suggests that businesses themselves do not practice teamwork, flexibility, and trustworthiness, which are characteristics they ask of their workers in the name of key skills or competencies. Both the business and labor perspective acknowledge that there is a tension between, on one hand, developing broad competencies that aren't applicable in specific jobs and, on the other, specific skills needed for a particular job but relevant for others.
25. Quotations from http://www.oecd.org/document/57/0,3343,de_2649_339 27_34474617_1_1_1_1,00.html. For more information about PIAAC, see http://www.oecd.org/document/35/0,3343,en_2649_39263238_40277475_ 1_1_1_1,00.html.

REFERENCES

Bain, Olga. 2001. "Russia: Towards Autonomous Personalities." In *Values Education for Dynamic Societies: Individualism or Collectivism*, ed. William Cummings, Maria T. Tatto, and John Hawkins, 21–58. Hong Kong: Comparative Education Research Centre.

Bloom, David E., and Joel E. Cohen. 2002. "Education for All: An Unfinished Revolution." *Daedalus*. Summer, 84–95.

Boli, John, and Francisco O. Ramirez. 1986. "World Culture and the Institutional Development of Mass Education." In *Handbook of Theory and Research for the Sociology of Education*, ed. John G. Richardson, 65–90. New York: Greenwood Press.

Bourdieu, Pierre. 1980. *Le Sense Pratique*. Paris: Editions de Minuit.

Bourdieu, Pierre. 1982. *Ce que parler veut dire: L'économie des échanges linguistique*. Paris: Faygard.

Brush, Lorelei, Cory Heyman, Stephen Provasnik, Marina Fanning, Drew Lent, and Johan DeWilde. 2002. *Qualitative Report: Description and Analysis of the USAID Girls' and Women's Education Activity Projects in Guatemala, Morocco and Peru*. Washington, DC: Office for Women and Development, U.S. Agency for International Development.

Callieri, Carlo. 2001. "The Knowledge Economy: A Business Perspective." In Rychen and Salganik, 2001, 228–231.

Carson, John. 2001. "Defining and Selecting Competencies: Historical Reflections on the Case of IQ." In Rychen and Salganik, 2001, 33–44.

Canto-Sperber, Monique, and Jean-Pierre Dupuy. 2001. "Competencies for the Good Life and the Good Society." In Rychen and Salganik, 2001, 67–92.

Cummings, William. 2001. "The Future of Values Education in the Pacific Basin." In *Values Education for Dynamic Societies*, ed. William Cummings, Maria T. Tatto, and John Hawkins. Hong Kong: Hong Kong University Press.

Delors, Jacques, et al. 1998. *Learning: The Treasure Within*. Report to UNESCO of the International Commission on Education for the Twenty-first Century. Paris: UNESCO.

Delors, Jacques, and Alexandra Draxler. 2001. "From Unity of Purpose to Diversity of Expression and Needs: A Perspective from UNESCO." In Rychen and Salganik, 2001, 214–221.

Farrugia, Jean-Patrick. 2001. "Competence Management as an Investment: A Business Perspective." In Rychen and Salganik, 2001, 232–235.

Fratczak-Rudnicka, Barbara, and Judith Torney-Purta. 2003. "Competencies for Civic and Political Life in a Democracy." In Rychen, Salganik, and McLaughlin, 2003, 71–89. Neuchâtel, Switzerland: Swiss Federal Statistical Office.

Gilomen, Heinz. 2003a. Concluding Remarks. In Rychen and Salganik, 2003a, 181–186.

———. 2003b. "Desired Outcomes: A Successful Life and a Well-Functioning Society." In Rychen and Salganik, 2003a, 109–134.

Goody, Jack. 2001. "Competencies and Education: Contextual Diversity." In Rychen and Salganik, 2001, 175–189.

Haste, Helen. 2001. "Ambiguity, Autonomy, and Agency: Psychological Challenges to New Competence." In Rychen and Salganik, 2001, 93–120.

Kegan, Robert. 1994. *In Over Our Heads: The Mental Demands of Modern Life*. Cambridge, MA: Harvard University Press.

Kegan, Robert. 2001. "Competencies as Working Epistemologies: Ways We Want Adults to Know." In Rychen and Salganik, 2001, 192–204.

Kelley, Frances. 2001. *Definition and Selection of Key Competencies in New Zealand.* http://www.portal-stat.admin.ch/deseco/sfso_deseco_ccp_newzealand_19122001.pdf.

Kitayama, Shinobu, and Sean Duffy. 2004. "Cultural Competence—Tacit, Yet Fundamental: Self, Social Relations, and Cognition in the United States and Japan." In *Culture and Competence: Contexts of Life Success*, ed. Robert J. Sternberg and Elena L.Grigorenko, 56–57. Washington, DC: American Psychological Association.

Levy, Frank, and Richard J. Murnane. 2001. "Key Competencies Critical to Economic Success." In Rychen and Salganik, 2001, 151–173.

Meyer, John W., and Ronald L. Jepperson. 2000. "The 'Actors' of Modern Society: The Cultural Construction of Social Agency." *Sociological Theory* 18 (1): 100–120.

Meyer, John W., Francisco O. Ramirez, and Yasemin N. Soysal. 1992. "World Expansion of Mass Education, 1870–1980." *Sociology of Education* 65 (2): 128–149.

Morris, Colin. 1972. *The Discovery of the Individual, 1050–1200.* London: SPCK.

National Education Goals Panel. 1999. *The National Education Goals Report: Building a Nation of Learners.* Washington, DC: U.S. Government Printing Office.

National Research Council, Commission on Behavioral and Social Science and Education. 1986. *Creating a Center for Education Statistics: A Time for Action*, ed. Daniel B. Levine. Washington, DC: National Academy Press.

Oates, Tim. 2003. "Key Skills/Key Competencies: Avoiding the Pitfalls of Current Initiatives." In Rychen, Salganik, and McLaughlin, 2003, 171–193.

Oliva, Attilio. 2003. "Key Competencies in and across Social Fields: The Employers' Perspective." In Rychen, Salganik, and McLaughlin, 2003, 97–99.

Organisation for Economic Cooperation and Development. n.d. *The Definition and Selection of Competencies: Executive Summary.* Paris: Author. https://www.pisa.oecd.org/dataoecd/47/61/35070367.pdf (English); https://www.pisa.oecd.org/dataoecd/36/55/35693273.pdf (French); https://www.pisa.oecd.org/dataoecd/36/56/35693281.pdf (German); http://www.deseco.admin.ch/bfs/deseco/en/index/03/02.html (Spanish).

Ouane, Adama. 2003. "Defining and Selecting Key Competencies in Lifelong Learning." In Rychen, Salganik, and McLaughlin, 2003, 133–142.

Perrenoud, Philippe. 2001. "The Key to Social Fields: Competencies of an Autonomous Actor." In Rychen and Salganik, 2001, 121–149.

Ridgeway, Cecilia. 2001. "Joining and Functioning in Groups, Self-Concept and Emotion Management." In Rychen and Salganik, 2001, 205–211.

Riordan, Trevor, and Gianni Rosas. 2003. "Key Competencies: The ILO's Perspective." In Rychen, Salganik, and McLaughlin, 2003, 91–95.

Ritchie, Laurell. 2001. "Key Competencies for Whom? A Labor Perspective." In Rychen and Salganik, 2001, 236–240.

Rychen, Dominique S. 2003. "Key Competencies: Meeting Important Challenges in Life." In Rychen and Salganik, 2003a, 63–108.

———. 2004. "Key Competencies For All: An Overarching Conceptual Frame of Reference." In Rychen and Tiana, 2004, 5–33.

Rychen, Dominique S., and Laura H. Salganik, eds. 2001. *Defining and Selecting Key Competencies.* Göttingen, Germany: Hogrefe & Huber.

———. 2003a. *Key Competencies for a Successful Life and a Well-Functioning Society.* Göttingen, Germany: Hogrefe & Huber.

———. 2003b. "A Holistic Model of Competence." In Rychen and Salganik, 2003a, 41–62.

————. 2004. *Definir y seleccionar las competencias fundamentales para la vida.* Trans. Letitia Ofelia Garcia Cortés. Mexico: D. F. Fondo de Cultura Económica.

————. 2006a. *Key Competencies for a Successful Life and a Well-Functioning Society.* Trans. Tashita Yoshihiro, Imanishi Kouzou, Nomura Nagomi, Hirasawa Yasumasa, Iwasaki Kumiko, Saruta Yuuji, and Natori Kazuyoshi. Tokyo, Japan: Akashi Shoten Co. Ltd.

————. 2006b. *Las competencias clave para el bienestar personal, social y económico.* Trans. José M. Pomares. Málaga: Ediciones Aljibe.

————. 2007. *Agire le competenze chiave: Scenari e strategie per il benessere consapevole.* Trans. Tiziana Abelli. Milano: FrancoAngeli.

Rychen, Dominique S., Laura H. Salganik, and Mary E. McLaughlin, eds. 2003. *Contributions to the Second DeSeCo Symposium.* Neuchâtel, Switzerland: Swiss Federal Statistical Office.

Rychen, Dominique S., and Alejandro Tiana, eds. 2004. *Developing Key Competencies in Education: Some Lessons from International and National Experience.* Paris: UNESCO, International Bureau of Education.

Sachar, Howard M. 1990. *The Course of Modern Jewish History.* New York: Vintage Books.

Sagan, Carl and Ann Druyan. 1992. *Shadows of Forgotten Ancestors: A Search for Who We Are.* New York: Ballantine Books.

Salganik, Laura H. 2001. "Competencies for Life: A Conceptual and Empirical Challenge." In Rychen and Salganik, 2001, 17–32.

Salganik, Laura H., and Maria Stephens. 2003. "Competence Priorities in Policy and Practice." In Rychen and Salganik, 2003a, 13–40.

Swartz, David. 1997. *Culture and Power: The Sociology of Pierre Bourdieu.* Chicago, IL: University of Chicago Press.

Trier, Uri Peter. 2003. "Twelve Countries Contributing to DeSeCo: A Summary Report." In Rychen, Salganik, and McLaughlin, 2003, 27–64.

Ullman, Walter. 1966. *The Individual and Society in the Middle Ages.* Baltimore, MD: The Johns Hopkins University Press.

Van Horn Melton, James. 1988. *Absolutism and the 18th Century Origins of Compulsory Schooling in Prussia and Austria.* Cambridge: Cambridge University Press.

Wax, Emily. 2004. "Ethiopian Rape Victim Pits Law against Culture." *The Washington Post,* June 7.

Weinert, Franz E. 2001. "Concept of Competence: A Conceptual Clarification." In Rychen and Salganik, 2001, 45–65.

World Bank. 2002. "Lifelong Learning in the Global Knowledge Economy: Challenges for Developing Countries, 2002." http://www1.worldbank.org/education/pdf/Lifelong%20Learning_GKE.pdf.

Contributors

Bala Ahmed is Assistant Chief Information Officer at the Bauchi State Ministry of Information in Nigeria. He has served as a class teacher, information officer, and headmaster at the Bauchi Local Education Authority, and as a class teacher at the Federal Government Girls College Bauchi.

James Carroll was ordained to the priesthood in 1969, and served as Catholic Chaplain at Boston University until 1974, when he left the priesthood to become a writer. He has published ten novels, most recently *Secret Father*, a *New York Times* Notable Book of 2003. His memoir, *An American Requiem: God, My Father and the War that Came Between Us*, won the 1996 National Book Award in Nonfiction. In 2001, he published *Constantine's Sword: The Church and the Jews, A History*, which was a *New York Times* bestseller, won numerous awards, and is the basis of a documentary film directed by Oren Jacoby. In 2004, he published *Crusade: Chronicles of an Unjust War*, a criticism of the War on Terrorism and in 2006, he published *House of War: The Pentagon and the Disastrous Rise of American Power*, which won the PEN-Galbraith Award. Since 1992, his op-ed column has appeared weekly in the *Boston Globe*. Carroll is a Trustee of the Boston Public Library and a member of the Dean's Council at Harvard Divinity School. He is Distinguished Scholar-in-Residence at Suffolk University, and a Fellow of the American Academy of Arts and Sciences.

Mohamed Charfi (deceased) was professor emeritus in law at the University of Tunis and a representative of the Tunisian democratic, secular opposition. He served as Tunisia's Minister of Education from 1989 to 1994, during which he introduced wide-ranging educational reforms that he believed were long overdue in Muslim countries. A student leader in the General Union of Tunisian Students in Paris in the 1960s, Charfi helped to found in Tunisia the progressive and democratic group called "Perspectives." Twenty years later, he became the first Vice President and then President of the Tunisian League for the Defense of Human Rights (1981–1989). He is the author of a number of books on legal and other themes, most recently *Islam and Liberty: The Historical Misunderstanding.*

Kai-ming Cheng is Chair Professor of Education and Senior Advisor to the Vice-Chancellor at the University of Hong Kong. He was Dean of Education (1992–1996) and Pro-Vice-Chancellor (1997–2003) at the University of Hong Kong. He was a visiting professor at Harvard University (1996–2006). He has undertaken extensive research and consultancies commissioned by major international organizations, working mainly on education in rural China and India, but his work also extended to higher education reforms in various parts of Asia and Africa. As a member of Hong Kong's Education Commission, he has been instrumental in the reform effort to overhaul the education system. He chaired the Advisory Committee on Teacher Education and Qualifications (2002–2008). He writes a column in the *Hong Kong Economic Journal.*

Joel E. Cohen is Abby Rockefeller Mauzé Professor of Populations at Rockefeller and Columbia Universities and head of the Laboratory of Populations at the Rockefeller University. He is also co-director of the American Academy of Arts and Sciences' project on Universal Basic and Secondary Education and co-editor (with David E. Bloom and Martin B. Malin) of *Educating All Children: A Global Agenda.* His research deals mainly with the demography, ecology, population genetics, epidemiology and social organization of human and nonhuman populations and with mathematical concepts useful in these fields. He is the author of numerous books and articles, including *How Many People Can the Earth Support?* He is a Fellow of the American Academy of Arts and Sciences and a member of the United States National Academy of Sciences.

William K. Cummings is Professor of International Education and International Affairs at the Elliot School of International Affairs at George Washington University. He has been involved in education and development work for over twenty-five years, including long-term residence in Ethiopia, India, Indonesia, Japan, and Singapore. His work has focused on evaluation and monitoring, policy analysis, sector assessment, management analysis, and teacher training. He has authored or edited over one hundred articles and twenty-four books or monographs on education and development, including *Education and Equality in Japan, Values Education for Dynamic Societies* and *The Institutions of Education.* He is past president of the Comparative and International Education Society.

George M. Ingram is Executive Director of the Education Policy and Data Center and Vice President at the Academy for Educational Development. He also serves as the Chairman of the U.S. Global Leadership Campaign, a consortium that advocates for greater resources for U.S. international affairs activities. He also serves on the board of the Eurasia Foundation and the Center for U.S. Global Engagement. Previously, he was the executive director of the Basic Education Coalition, and earlier served as deputy assistant administrator at the U.S. Agency for International Development and a senior staff member of the House Committee on Foreign Affairs.

Rebecca Jacobsen is an assistant professor in the College of Education at Michigan State University. She has written on the role of the voice of the people in education policy and the public's opinions on the goals of public education. Her current research investigates the way in which accountability policies can be used to narrow the achievement gaps across all goals of public education.

Ana Carolina Letichevsky is an expert in educational assessment and program evaluation and is active on both regional and national levels in Brazil. She heads the Department of Statistics at Cesgranrio Foundation and is a professor of the professional Master Course on Evaluation at Cesgranrio Foundation. She teaches statistics at the Pontifical Catholic University of Rio de Janeiro (PUC-Rio). She has published mainly in the areas of statistics and evaluation.

Beryl Levinger is Distinguished Professor at the Monterey Institute of International Studies, an affiliate of Middlebury College. Her academic focus is on the interplay between human and organizational capacity development. She also directs the Development Project Management Institute, which prepares professionals to contribute to achievement of the Millennium Development Goals. She has worked in the field of international development and education for over forty years, serving as President of AFS Intercultural Programs and Senior Vice President of CARE. She is also past Vice Chair of InterAction, a consortium of more than 150 internationally focused nongovernmental organizations based in the United States. She has been a consultant to major nongovernmental and multilateral organizations and, for the past eight years, has been Research Director of Save the Children's annual *State of the World's Mothers Report.*

Claudia Madrazo is the founder and director of La Vaca Independiente (The Independent Cow), an organization created in 1992 in Mexico City to promote the integration of art into daily life. She created the *DIA* program (Development of Intelligence through Art), into which 25,000 teachers have been incorporated and from which more than 500,000 students have benefited. Today it focuses on educational innovation and the promotion of human development through art. She is the author of nine books and several essays and articles. She participates in several Mexican non-profit organizations in the areas of art, education, social development and ecology. She sits on the board of Museo del Barrio in New York, the Cornell Lab of Ornithology, and Alliance for a New Humanity.

Kishore Mahbubani is the first Dean and Professor in the Practice of Public Policy at the Lee Kuan Yew School of Public Policy at the National University of Singapore. With the Singapore Foreign Service from 1971 to 2004, he had postings in Cambodia (where he served during the war in 1973–1974), Malaysia, and Washington, DC, and he served two stints as Singapore Ambassador to the United Nations. He also served as President of the United Nations Security Council in January 2001 and May 2002. He was Permanent Secretary at the Foreign Ministry from 1993 to 1998. The Foreign Policy Association Medal was awarded to him in June 2004. He was also listed as one of the top one hundred public intellectuals in the world by *Foreign Policy* and *Prospect* magazines in September 2005. He is the author of *Can Asians Think?*, *Beyond the Age of Innocence: Rebuilding Trust between America and the World*, and *The New Asian Hemisphere: The Irresistible Shift of Global Power to the East*, which was published recently.

Martin B. Malin is Executive Director of the Managing the Atom Project at the John F. Kennedy School of Government, Harvard University. He was staff director of the project on Universal Basic and Secondary Education at the American Academy of Arts and Sciences. He is co-editor of *Educating All Children: A Global Agenda*. His writing has focused on American foreign policy, international relations in the Middle East, and arms control. He has taught at Columbia University, Barnard College, and Rutgers University.

Deborah Meier has spent more than four decades working in public education as a teacher, principal, writer, advocate, and leader of the school reform movement in the United States. For twenty years, Meier helped revitalize public schools in New York City's East Harlem district. In 1974, she founded Central Park Elementary School (CPE), a highly successful alternative school emphasizing active learning. Within the next dozen years, Meier opened two other Central Park elementary schools and one secondary school (CPESS). At these schools, Meier fostered democratic community, gave teachers greater autonomy in the running of a school, gave parents a voice in what happens to their children in schools, and promoted new approaches to assessment. In the 1990s she started a public "pilot" school in Boston, Mission Hill, to explore the ideas again in a K–8 school. She is the author of many books, including *The Power of Their Ideas: Lessons to America from a Small School in*

Harlem and *In Schools We Trust*. She was a founding member of the Coalition of Essential Schools and received the MacArthur Fellowship in 1987. Currently she is a senior scholar at New York University.

Mary Joy Pigozzi is Senior Vice President and Director of the Global Learning Group at the Academy for Educational Development (AED), where she is leading new initiatives for educational quality improvements, collaborating on education in fragile states, and overseeing the AED Information Technology Applications Center, the Systems Services Center, and the Education Policy and Data Center. She joined AED in 2006, having served most recently as Director of the Division for the Promotion of Quality Education at UNESCO in Paris. Prior to that, she was Senior Advisor for education at UNICEF in New York.

Stephen J. Provasnik is a research scientist at the Institute of Education Sciences at the National Center for Education Statistics (NCES). Currently, he is the U.S. National Research Coordinator for the Progress in International Reading Literacy Study (PIRLS) and assists with the Programme for the International Assessment of Adult Competencies (PIAAC). He has worked closely with NCES on the production of *The Condition of Education*, and has authored reports on U.S. community colleges, U.S. high school course taking, mobility in the U.S. teacher workforce, and the status and performance of U.S. minority students. Before joining NCES, he worked as a senior research analyst at the American Institutes for Research. He has worked as a Washington correspondent for the Japanese national newspaper, *The Yomiuri Shimbun*, and has taught writing and rhetoric at DePaul University and high school English in the Japanese public school system.

Vimala Ramachandran is a partner in the Educational Resource Unit in New Delhi, India, a research and consulting group that works in an interdisciplinary manner on issues in education, health, rights, livelihood and sustainable development. She was the first National Project Director of Mahila Samakhya (1988–1993), an NGO dedicated to the empowerment of Indian women. She is the author of *Getting Children Back to School: Case Studies in Primary Education* and *Gender and Social Equity in Primary Education: Hierarchies of Access*.

Hamadi Redissi is professor in Public Law and Political Science, Faculty of Law and Political Science at the University of Tunis and was a visiting scholar at Yale University in spring 2008. He is the author of several publications, including *L'exception islamique*, *Les Politiques en Islam: le Prophète, le Roi et le Savant*, and *Religion and Politics: Islam and Muslim Civilisation* (in collaboration with Jan-Erik Lane). His most recent publication is on the history of Wahhabism, *Le Pacte de Nadjd. Comment l'islam sectaire* *est devenu l'islam.* He is also an editor in Arabic of Maghribi manuscripts refuting Wahhabism in the nineteenth century (in collaboration with Asma Nouira), *Al-Radd 'alâ al-wahabiyya fil qarn al-tasa' 'ashar—Nusus al-gharb al-islami namuthajan.*

Fernando Reimers is Ford Foundation Professor of International Education at the Graduate School of Education at Harvard University. His research and teaching focus on the effects and implementation of education policies that intend to support the academic success of low-income children. He has advised governments, private groups and international agencies on issues of educational change and social inequality. He serves on the college of fellows of UNESCO's International Bureau of Education and on the Board of Directors of the New England Council of Latin American Studies. Prior to joining the Harvard Faculty he worked at the World Bank, the Harvard Institute for International Development and at the Universidad Central de Venezuela.

Richard Rothstein is a research associate of the Economic Policy Institute. From 1999 to 2002 he was the national education columnist of *The New York Times.* He is the author of *Class and Schools: Using Social, Economic and Educational Reform to Close the Black-White Achievement Gap; The Way We Were? The Myths and Realities of America's Student Achievement* and other articles and books on education policy.

Laura Hersh Salganik is the director of the Federal Statistics Program at the American Institutes for Research. She has worked on a number of projects under the umbrella of the OECD to improve the quality of international education statistics, most recently the DeSeCo Project (Definition and Selection of Competencies: Theoretical and Conceptual Foundations). DeSeCo's goal was to identify a small set of key competencies, based on a theoretical understanding of how such competencies are defined, that are needed by all individuals and that contribute to valued outcomes for individuals and societies in the OECD and potentially beyond. Its work is being used as the overarching framework for the OECD's Programme for the International Assessment of Adult Competencies (PIAAC). She is the co-editor of *Defining and Selecting Key Competencies* and *Key Competencies for a Successful Life and a Well-Functioning Society.*

Marcelo M. Suárez-Orozco is Courtney Sale Ross University Professor of Globalization and Education at the Steinhardt School of Education at New York University, where he holds the title of University Professor. His basic research is on conceptual and empirical problems in the areas of cultural psychology and psychological anthropology with a focus on the study of immigration and globalization. He is author of numerous scholarly essays, books, and edited volumes including *Globalization: Culture* *and Education in the New Millennium*, *Latinos: Remaking America*, and the six-volume *Interdisciplinary Perspectives on the New Immigration*. Previously, he was Victor S. Thomas Professor of Education at Harvard. In 1997, along with Carola Suárez-Orozco, he co-founded the Harvard Immigration Projects and began to co-direct the largest study ever funded in the history of the National Science Foundation's Cultural Anthropology division—a study of Asian, Afro-Caribbean, and Latino immigrant youth in American society.

Camer Vellani is Distinguished University Professor Emeritus at the Aga Khan University and a physician with broad interests in education and healthcare. He was associated with the development of the Aga Khan University in 1979 and served as its Rector from 1997 to 2001. In that capacity he was involved in planning of the University's future development envisioned by the Chancellor's Commission, which included the Human Development Program and the Institute for the Study of Muslim Civilizations. Planning for the University's Examination Board and subsequent membership of a national task force on improvement of higher education in Pakistan refined his understanding of the practice of education and the continuum of learning.

Index

Note: Abbreviations are: n., nn. = note, notes; t.= table; f. = figure

A

Abdherazak, (also Adb Al-Raziq), Ali, 157, 158–59

Abduh, Mohammed, 29, 157, 158–59, 170

access to education, 3, 10–11, 29, 31–32, 43, 69–70, 83, 90–91, 94, 98, 102, 104–6, 116, 236–237, 240, 243, 249; access to materials, 6, 90, 188, 196–200, 240, 250; geographic access, 11, 98, 102; participation opportunity concept, 85. *See also* universal education

accountability: of educational systems, 107–9, 116, 179, 230–31; failures in, 225; restricting areas of, 226–27; of schools, 188–90

adult literacy, 280. *See also* literacy

Adult Literacy and Lifeskills Survey (ALL), 280

affective or values dimensions, 60. *See also* self-knowledge and affective development; love

Afghanistan, 150, 153

Africa, 35, 70

Ahmed, Bala, 10, 28, 88

Al-Jazira, 163

allochthonous social practices, 206–7, 209

American Academy of Arts and Sciences, 3

American Federation of Labor, 16–17

American Institutes of Research, 126

Amin, Qacem, 157, 160

Amnesty International, 199

ancient perspectives on education: Buddha, Buddhist, 12–13; Confucius, 12–13, 18; Jesus, 142–143; Plato, 12–14, 17, 27, 150; Socrates, Socratic spirit, 17, 26–27, 68

Arabic language, 28, 88–89, 149, 152, 166–67, 171

Arab-Muslim identity, 150, 151. *See also* Muslim societies

Arab unity, 151

art education (also arts), 23, 29–30, 34–35, 58–60, 128–29, 135, 195, 199, 220, 225, 230t. *See also dia* Program

assessment 3–4, 8–11, 25–27, 31, 34–35, 50, 53, 90–91, 98, 165, 172, 176, 178, 197, 213, 215–23, 223n.4, 225–26, 228–230, 236, 244, 247; in Brazil, 220–23; in Mexico, 115–16, 121; in Pakistan, 99–102; measurement of learning outcomes, 60, 243–44, 245n.5; methodological questions, 217–20; screening, 56. *See also* accountability

Australia, 62–63n.20

authoritarian teaching methods, 17

autonomy, 264, 271–73, 275; acting autonomously, 263–65, 271–72; inculcating as an educational goal, 22, 32, 75, 106, 123, 208, 260, 261; support of educational autonomy in Arab tradition, 171, 172, 173n.19

Averroés, 155, 165, 168

B

Ba'ath Party, Ba'athism, 151

American Academy of Arts & Sciences

The Academy was founded during the American Revolution by John Adams, James Bowdoin, John Hancock, and other leaders who contributed prominently to the establishment of the new nation, its government, and its Constitution. Its purpose was to provide a forum for a select group of scholars, members of the learned professions, and government and business leaders to work together on behalf of the democratic interests of the republic. In the words of the Academy's Charter, enacted in 1780, the "end and design of the institution is . . . to cultivate every art and science which may tend to advance the interest, honour, dignity, and happiness of a free, independent, and virtuous people." Today the Academy is both an honorary learned society and an independent policy research center that conducts multidisciplinary studies of complex and emerging problems. Current Academy research focuses on science and global security; social policy; the humanities and culture; and education. The Academy supports young scholars through its Visiting Scholars Program and Hellman Fellowships in Science and Technology Policy, providing year-long residencies at its Cambridge, Massachusetts, headquarters. The Academy's work is advanced by its 4,600 elected members, who are leaders in the academic disciplines, the arts, business, and public affairs from around the world.